Optimise

Student's Book

B2

macmillan
education

LISTENING	SPEAKING	USE OF ENGLISH	WRITING
Predicting missing information Sentence completion	Talking about habits and routines Interview ▶ Talk2Me	Word formation Open cloze	Creating an appropriate style An article
Listening for agreement and disagreement Multiple choice (extracts)	Agreeing and disagreeing (1) Collaborative task ▶ Talk2Me	Word formation Sentence transformation	Expressing and justifying opinion An essay
Listening for opinion and attitude (1) Multiple matching	Comparing and contrasting Photo task ▶ Talk2Me	Word formation Multiple-choice cloze	Making recommendations A review
Listening for synonyms (1) True/false	Expressing and justifying opinions Discussion ▶ Talk2Me	Word formation Sentence transformation	Giving reasons and examples (1) A letter / An email
Listening for relevant information Multiple choice (single extract)	Talking about experiences Photo task ▶ Talk2Me	Word formation Open cloze	Formality (1) A letter / An email
Avoiding unneccessary detail Sentence completion	Making suggestions Collaborative task ▶ Talk2Me	Word formation Multiple-choice cloze	Making suggestions A letter / An email
Listening for purpose Multiple choice	Expressing preference and giving reasons Photo task ▶ Talk2Me	Word formation Sentence transformation	Creating a good narrative A story
Predicting and anticipating Multiple matching	Qualifying your opinion Discussion ▶ Talk2Me	Word formation Open cloze	Giving reasons and examples (2) An article
Recognising difference in meaning True/false/not stated	Speculating and expressing uncertainty Interview ▶ Talk2Me	Word formation Multiple-choice cloze	Using descriptive language A story
Understanding responses to questions Multiple choice	Reaching a decision Collaborative task ▶ Talk2Me	Word formation Open cloze	Introducing and concluding An essay
Listening for synonyms (2) Sentence completion	Talking about hopes and ambitions Interview ▶ Talk2Me	Word formation Sentence transformation	Formality (2) A letter / An email
Listening for opinion and attitude (2) Multiple choice (extracts)	Agreeing and disagreeing (2) Discussion ▶ Talk2Me	Word formation Multiple-choice cloze	Using your imagination A review

▶ USE OF ENGLISH p 144–145 ▶ WRITING p 146–147

Student's Resource Centre

- *Talk2Me* videos
- Speaking test videos
- *Optimise your grammar* worksheets
- *Optimise your vocabulary* worksheets
- *Say it right* pronunciation worksheets
- Culture and CLIL worksheets
- Class and Workbook audio

READING | Gapped text | A magazine article

1 **In pairs or as a group, answer the questions.**

1 What's your favourite film? Why do you like it?

2 What types of people work in the film industry?

2 **Read the article quickly to get a general idea of what it's about. Choose the sentence that best summarises each paragraph.**

Paragraph 1	____	Paragraph 5	____
Paragraph 2	____	Paragraph 6	____
Paragraph 3	____	Paragraph 7	____
Paragraph 4	____		

a) You need to choose an idea that works with the resources you have available.

b) Show your movie to lots of people and see what you learn from the experience.

c) Some young people make films while the rest of us just watch them.

d) Solving problems and never giving up are important skills.

e) You should see what a few people think of your movie once you've finished.

f) Film-making classes might help you to think about what's possible.

g) Only you can make your movie, no-one else.

3 **Look at the sentences in Exercise 4 that have been removed from the text. Write all the reference words. The first one has been done.**

They _____

_____

_____

_____

_____

OPTIMISE YOUR EXAM

Gapped text

● Look out for words such as pronouns that refer to things or people in the main text and the gapped sentences.

● Look carefully at the sentences before and after the gap and try to find reference words that are connected. Remember that a pronoun could refer to something two or more sentences away from the gap.

Stop watching movies and start making them!

E very time you see a trailer for the latest 3-D blockbuster, it can seem as if making successful films is something that only happens in Hollywood. You need years of experience, a huge budget, an all-star cast and fantastic special effects, right? Wrong! You might be surprised to hear that some of the most exciting screenwriters and directors in the industry are young people, whose passion for storytelling is producing original new films without the million-dollar budgets or CGI sequences.

Being a teenage director is probably the toughest challenge of all. Often, no-one takes you seriously, and everyone wants to tell you how to make your movie. Luke Jaden, a young film-maker from Detroit, USA, has already written and directed four critically-acclaimed films and documentaries. 'Nobody can do it for you … You're the only one with your particular vision,' Luke says. [1] Use whatever equipment and money you have available and get started.

However, that might be easier said than done. In one sense, all you need is the smartphone in your pocket, an idea and some willing friends. But how do you make sure that the end result doesn't just look like you and a group of friends messing around? You need a few key skills, one of which is making sure your plan works. [2] They're the ones who can make action movies and large-scale epics. Your story may be more low key and your movie may be shorter, but that doesn't mean it can't be great.

And then there's the technical side. Many young film-makers enrol on a course to learn the basic skills, and it's easy to find advice and information on courses online. [3] Sometimes that may mean accepting the limitations that you are forced to work with. It's not always easy to record high-quality sound, for example, so why not think about making a silent movie? A film-making course teaches you to explore possibilities like this.

Film-making is also in some ways a test of your character and your ability not to panic or give up. You have to learn to overcome problems, because there are always problems! And you have to learn to work with what you've got. [4] As Luke Jaden says: 'No matter where you are located on this earth, you can film.' Only

"Your story may be more low key and your movie may be shorter, but that doesn't mean it can't be great."

those people who are really determined will get to the point where they have an edited film in their hands.

Once you've got your film, then what? Many people don't realise how important it is to test screen your film. [5] That doesn't mean that you have to change your vision to keep people happy. However, watching your movie with 20 or 30 other people who weren't part of the film-making process can help you to see it in a different way. Seeing where they laugh and where they seem to lose interest can help you edit your film more effectively.

After that, it's time to think about how you get your movie in front of a wider audience. Film festivals and competitions are a great way to do this. [6] They provide a fantastic opportunity to see your work on the big screen and get feedback on what is successful (or not!) in your work. And the lessons you learn along the way will make your next movie even better!

---

4 ◁))) 1.01 **Read the text again. Choose which sentence A–G fits each gap 1–6. There is one extra sentence you do not need.**

A They'll teach you how to plan, shoot and edit your film to get the best results.

B This involves showing it to a small audience to see how they react.

C It's a problem that makes many young film-makers question why they are trying to make a movie.

D There's no point taking Hollywood on at its own game.

E They are often free to enter and many of them focus on movies made by teenage film-makers.

F One piece of advice he offers to young people wanting to get into film-making is to just go for it.

G You'll get nowhere if you wait until you find the perfect place to shoot or get perfect weather.

5 **Find these words and phrases in the text. Work out what they mean from the context.**

blockbuster (n) | budget (n) | cast (n)
determined (adj) | enrol (v) | epic (n)
messing around (phr v) | overcome (v)
special effects (n) | trailer (n) | willing (adj)

👤

THINK | RESEARCH | CULTURE | LEARN | ME

What type of things do you and your friends like to film?

What was the last thing you filmed?

Would you like to have a go at film-making?

Grammar in context

Look at these sentences from the article on page 5. Underline any countable nouns and circle any uncountable nouns.

1 *Many young film-makers enrol on a course to learn the basic skills.*

2 *It's easy to find advice and information on courses online.*

3 *They provide a fantastic opportunity to see your work on the big screen and get feedback on what is successful.*

✓ REMEMBER

- Countable nouns have both singular and plural forms and can be counted. We use *a/an* (singular, not specific or mentioned for the first time), *the* (singular or plural, specific) or no article (plural, not specific) with countable nouns.

- Uncountable nouns can't be counted and don't have a plural form (although a few uncountable nouns are in plural form and take a plural verb, e.g. *jeans*). We don't use an article with uncountable nouns when we are being general. We use *the* when we are being specific.

- Uncountable nouns are often materials (e.g. *glass*), abstract ideas (e.g. *information*) or collections (e.g. *luggage*).

- Some nouns can be either countable or uncountable, with a change in meaning (e.g. *hair*, *a hair*).

▶ **See Grammar reference, Unit 1,** page 148

---

1 **Look at the list of words. Put them into the correct noun category: countable, uncountable or both. If a noun can be both, explain any difference in meaning.**

baggage	book	clothes	coffee
entertainment	equipment	film
glass	house	interest	knowledge
leisure activity	metal	money	music
news	table	time	trousers	truth

countable	uncountable	both

2 **Insert articles in the sentences where appropriate.**

1 I went to great show at theatre last week with group of friends.

2 Music is big part of my life and I like listening to latest tracks on radio.

3 Lisa saw great interview on internet with local TV presenter.

4 Would you prefer to be actor or musician, or does working in entertainment not interest you?

5 Way we get our entertainment is changing quickly and lots of people watch films online now.

6 I'd rather go to cinema and see movie than stay at home and watch programme on TV.

3 **Write one word in each gap to complete the text. If no word is necessary, put a dash (–).**

Acting in your free time

If you have (**1**) _____ decent theatre in your town, then there's (**2**) _____ good chance that they offer drama workshops for anyone who is interested in giving acting (**3**) _____ go. And they're not just for (**4**) _____ stars of tomorrow who are thinking of working in (**5**) _____ media. Many young people who get involved in drama as (**6**) _____ free-time activity usually gain a lot from (**7**) _____ experience.

What are (**8**) _____ benefits of getting involved in something like (**9**) _____ acting? First of all, it's (**10**) _____ great way to meet new friends. And drama brings people closer because it involves taking (**11**) _____ risks together. Acting in front of an audience can be scary, but sharing that fear of (**12**) _____ failure with someone else makes it easier.

Secondly, acting teaches you to consider your emotions carefully. This can be a good thing for teenagers going through (**13**) _____ emotionally challenging period of their lives. It will definitely make you a more confident person.

THINK | RESEARCH | CULTURE | LEARN | ME

How popular is acting as a free-time activity in your area? Would you like to try it?

Why do you think people enjoy it?

Words connected with *TV* and *cinema*

1 🔊 1.02 **Complete the table with the words and phrases. Explain what each one means. Listen and check.**

> audience | box office | broadcast
> cast | channel | credits | director
> flop | on demand | programme
> reality show | release | satellite
> screenplay | series | sitcom | viewer

TV	cinema	both

2 **Write a word or phrase from Exercise 1 in each gap in the correct form.**

1 I can't wait for the new *James Bond* film to be _____ !

2 There's a new _____ on Channel 7 tonight about six teenagers trying to make it in the music business.

3 Did you know his last movie was a complete _____ and lost a lot of money?

4 I'm sure it'll say what the actor's name is in the _____ .

5 Amy might not like the show, but ten million _____ can't all be wrong!

6 The last *Star Wars* film was a huge success – it made millions of dollars at the _____ .

7 The channel lets you watch some programmes _____ for a month after they're on TV.

8 The actors did their best in the movie, but I don't think the _____ did a very good job of bringing it all together.

Phrasal verbs

3 🔊 1.03 **If a word in bold is correct, put a tick. If it's incorrect, write the correct word. Listen and check.**

1 What time does the new reality show *come* **up**? I don't want to miss it. _____

2 Jen's just going to *chill* **out** this weekend and watch a few episodes of her favourite TV series. _____

3 In last week's drama class we started *acting* **out** a new play. _____

4 This programme is boring. Why don't you *turn* **down** and see what else is on? _____

5 My schoolwork *takes* **up** so much time that I don't really watch much TV. _____

6 Tim likes to *hang* **off** with his friends at the weekend and play video games. _____

7 I *sat* **through** the film all the way to the end, even though I really wasn't enjoying it. _____

Collocations with *do, have, make* and *take*

4 🔊 1.04 **Complete the phrases with *do, have, make* or *take*. There may be more than one correct answer for some gaps. Listen and check.**

1 _____ a break
2 _____ a good time
3 _____ a difference
4 _____ a holiday
5 _____ time off work
6 _____ nothing all day
7 _____ an effort
8 _____ part in
9 _____ someone a favour
10 _____ your best
11 _____ work to do
12 _____ your time

5 **Choose six phrases from Exercise 4. Write a sentence for each one, showing how it is used.**

• SAY IT **RIGHT**

> **Resource centre: Unit 1**
> Stress in phrasal verbs (1)

> THINK | RESEARCH | CULTURE | LEARN | ME
>
> How often do you watch on-demand TV? What difference has it made to TV watching in your country?
>
> Are TV series in your language more popular than those in English? What are the main differences between them?

1 Look at the photos and ask and answer the questions.

1 What do you think is happening in the photos?
2 Have you ever been to the circus? If so, what was it like? If not, what do you imagine it is like?

2 Look at Exercise 4 and quickly read all the sentences. For sentences 1–3 below think of different words or short phrases that might fill each gap.

1 Jamie became interested in circuses when _____ took him to see a performance.
2 The most difficult thing at the beginning was a lack of _____ .
3 Most people don't realise that you need to be _____ to be a good performer.

3 Write the number of the gap in Exercise 4 that each word or short phrase could possibly fill. There may be more than one correct answer for some gaps.

1 carefully _____
2 his mother _____
3 an acrobat _____
4 stand on his head _____
5 exciting _____
6 shocked _____
7 confident _____
8 exercising _____
9 sleep _____
10 the park _____

▶ Workbook Unit 1: Listening, page 8, exercises 1, 2, 3

OPTIMISE YOUR **EXAM**

Sentence completion

● Before you listen, read through the sentences so you know what to expect.
● Try to guess what kind of words or phrases could complete the gap so that you can listen for the right information, e.g. pronouns, adjectives, places.

4 🔊 1.05 Listen to a teenager called Jamie Moody talking about learning circus skills as a free-time activity. Complete sentences 1–10 with a word or short phrase.

1 Jamie became interested in circuses when _____ took him to see a performance.
2 Jamie's family were _____ at first when he said he wanted to take up the activity.
3 The most difficult thing at the beginning was a lack of _____ .
4 Jamie's circus skills teacher suggested _____ as a way of getting in better shape.
5 Jamie tries to do things _____ when he starts to learn a new routine.
6 Regularly performing in _____ helps Jamie stay in practice and learn new routines.
7 Jamie uses the word _____ to describe the reaction to his first performance.
8 The next skill Jamie wants to learn is how to _____ so that he can include that in his performances.
9 Most people don't realise that you need to be _____ to be a good performer.
10 In the future, Jamie hopes to work as _____ because it would use all his skills.

5 🔊 1.05 Listen again and check your answers to Exercise 4. Don't leave any gaps empty.

THINK | RESEARCH | CULTURE | LEARN | ME

The words and phrases in Exercise 3 showed you what kind of word or phrase to listen for. Did that help you do Exercise 4? Explain how you found the correct answers.

Grammar in context

Look at these sentences from the audio in the listening lesson. Choose the correct phrase to complete each sentence.

1 *I have quite an unusual free-time activity, I suppose, but it's ____ fun.*

   a) much   **b)** a lot of   **c)** lots

2 *____ my family know anything about the circus.*

   a) None   **b)** No-one   **c)** None of

 REMEMBER

- Quantifiers show the number or amount of something. Some can be used with both countable and uncountable nouns (e.g. *a lot of / lots of*), some only with countable nouns (e.g. *a few / few*) and some only with uncountable nouns (e.g. *a little / little*).

- Some quantifiers (*all, both, each, either, every, many, much, neither, some*) can come immediately before a noun. – *all* people

- When we want to use these quantifiers before an article, a possessive or a pronoun, we use *of*. – *all of* my friends, *both of* the people, *neither of* us. With *all* and *both*, we can leave out *of* before an article or a possessive, but not before a pronoun.

- When we want to use *every* before an article, a possessive or a pronoun, we use *one of*. – *every one of* my friends

- With *no* and *none*, we use *no* when we are talking generally and *none* before an article, a possessive or a pronoun. – *No phones are allowed*. *None* of the phones was black.

▶ **See Grammar reference, Unit 1,** page 148

1 Choose the correct word or phrase to complete each sentence. In one sentence, both options are correct.

1 Could you give me **an / some** information about this dance class?

2 Nowadays, I only have time for **a little / a few** activities.

3 I got **lots of / several** advice about the best camera to buy for my photography course.

4 I'm afraid that **neither / neither of** us has any interesting hobbies.

5 **No / None of** my school friends is interested in painting as a leisure activity.

6 **Each / Each of** person I invited to come to the cinema with me was busy.

7 **Both / Both of** my parents love watching plays at the theatre.

8 I think **all / all of** young people would benefit from getting involved in drama.

2 Complete the second sentence so it has a similar meaning to the first. Do not change the word given. Use two to five words, including the word given.

1 Do you have a lot of free time?   **MUCH**

   Do you _____ free time?

2 We don't have much time before the gig.   **ONLY**

   There _____ left before the gig.

3 Olivia has few interests outside school.   **MANY**

   Olivia _____ interests outside school.

4 Andy and I don't like the new sitcom.   **US**

   _____ the new sitcom.

5 Abi advised me what equipment I needed to buy.   **BIT**

   Abi _____ advice on what equipment I needed to buy.

6 I asked some of my friends to come over to watch the latest Divergent film.   **FEW**

   I invited _____ to come over to watch the latest Divergent film.

3 Find and correct six mistakes in the text.

HOME • ABOUT ME • ARCHIVE • LINKS

It's here!

I've got a really exciting news! I've finally got my drone! For those of you who don't know, drone flying is becoming really popular. In the past, little people had drones, but now more and more of my friends are getting them – including me! My friend and I are going out this weekend to try it out and neither us can wait!

Of course, you have to remember few things if you're going to fly a drone. Safety is very important, so make sure you can see your drone at all of times. Also, remember that privacy is important to a lots of people, so don't fly over people's gardens or crowded public places taking photos. I'll post pics here when I get it up in the air!

THINK | **RESEARCH** | CULTURE | LEARN | ME

Find out more information about drone flying as a leisure activity. Tell the rest of the class what you find out.

1 SPEAKING | Interview

Flipped classroom

1 ▷ **Watch the *Talk2Me* video and answer the questions.**

1 How much free time do the people have per week?

2 Do the people do more indoor or outdoor activities?

3 How many of the people watch TV on demand?

2 ▷ **Watch the video again. Underline the expressions in the *Phrase expert* box that you hear on the video.**

PHRASE EXPERT

(at least) once/twice/three times a week/month |
I don't often/ever … because … |
In an average / a normal week, I … |
I usually/normally/sometimes/never … |
My usual/normal routine involves (+ *-ing*) … |
On average / In general, I … | quite often

3 **In pairs or groups, answer the questions.**

- Do you have a fixed routine each week, or do you do different things every day?
- Do you plan your weekends carefully or just let things happen? Explain why.
- Which activities do you tend to do with your friends?
- Which activities do you tend to do with your family?
- Which activities do you tend to do alone?

4 **Write a word or short phrase in each gap to complete the sentences.**

1 In a _____ week, I spend four hours playing video games.

2 _____ average, I study at home for an hour a day.

3 I go to the cinema at _____ once a month.

4 I'd say that in an _____ month I meet my friends most weekends.

5 During the week, my _____ routine _____ going to school, doing homework and watching TV.

5 **Complete the table. Write how often you do each of these activities (e.g. *every day, once a week, never*, etc.). Add two more activities and write how often you do them.**

activity	how often you do it
watch TV	
go to the cinema	
go to the theatre	
meet up with my friends	
go scuba diving	
go out to eat	
chat on social media	
play video games	
listen to music	

OPTIMISE YOUR EXAM

Interview

- Remember that we use the present simple tense to talk about repeated actions that we do or don't do often or regularly.

6 **In pairs, ask and answer these questions.**

- How much free time do you usually have each week?
- What kind of things do you like doing in your free time?
- What is a typical weekday like for you?
- How often do you listen to music?
- What sports do you do? How often do you do them?

1 **Look at the words in capitals in Exercise 2 and answer the questions.**

1 The first four words are verbs. Can you form any adjectives from them?
_____

2 Which two words are adjectives? What nouns can you form from them?
_____ _____

3 Which two words can form nouns ending in -nce? _____ _____

▼ OPTIMISE YOUR **EXAM**

Word formation
● Use the words before and after the gap to help you decide what part of speech you need, e.g. a preposition is often followed by a noun.

2 **Write a form of the word in capitals in each gap to complete the text.**

Cosplay

One free-time activity that brings (**1**) _____ and enjoyment to thousands of young people around the world is cosplay. Cosplayers create or buy costumes that copy the (**2**) _____ of their favourite character from video games, movies, TV series or comic books. They wear these (**3**) _____ costumes to attend conventions, such as Comic Con, and other meetings with other cosplayers. Although many people don't know about the (**4**) _____ of this activity, among gamers it is increasing in (**5**) _____ .

One of the main (**6**) _____ you have to make as a cosplayer is which character you want to look like. The possibilities are (**7**) _____ and new characters appear all the time as new video games and comics come out. Whether you go for a classic character or someone from the (**8**) _____ game, cosplay can be a fantastic activity for the superhero in you!

PLEASE
APPEAR

IMPRESS
EXIST
POPULAR

DECIDE
END

LATE

3 **Read the text in Exercise 4 quickly. Answer the questions.**

1 Which two gaps test your understanding of phrasal verbs? ____ , ____
2 Which gap needs to be filled with an article? ____
3 Which gap tests your understanding of quantifiers? ____
4 Which gaps test collocations? ____ , ____ , ____ , ____

▼ OPTIMISE YOUR **EXAM**

Open cloze
● Read the title and the text quickly for general understanding.
● Decide what kind of word is needed in each gap, e.g. a preposition, auxiliary verb (*has*, *is*), noun.
● Remember to write only one word in each gap, so do not use a contraction (*isn't*, *didn't*).

4 **Write one word in each gap.**

Scuba diving

One of the more unusual free-time activities that a few young people take part (**1**) _____ is scuba diving. This involves diving underwater using a self-contained underwater breathing apparatus (or 'scuba'). It can be very demanding and the activity (**2**) _____ up a lot of time, but it can also be very rewarding. For those who are willing to (**3**) _____ the effort, scuba diving can be (**4**) _____ absolutely fascinating experience.

Most people start by joining a scuba diving club. There, they can hang (**5**) _____ with experienced divers and begin to learn what is involved in scuba diving. The important thing is to (**6**) _____ your time and learn as much as you can before you make your first dive. You have to remember that scuba diving can be very dangerous and it's important to (**7**) _____ your best to prepare for any dive. Only a (**8**) _____ people out of the many who join a club go on to become expert divers.

1 In pairs or as a group, answer the questions.

1 What do you think the person in the photo is doing?

2 How difficult do you think this activity is?

2 Read this article and answer the questions in your own words.

Slacklining: An unusual activity

Have you ever seen someone balancing on a rope between two trees? If so, you've seen someone slacklining. It's an activity my cousin and I have done for a couple of years, and it's great fun!

You need a special rope made out of nylon and you also need something to pull the rope tight. Take my advice and buy a kit – it's the easiest way! Slacklining involves balancing on the rope and doing tricks. Popular tricks include walking along the rope, jumping and bouncing. It's hard at first, but practice makes perfect!

Why is it unusual? Well, first of all, not many people know about this activity. Secondly, it's unusual because you can do it with your friends anywhere you can find a couple of trees! It's lots of fun to practise tricks together, and you'd be amazed at how many people stop and talk to you about it.

So, why not give it a go? Find out more about slacklining online. There might even be a club near you. You won't regret it, even if you get a few bruises while you're learning!

1 What is slacklining?

_____

2 What does the writer say this activity involves?

_____

3 What does the writer say is enjoyable about this activity?

_____

3 Read the questions and choose the correct answers. There may be more than one correct answer for some questions.

1 How formal is the language the writer uses?

a) quite formal

b) fairly informal

c) very informal

2 How would you describe the style the writer uses?

a) friendly

b) serious

c) academic

3 Which of these things does the writer use to help create the style?

a) complex sentences

b) exclamation marks

c) rhetorical questions

4 Read this paragraph that the writer didn't include in the article. Rewrite it using your own words and a more appropriate level of formality and style. Use the words and phrases in the box to help you.

| came up with | catch on | fun |
| have you ever wondered ...? | | |

Slacklining originated from tightrope walking, which was commonly included in circus performances. During the 1970s, climbers developed slacklining as a pleasurable way to improve balance. The activity became increasingly popular and impressive tricks were created.

OPTIMISE YOUR EXAM

An article

- Remember that the style of an article is different from an essay. An article can usually be more informal.

- Think about who you are writing to. Address your reader directly and use imperatives to tell your reader what you think they should do.

- Remember that you may have to describe something briefly first and give an opinion about it in your conclusion.

5 Look at this writing task and make notes to answer the questions. Use your imagination if necessary.

You see this advert in an English-language magazine for teenagers.

> ### Articles wanted
> We're planning a special issue on unusual leisure activities, and we want your articles!
> Do you, or does anyone you know, have an unusual free-time activity?
> Tell us about it. Describe the activity and what it involves. Explain what makes it unusual and why it's enjoyable. Would you recommend it?
> We'll print the best articles in our special issue!

Write your **article**.

- Who does this activity: you or someone else? Be specific.

- What is the unusual leisure activity?

- What does this activity involve?

- Do you need any special equipment?

- Why is it unusual?

- Why is it enjoyable?

6 **Plan** Make a paragraph plan.

Part	Purpose	Useful phrases	My notes
Title	show clearly what you are writing about		
Paragraph 1	engage the reader and briefly describe the free-time activity and your / someone else's involvement	*Have you ever …?* *Are you one of those people who …?* *Do you ever …?* *I've been doing it for …*	
Paragraph 2	describe the activity in more detail, saying what it involves and any special equipment you need	*You don't need much, just …* *You need a few pieces of equipment, such as …* *The activity involves …* *You also have to …*	
Paragraph 3	explain what makes the activity unusual and why it's enjoyable	*One of the unusual aspects of this activity is …* *Very few people have heard of this free-time activity so …*	
Paragraph 4	suggest your readers try this unusual activity	*Take my advice …* *Give it a go!* *Go online and find out about …*	

7 **Write** Write your article in an appropriate style. Write 140–190 words.

8 **Check** Before you hand in your article, complete this checklist.

Checklist

- ◯ I've given my article a title.
- ◯ I've written at least four paragraphs.
- ◯ I've included all the information I was asked to.
- ◯ I've given a brief description and engaged the reader.
- ◯ I've used an appropriate style for an article.
- ◯ I've checked my spelling and grammar.

▶ **Writing reference,** page 169   ▶ **Workbook Unit 1:** Writing, page 10, exercises 1, 2, 3, 4 and Progress check 1, page 11

2 Learning about learning

1 **In pairs or as a group, answer the questions.**

1 What do you do in the hour or two before you go to bed at night?

2 How many hours' sleep do you get at night? Do you think it's enough?

3 Do you usually wake up in the morning feeling refreshed?

2 **Read the article quickly and tick the ideas that are mentioned.**

1 activities before bedtime ☐
2 not getting enough sleep ☐
3 food, drink and diet ☐
4 light and dark ☐
5 different types of bed ☐
6 electronic equipment ☐
7 TV distractions ☐
8 scientific experiment ☐

3 **Choose the correct word or phrase and give a reason based on the context.**

1 The phrase 'forbidden zone' in paragraph 2 is probably connected with the idea of **forcing** / **not allowing** someone to go to sleep because …

2 The word 'alert' in paragraph 2 is probably closest to the word 'sleepy' / 'awake' because …

3 The phrase 'sleep deprivation' in paragraph 3 probably means 'getting too much sleep' / 'not getting enough sleep' because …

4 The word 'trigger' in the final paragraph probably means 'start' / 'stop' because …

OPTIMISE YOUR EXAM

Multiple choice

• Some questions test the meaning of a word or expression. You can't use a dictionary in an exam, so try to guess the meaning from context. Use these ideas to help you:

Is the word/phrase similar to a word in your language?

Read the sentences before and after the word. Is there a similar or opposite word/phrase that explains it?

Can you find it repeated later in the text?

• Try to work out its approximate meaning BEFORE you look at the four options.

Teenagers, sleep and learning

What we know about teenagers' need for sleep, and how sleep affects learning

What do you do in the hour before your bedtime? How many hours' sleep do you get at night? Do you wake up in the morning feeling refreshed? These are some of the questions researchers have been asking teenagers all round the world in order to better understand teenagers' sleep patterns, and how those patterns can affect learning at school.

Sleep patterns change depending on your age. Most younger children get a good night's sleep and wake up fresh and energised the next day. In contrast, teenagers' body clocks change, creating a 'forbidden zone' for sleep at around 9 or 10 pm. It's propping them up just as they should be feeling sleepy. Later on, in middle age, the clock changes again, making it hard for parents to stay awake just when their teenage kids are at their most alert.

To make matters worse, recent research has shown that using an electronic device in the hour before going to bed greatly affects sleep patterns. According to studies, teenagers who used a computer or mobile phone before bedtime were much more likely to need more than an hour to fall asleep, and were also more likely to sleep several hours less each night. Teens

who used other electronic devices such as an MP3 player, tablet, game console or TV also experienced some sleep deprivation. Greg Dickson, 16, is a prime example. 'I usually chat to a few mates on WhatsApp before bed, and maybe watch a couple of videos on YouTube or Vimeo,' he says. 'I don't feel like going to sleep after that. And I really don't feel like getting up the next morning and spending the day in the classroom either!'

But how does this lack of sleep affect learning? In experiments carried out in North America, students were taught a series of skills and then slept for various lengths of time. For example, some students were trained to catch a ball attached by a string to a cone-like cup. The more they practised, the faster and more accurate they became. The students who then had a good sleep improved further. The other students who got less than six hours' sleep either didn't improve or actually fell behind. What this shows is that the brain consolidates and practises what has been learnt while you're asleep. This means sleep after learning is as important as getting a good night's rest before a test or exam.

Because of this, some researchers, such as Professor Paul Kelley from Oxford University, are pushing for later school start times. He's suggested that children aged 8 to 10 should start school at 8:30 am or later, 16-year-olds should start at 10 am and 18-year-olds as late as 11 am.

Other researchers are exploring the effect of light in setting sleep patterns, as darkness seems to trigger the release of melatonin, often called 'the sleep hormone', and light emitted from electronic devices tricks the brain into thinking it should be active rather than winding down. The solution here may involve the introduction of a 'digital sunset', where music, social media and all electronic devices are turned off a couple of hours before bed, similar to how the sun sets in the evening. And, finally, try not to binge-sleep at the weekend – if you're used to getting up at 6:30 am during the week, you shouldn't sleep until noon on a Saturday. That simply confuses the body.

4 ◁))) 1.06 **For questions 1–6, choose the answer (A, B, C or D) which you think fits best according to the text.**

1 What does 'propping them up' in paragraph 2 mean?
  A making them even more tired
  B keeping them energised and awake
  C stopping them from thinking clearly
  D supporting and encouraging them

2 What does Greg Dickson's quote demonstrate?
  A Many teenagers are careful to limit their usage of electronic devices.
  B It makes no difference whether you use a tablet or a mobile phone.
  C It's very common for teenagers to use the internet at night.
  D It's important to have close friends when you're a teenager.

3 What is the experiment with the ball designed to show?
  A The more you practise something, the better you become at it.
  B If you don't sleep well after learning something, you might lose the skill.
  C Testing is an essential part of the learning process.
  D Some people are much better at physical tasks than others.

4 What point does the writer make in paragraph 4?
  A The most important thing is to sleep well before an exam.
  B Teenagers' brains are more complex than scientists thought.
  C Teenagers should be encouraged to sleep at school.
  D We continue to learn things while we are sleeping.

5 What is suggested about melatonin in the final paragraph?
  A It is only produced when we are asleep.
  B It is most effective in a brightly lit room.
  C It naturally helps the human body feel sleepy.
  D Most teenagers don't produce enough of it.

6 The writer uses the word 'binge-sleeping' in the final paragraph to describe
  A only getting up when you feel refreshed.
  B getting up but still feeling tired.
  C getting a lot less sleep than usual.
  D getting a lot more sleep than usual.

Grammar in context

Look at the article on page 15 and find examples of each of the following:

1 present simple (question and negative)
2 past simple (negative and irregular form)

> ✓ **REMEMBER**
>
> ● We use present simple and past simple to describe: general truths and facts, permanent situations, states, how often things happen.
> ● We use past simple to describe single, completed actions and situations.
>
> ▶ **See Grammar reference, Unit 2,** page 149

1 **Put the verbs into the correct tense. Sometimes there is more than one answer.**

1 This new vocabulary app _____ (**be**) great – every day I _____ (**learn**) new English words!

2 Last year I _____ (**go**) to Germany on a language exchange and I really _____ (**enjoy**) myself a lot!

3 These days, students _____ (**not / usually / stand**) up when a teacher enters a room, do they?

4 Why _____ (**you / not / come**) to guitar practice today, Dan? _____ (**you / be**) ill?

5 Don't worry – you won't take the exam until your teacher _____ (**say**) you're ready.

6 Hurry up! The workshop _____ (**start**) in two minutes and they _____ (**not / like**) it when _____ (**we / be**) late!

> ✓ **REMEMBER**
>
> ● We use *used to* to describe a past habit or state – *We **used to** have PE twice a week, but now it's only once a week.*
> ● We use *would* to describe a past habit but NOT a past state – *We **would** usually do experiments in the school lab.*
> ● We use *be used to* to describe a situation that is familiar and not strange. – ***Are** you **used to** getting the bus to school every day, or is it still a bit strange?*
> ● We use *get used to* to describe the process of a situation becoming familiar and not strange. – *It took me about 3 months to **get used to** going to a new school.*
>
> ▶ **See Grammar reference, Unit 2,** page 149

2 **If a phrase in bold is correct, put a tick. If it's incorrect, rewrite it correctly.**

1 At my dad's school, the boys **used to wearing** shorts until they were 11 years old. _____

2 At the age of 11, they **would start** wearing long trousers. _____

3 **Did you used to use** to write your school essays by hand? _____

4 I **never use to like** physics but I do now.
_____

5 We've had a lot of practice doing exam tasks, so I **really used to doing** them now. _____

6 Until recently, we did our homework in a notebook, so **I'm still getting used to do** it all on a tablet. _____

3 **Write one word in each gap to complete the text.**

GÖBEKLI TEPE

Learning is part of our everyday life and work and experts such as scientists (**1**) _____ used to changing their minds when they learn new evidence that questions their accepted ideas. This is particularly true with archeology, and the excavation of Göbekli Tepe in Turkey is a good example.

Archeologists used to (**2**) _____ believe that before humans first started farming, people did (**3**) _____ have enough spare time or energy to build temples and other religious sites as they (**4**) _____ too busy hunting and gathering food. They believed that the development of agriculture led to the building of towns, which in turn made it possible to build large religious monuments.

The findings at Göbekli Tepe have changed that view. Recent excavations suggest that stone-age hunter-gatherers (**5**) _____ in fact able to work together to build incredible religious sites – before farming, before cities, and thousands of years before the invention of the wheel. So when (**6**) _____ our ancestors build Göbekli Tepe? The evidence suggests that it (**7**) _____ more than 11,000 years ago!

Words connected with *studying* and *learning*

1 🔊 1.07 **Write a word from the box in each gap. Don't use all the words. Listen and check.**

> certificate | degree | licence | qualification

1 This allows you to do something, such as drive a car. _____

2 This is a piece of paper showing you've achieved something. _____

3 This is a course of study that you take at university. _____

> pass | revise | take

4 We've got a test tomorrow so I'm going to _____ tonight.

5 Jason's going to _____ his first guitar exam next month even though we're not sure he'll _____ .

> coach | instructor | lecturer

6 This person teaches at a university. _____

7 This person trains a sports player or team. _____

8 This person teaches you how to do something, such as drive a car. _____

> graduate | pupil | undergraduate

9 This person has successfully completed a course at university. _____

10 This person is studying at university. _____

Phrasal verbs

2 🔊 1.08 **Match each phrasal verb with a meaning from the box. Use each meaning twice. Listen and check.**

> approach | create | discover/find
> finish/complete | increase

1 If you don't know a word, *look* it *up* in a dictionary. _____

2 I want to *set up* a computer-coding club at school. _____

3 Alex *crept up behind* Jake while he was doing his homework and surprised him. _____

4 There's only five minutes left, so *hurry up*! _____

5 Laura *thought up* a ridiculous excuse about why she hadn't written her essay. _____

6 When a student returns after being ill, they have to *catch up with* the rest of the class. _____

7 Go online and see what information you can *dig up* about the Romans for the class project. _____

8 I was going to do my presentation just on Antarctica, but I *ended up* doing it on the Arctic as well. _____

9 *Speak up*, Simon! We can't hear you at the back. _____

10 Who's *used up* all the glue? There's none left! _____

Words + prepositions

3 🔊 1.09 **Write one preposition in each gap to complete the sentences. Use the words in italics to help you. Listen and check.**

1 My brother's just *qualified* _____ a nurse and we're all really proud.

2 There's nothing *wrong* _____ decid*ing* you don't want to go to university.

3 I'm going to quit the swimming team for a while as I have to *concentrate* _____ my studies.

4 Warren's *decided* _____ becom*ing* a pilot and now wants to be a surgeon.

5 How *interested* are you _____ watch*ing* a documentary about archeology?

6 We need to find someone who's *experienced* _____ teach*ing* young children.

7 If you don't *pay attention* _____ anything I say, you're not going to learn anything!

8 All his explanation *succeeded* _____ do*ing* was to confuse me further!

9 The new education laws were *criticised* _____ not address*ing* the problem of class sizes in secondary schools.

10 I'm so *bored* _____ do*ing* homework – I can't wait to meet my friends afterwards.

1 **In pairs or as a group, ask and answer the questions.**

1 What different skills have you learnt to do in the last few years?

2 How keen are you to try things you haven't done before (e.g. rock-climbing, Zumba)?

2 ◁))) 1.10 **For each dialogue, decide if Zach completely agrees (A), completely disagrees (D) or partly agrees (P) with Alex.**

1 **Alex:** It's not as easy as it looks, is it?

Zach: No, it isn't! ____

2 **Alex:** You don't seem to have that problem though.

Zach: Oh, I wouldn't say that. ____

3 **Alex:** I had no idea you could do that.

Zach: Me neither! ____

4 **Alex:** I thought she'd done a really good job.

Zach: Yeah, to some extent, I suppose. ____

5 **Alex:** I can't imagine why he's the new instructor.

Zach: I can't see why not. ____

3 **Look at Exercise 4. Which questions ask about agreement and disagreement?**

OPTIMISE YOUR EXAM

Multiple choice (extracts)

- When you're asked what two people agree or disagree about, you may hear all the ideas expressed in the three options.

- Don't decide on your answer too quickly. Listen to the complete extract twice. Sometimes the correct answer comes in the middle or at the end.

- Remember that a negative (e.g. *Me neither!*) doesn't always mean someone disagrees, and a positive (e.g. *Yes*) doesn't always mean they agree.

---

4 ◁))) 1.11 **You will hear people talking in eight different situations. For questions 1–8, choose the best answer (A, B or C).**

1 You hear two friends talking about doing an online course.

What do they agree about?

A doing a similar course in the future

B how much they have learnt

C the quality of the teaching

2 You overhear a girl talking on the phone about a new arts and sports centre.

What does she think her friend would most enjoy?

A dance classes

B aerobics sessions

C acting lessons

3 You hear two teachers talking about an exam.

What do they agree about it?

A All the students found it challenging.

B It was harder than last year's exam.

C It had some questions that were unfair.

4 You hear part of an interview with a professional magician.

What is she doing?

A describing her working day

B promoting a series of events

C justifying her choice of career

5 You hear a boy talking about learning to ride a bike.

What does he remember most clearly?

A his father's support

B his sister's enthusiasm

C his mother's pride

6 You hear two friends talking about revising for an exam.

What do they disagree about?

A where they should do their revision

B who they should study with

C whether they have enough time

7 You hear a teacher talking about a charity event.

Why is she talking to her class?

A to encourage them to continue raising money

B to inform them about the outcome

C to remind them why the event was held

8 You hear two friends talking about an adventure weekend.

What do they both agree to do next?

A Find out prices.

B Invite other friends to come with them.

C Ask their parents for permission.

5 ◁))) 1.11 **Listen again and check your answers.**

Grammar in context

Look at these sentences from the audio in the listening lesson and answer the questions.

I've already signed up for their Monday-night dance class.

1 Why does the speaker use present perfect simple and not past simple here?

I couldn't wait to tell my mum I'd learnt how to do it.

2 Why does the speaker use past perfect simple and not past simple here?

REMEMBER

We use present perfect simple for:

- situations that started in the past and are still true.
- a series of actions continuing up to now.
- completed actions at an unspecified time in the past.
- completed actions where the present result is important.

We use past perfect simple for:

- situations and completed actions before a specific moment in the past.

We usually use present perfect simple after the phrase *It's the first/second time …*

We usually use past perfect simple after the phrase *It was the first/second time …*

We often use time words, such as *already, yet, before, since, ever, never, just, still*, with present and past perfect. We often use *so far* with present perfect, and *up to that point* with past perfect.

▶ **See Grammar reference, Unit 2,** page 150

1 **Put the verbs into the correct tense (present perfect simple, past simple or past perfect simple). There may be more than one correct answer for some gaps.**

1 Chris _____ (**decide**) to give up the piano and he _____ (**just / buy**) a guitar.

2 It wasn't the first time I _____ (**read**) some instructions and not understood them.

3 Is it really the first time Angela _____ (**ever / fail**) a test?

4 We _____ (**not / be**) in Germany long when I _____ (**realise**) my spoken German wasn't as good as I _____ (**think**) it was.

5 So far in this course, we _____ (**look**) at how the brain processes information.

6 I _____ (**want**) to show you a video online today, but someone _____ (**change**) the Wi-Fi password.

2 **Write a time word in each gap.**

1 Have you _____ had a dream where you took a test you hadn't revised for?

2 Jo's had her driving licence _____ May.

3 I'd never taken an important exam _____ so I was extremely nervous.

4 You can't have finished your homework _____ . You've only _____ started!

5 Haven't you done your report _____ ? Hurry up then!

6 I've won three swimming trophies _____ far, and I'm hoping to get another one this year.

7 That was an amazing vocal performance, especially since you've _____ had singing lessons.

8 We wrote an essay three weeks ago but Mr Blake _____ hasn't given it back with our marks!

3 **Write one word in each gap.**

What Einstein taught us

You (**1**) _____ almost certainly heard of Albert Einstein, but do you know why he was so important? Before Einstein, scientists (**2**) _____ all thought that time was constant. In other words, that three seconds is three seconds wherever you are in the universe, and whatever you're doing. Einstein showed that's not true and that how time passes is related to how fast you're moving. No-one had (**3**) _____ suggested this before Einstein.

But (**4**) _____ anyone ever tested this incredible idea? The answer is yes, they (**5**) _____ . They've tested and proved it many times (**6**) _____ Einstein first came up with it in the early 1900s. For example, scientists have taken two atomic clocks, both showing exactly the same time, and have (**7**) _____ one round the world in a plane. It ran a little bit faster than the clock which (**8**) _____ remained stationary on the ground. Today, clocks in GPS systems and satellites have to take this theory into account.

THINK | RESEARCH | CULTURE | **LEARN** | ME

Do you have tenses similar to the present perfect simple and past perfect simple in your language?

If so, are they used in the same way as English or in different ways?

Talk 2 Me

Neither do I ...

1 ▷ Watch the *Talk2Me* video and answer the questions.

1 What places for school trips are mentioned?

2 Which type of trip would the people prefer to go on?

3 What do the people say students can learn from going on school trips?

2 ▷ Watch the video again. Circle the expressions in the *Phrase expert* box that you hear on the video.

> **PHRASE EXPERT**
>
> Absolutely! | But don't you think that …? |
> Do you really think so/that? | I agree/disagree
> because … | I'm sorry, but I (really) don't agree
> because … | I suppose so, but … |
> Me neither | Me too! | Neither do I | So do I |
> Yes, but what about …? | You're right about
> that … | You've got a point, but …

3 In pairs or groups, answer the questions.

- What was the last school trip you went on?
- What was the best thing about it?

4 In pairs or as a group, make notes about the benefits of the different places for going on a school trip.

1 a theme park
   get to know classmates better

2 a zoo

3 a science museum

4 an adventure activity centre

5 an art gallery

5 Correct the underlined mistakes in the phrases for agreeing and disagreeing.

1 I'm sorry but I don't <u>disagree</u>. ___*agree*___

2 I don't agree with him. <u>So</u> do I. _____

3 But <u>can't</u> you think that … _____

4 You've got a <u>problem</u>, but … _____

5 I <u>agree</u> so, but … _____

6 I think it's a great idea. <u>Neither</u> do I. _____

OPTIMISE YOUR EXAM

Collaborative task

- Use phrases that show you agree, disagree or partly agree with your partner.
- You don't have to agree with your partner. If you don't agree, be polite and then explain why. Give reasons and examples when you talk about your ideas.

6 Talk in pairs for two minutes. Follow the instructions.

Imagine that a secondary school is organising a trip for its students. Talk about what students might learn by going on a school trip to these places.

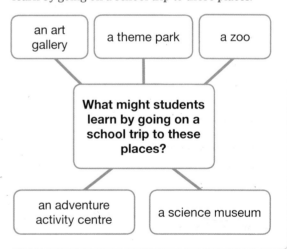

an art gallery · a theme park · a zoo

What might students learn by going on a school trip to these places?

an adventure activity centre · a science museum

7 Talk for a minute and decide which two places would be the best places to visit. Try to disagree with each other about one thing and expand your ideas!

• SAY IT RIGHT

> **Resource centre: Unit 2**
> Stress in phrases for agreeing and disagreeing

1 Look at the words in capitals in Exercise 2 and answer the questions.

Which of them …

1 isn't a noun or a verb? _*adjective*_
2 has a noun form ending in -*ship*? _*championship*_
3 has an adjective form ending in -*ful*? _*successful*_

Word formation

- Always read the whole sentence carefully to see if you need to form a word with a negative meaning, e.g. (*im*)*possibility*, (*dis*)*ability*, (*il*)*logical*, (*un*)*fortunately*.

2 Write a form of the word in capitals in each gap to complete the text.

Feats of memory

How good is your memory? Do you have (1) _*difficulties*_ remembering long strings of numbers? Some people are very good at it. If you're one of them, and if you're (2) _*competitive*_ , you might want to take part in one of the numerous memory (3) _*championships*_ that are held round the world. **DIFFICULT** **COMPETE** **CHAMPION**

You probably recognise this symbol: π. It's a number called pi, which has some interesting (4) _*mathematical*_ properties. Its digits continue for ever (3.14159265 ,…) and don't repeat in a pattern. **MATHS**

Some people have (5) _*successfully*_ managed to memorise a lot of the digits of pi. In 2015, 25-year-old Rajveer Meena remembered 70,000 digits correctly, which took him just over nine hours to recite. **SUCCESS**

Although memorising that amount of (6) _*information*_ may seem absolutely (7) _*unbelievable*_ , there are methods to help you. Memory experts recommend matching each thing you need to remember with a shape or colour or place, and creating a visual (8) _*relation*_ between each one. **INFORM** **BELIEVE** **RELATE**

3 Look at the sentences in Exercise 4 and answer the questions.

1 Which of them rely on knowing the structure *used to* + bare infinitive?

_____

2 Which of them rely on knowing the structure *be/get used* + -*ing* form?

_____

Sentence transformation

- Remember that contracted forms such as *didn't*, *haven't*, etc. count as two words (*did not*, *have not*). The exception is *can't*, which is short for *cannot*.

4 Complete the second sentence so it has a similar meaning to the first. Do not change the word given. Use two to five words, including the word given.

1 In the past, we didn't usually use computers in class. **USE**
We _*didn't use to*_ use computers in class.

2 I thought I'd get the geography prize but I actually got the biology prize. **UP**
I thought I'd get the geography prize but I actually _*ended up with*_ the biology prize.

3 It's been over two years since Sam last took exams. **TAKEN**
Sam _*hasn't taken exams for*_ over two years.

4 They started the aerobics club in the school gym. **UP**
The aerobics club _*was set up*_ in the school gym.

5 It took me about two years to become comfortable with speaking French in public. **USED**
It took me about two years to _*get used to speaking*_ French in public.

6 I don't know how he managed to remember so many numbers. **SUCCEEDED**
I don't know how he _*succeeded in remembering*_ so many numbers.

🌐 THINK | **RESEARCH** | CULTURE | LEARN | ME

Search online to find out about some different ways to improve your memory. Tell the class what you discovered.

1 **In pairs or as a group, answer the questions.**

1 Look at the photos. What is happening?
2 Have you ever taught your parents or other family members anything?

2 **Read this essay and complete the essay question.**

'Teenagers _____ .' Do you agree?

Some people think teenagers are bad at teaching because they are too young and inexperienced. While it's true they are not old enough to work at a school, I would argue that teenagers can teach people many different things.

One area where teenagers often have an advantage over older people is new technology. For example, my parents often ask me for help and advice about smartphones, computers, tablets and apps. Whereas adults sometimes seem to struggle with new gadgets, it seems to me that teenagers understand them almost instantly – and can teach others how to use them.

In my view, another area where teenagers lead the way is in environmental awareness. My friends, for example, understand green issues more than their parents, and are often good at persuading them to change their ways, for instance with recycling. Similarly, teenagers often have specific interests and skills which they can teach. My sister loves fashion, for example, and often helps my dad choose stylish clothes.

In conclusion, I disagree with the idea that teenagers make bad teachers. In my experience, I have seen them successfully teach and influence many people.

3 **Find these phrases in the essay. Tick the ones which highlight that the writer is expressing their own opinion.**

1 Some people ☐
2 I would argue that ☒
3 … it seems to me that ☐
4 In my view, ☐
5 Similarly, ☐
6 In conclusion, ☐
7 I disagree with ☑
8 In my experience, ☑

4 **The writer of the essay expresses opinions and justifies them by giving reasons and examples. In pairs or groups, note down the reasons and examples mentioned.**

main point:	reason and/or example given to justify it:
teenagers are good at teaching	
how to use modern technology	
green issues	
particular interests or skills	

OPTIMISE YOUR **EXAM**

An essay

● When you write an essay, you can use these phrases to show your opinion: *I would argue that, It seems to me, In my view, In my opinion …*

● Try to justify your opinions by giving reasons and/or examples. Some useful words and phrases to connect your ideas are: *because, since, as, this is why, for example, such as, that is …*

5 Look at this writing task. In pairs or as a group, discuss the questions after the task.

In your English class you have been discussing how schools prepare teenagers for the future. Your English teacher has asked you to write an essay for homework.

'Schools don't prepare teenagers well enough to be adults in the modern world.' Do you agree?

Notes
Write about:

1 everyday tasks, such as cooking, car maintenance, etc.
2 getting a job
3 .... (your own idea)

- How well do you think schools prepare teenagers to be adults in the modern world?
  a) extremely well   **b)** well enough   **c)** not well enough

- You have to write about everyday tasks, such as cooking and car maintenance.
  How well do schools prepare people for those kinds of tasks?

- You have to write about the idea of getting a job. What are the main points to make here?

- You have to come up with your own idea too. What could this idea be?

6 Plan Make a paragraph plan.

Part	Purpose	Useful phrases	My notes
Paragraph 1	introduce your essay and state your opinion	I would argue that … It seems to me that … In my view, In my opinion,	
Paragraph 2	your thoughts about how schools prepare students to do everyday tasks	I agree/disagree with … While … Whereas … For example/instance, Similarly,	
Paragraph 3	your thoughts about how schools prepare students to get a job _____ (your own idea)		
Paragraph 4	conclusion	In conclusion, To conclude, To sum up,	

7 Write Write your essay in an appropriate style. Write 140–190 words.

8 Check Before you hand in your essay, complete this checklist.

Checklist ✓

- ◯ I've written at least four paragraphs.
- ◯ I've expressed and justified my opinions.
- ◯ I've discussed the ideas of everyday tasks and getting a job.
- ◯ I've also discussed my own idea.
- ◯ I've concluded my essay appropriately.
- ◯ I've checked my spelling and grammar.

UNITS 1–2

GRAMMAR AND VOCABULARY

1 Write a form of the word in capitals in each gap.

21ST CENTURY SCRABBLE

When the spelling board game Scrabble first made an **(1)** _____ over 70 years ago, it wasn't an immediate **(2)** _____. But over time it has become one of the biggest board games in the world and is now sold in 121 countries. There are many **(3)** _____ and every year the world's best players enter the World Scrabble **(4)** _____.

With the introduction of versions of the game for smartphones and on Facebook, Scrabble's **(5)** _____ has grown with younger players in recent years. It is now possible to play a game against anyone in the world providing both players are connected to the internet.

Why do people get so much **(6)** _____ out of using a few letters to spell out words on a board? Some people **(7)** _____ that Scrabble's winning formula is its simplicity. It doesn't require you to have any **(8)** _____ skills to play the game. In fact, if you can read this text, you can play Scrabble.

APPEAR
SUCCEED
COMPETE
CHAMPION

POPULAR

PLEASE
BELIEF
IMPRESS

___/8

2 Write a form of *do*, *make*, or *take* in each gap.

1 We _____ our time because we wanted to make sure we hadn't made any mistakes.
2 I find having someone to study with really _____ a difference.
3 You _____ your best – now we just have to wait for your exam results.
4 Dan _____ part in a whole range of activities since he joined the club.
5 It was the first time Lauren and Will _____ me such a big favour.

___/5

3 Match 1–5 to a)–f) to make words and phrases. There is one extra word you do not need.

1 screen ___   a) demand
2 special ___   b) buster
3 on ___   c) maker
4 block ___   d) play
5 box ___   e) office
            f) effects

___/5

4 Choose the correct word.

1 They found the programme boring so they turned **over / off** to watch something else.
2 We'd said we'd go to the cinema, but we ended **up / with** just staying in.
3 I'm thinking of **taking / setting** up an online group for people our age who like photography.
4 On Sundays, I usually just hang **off / out** with my friends in the park.
5 Homework takes **up / down** most of my time in the evenings at the moment.
6 You haven't got school tomorrow, so you can **lie / laze** in if you want to.
7 After missing several lessons, it took Angie quite a while to **catch / hold** up.

___/7

5 Write one word in each gap.

1 Can everyone pay careful attention _____ this, please?
2 You can't criticise Lizzie _____ trying her best.
3 My sister's just qualified _____ a dental hygienist.
4 There's nothing wrong _____ using a dictionary if you don't know the meaning of a word.
5 You need to concentrate _____ your studies and spend less time online.
6 I've decided _____ becoming a doctor. I want to be a vet instead.
7 I'm not very experienced _____ organising events, so could you help me?
8 I don't know how you succeeded _____ persuading Adam to lend you his favourite jacket!

___/8

6 Choose the correct word or phrase.

1 The teacher was very angry because **no / none** of the students had done their homework.

2 Have you heard **a / any / many** news about the new games console that's coming out?

3 After spending so much on going out, Lauren's got **few / a few / little** money left over to buy new trainers.

4 I think **all / all of** young people would benefit from getting involved in drama.

5 I have enough free time for **either / either of** a sport or going to Zumba tonight, but not both.

___/5

7 Complete the second sentence so it has a similar meaning to the first. Do not change the word given. Use two to five words, including the word given.

1 Not many people came to the party.   **ONLY**
There _____ people at the party.

2 For a long time, Emma found living in a foreign country difficult.   **USED**
It took a long time for Emma _____ in a foreign country.

3 It was my second time in a helicopter.   **BEEN**
It was the _____ in a helicopter.

4 Do you really think that aliens exist?   **EXISTENCE**
Do you really believe _____ aliens?

5 If you really try hard, you'll succeed.   **EFFORT**
If you really _____ , you'll succeed.

6 I'm trying to think of a good excuse!   **COME**
I'm trying to _____ a good excuse!

___/12

Total score   ___/50

▼

EXAM SKILLS

Tick the statements that are true for you. Review the skills in the unit if you need more help.

I can …	Unit/page
☐ understand pronoun references in a magazine article	Unit 1 p4
☐ predict missing information in a short talk	Unit 1 p8
☐ talk about habits and routines	Unit 1 p10
☐ identify negative forms and decide which kind of word is missing	Unit 1 p11
☐ create an appropriate style in an article	Unit 1 p12
☐ deduce meaning from context in an online article	Unit 2 p14
☐ listen for agreement and disagreement in conversations	Unit 2 p18
☐ use phrases for agreeing and disagreeing in a collaborative task	Unit 2 p20
☐ understand negative forms and remember that contracted forms are generally two words	Unit 2 p21
☐ express and justify opinions in an essay	Unit 2 p22

READING | Multiple matching | A science article

1 In pairs or as a group, answer the questions.

1 Think of some famous inventors and their inventions.

2 What are some of the best inventions of the last 50 years? Write them here.

_____

_____

_____

2 Read the text quickly. Choose the best heading for each paragraph.

1 Paragraph A:
Light power / Heat power

2 Paragraph B:
A new medicine / A new way to get medicine

3 Paragraph C:
A new way to speak / A new way to hear

4 Paragraph D:
Better protection / Better behaviour

3 Decide if each idea is mentioned in the paragraph or not. Write *Yes* or *No*.

1 Paragraph A:
when she had the initial idea _____

2 Paragraph B:
how long it took her to create the invention _____

3 Paragraph C:
how much the invention costs _____

4 Paragraph D:
what inspired his idea _____

OPTIMISE YOUR EXAM

Multiple matching

● Read each question carefully, then scan from the start of the text looking for information connected to each question. Then read that section more carefully to make sure it answers the question.

● Be careful! Some words in the questions may be exactly the same as words in the text. For example, the word 'beneficial' appears in question 1 and Paragraph B – but this might not help you choose the right answer.

YOUNG INVENTORS

Four young people are leading the way with their new inventions.

A ANN MAKOSINSKI

Ann Makosinski has been creating useful 'clean technology' gadgets for several years. At just 15, Ann brought out the Hollow Flashlight, a torch powered by the heat of someone's hand, which won her a prestigious award at the Google Science Fair. The inspiration for the invention came from a friend in the Philippines, who found it difficult to do homework in the evening because they didn't have electricity at home. Ann has described her eureka moment: 'I thought, why not body heat? We have so much heat radiating out of us and it's being wasted.' It then took months of hard work designing and fine-tuning the torch before she had a working model. Now, Ann is taking her ground-breaking technology one stage further. Her latest invention, the E-Drink, allows devices such as mobile phones to be charged using nothing more than the heat generated from a hot drink.

C ARSH SHAH DILBAGI

It's been estimated that nearly 1.5% of the human population has some kind of medical condition prohibiting them from communicating verbally. Many of them, such as the world-famous scientist Stephen Hawking, use devices to create artificial speech. However, these are often expensive, bulky and slow. 19-year-old **Arsh Shah Dilbagi** thinks he has the solution. Arsh's invention, called TALK, converts human breath into language. Users breathe into a microphone, essentially creating dots and dashes, as in Morse Code. The system recognises the code and converts it to words, which are then spoken out loud by the machine. Arsh believes his system is three times faster than existing devices which rely on tracking eye movement, and much more affordable. He's under no illusions how beneficial this could be, describing it as having 'the potential to change the world'.

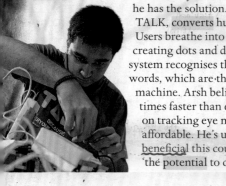

B KYLIE SIMONDS

Kylie Simonds is the 14-year-old inventor of the I-Pack. This colourful, lightweight and practical backpack is specifically designed for seriously ill children who have to receive medicine intravenously (in other words, via a needle into the blood stream). Kylie knows all too well what this experience is like: three years ago she was diagnosed with cancer. While receiving her IV (intravenous) medicine, Kylie had to push a heavy metal pole around. This held the IV bag, and had wires dangling which were easy to trip over. Now recovering from her ordeal, Kylie wants to make life easier for children in a similar situation. Her design has won praise from medical practitioners and patients. Kylie's currently raising the money required to manufacture the I-Pack commercially.

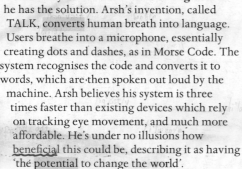

D RYAN BECK

In certain sports such as ice hockey or American football, players wear head protection such as helmets in order to prevent serious injury to the head in the event of a fall or blow. However, head injuries and concussion are, unfortunately, still common problems for helmet-wearers – as 16-year-old **Ryan Beck**, from San Diego, USA, recognised while he was watching a particularly vicious game of American football. It was this particular game which inspired him to develop a safer and stronger kind of helmet, offering greater protection to the part of the brain called the 'temporal lobe' in the case of a head-on collision during a game. The secret is in a layer of external padding made of a particular kind of foam, which is then covered in neoprene (the same type of rubber which is used to make wetsuits). Ryan's helmet could reduce the impact on the brain by as much as 55%. He's considering patenting his invention to protect his idea.

4 🔊 1.12 **Read the text. For each question, choose from the people A–D. The people may be chosen more than once.**

Which person

would have personally found their invention beneficial?	1
proudly claims that their invention is extremely important?	2
has received approval from people working within the relevant industry ?	3
witnessed aggression, which then inspired their invention?	4
needed time and effort to put their idea into practice?	5
created something based on a much older means of communication?	6
has focused on increasing speed and reducing cost?	7
received a prize for their contribution to technology?	8
has developed something which improves safety through increased strength?	9
wanted to find a solution for a particular person's problem?	10

5 **Find these words and phrases in the text. Work out what they mean from the context.**

bulky (adj)	converts (v)	collision (n)
dangling (v)	eureka moment (n)
fine-tuning (n)	ground-breaking (adj)
impact (n)	ordeal (n)	patenting (v)
potential (n)

THINK | RESEARCH | CULTURE | LEARN | ME

Which of the inventions do you think is the most useful?

In which area (e.g. health, sport) would you like to invent something that could change the world?

▶ **Workbook Unit 3:** Reading, pages 20–21, exercises 1, 2, 3

Grammar in context

Find these extracts in the text on page 27. Explain why each verb in bold is in a continuous tense.

1 *Ann Makosinski **has been creating** useful 'clean technology' gadgets for several years.*

2 *… as 16-year-old Ryan Beck recognised while he **was watching** a particularly vicious game of American football.*

REMEMBER

We use continuous tenses for:

● actions or situations in progress at a particular moment – *What **were** you **doing** when I called?*

● temporary actions or situations – *I'm **living** here for a few months.*

● unfinished actions or situations – *I've **been working** on a new invention recently.*

● annoying habits – *You're always **criticising** me.*

● events continuing up to a particular moment or stopping just before it – *I'm tired because I've **been studying** all evening.*

▶ See Grammar reference, Unit 3, page 150

---

1 **If a tense in bold is correct, put a tick. If it's incorrect, write the correct tense and explain why.**

1 What **is** Sally **doing** with that machine?
_____

2 You look out of breath. **Have** you **run**?
_____

3 I**'m studying** graphic design for six months now.
_____

4 When we were children, my brother **was** always **play** tricks on me. _____

5 They**'ve been creating** a new version of the iPhone at the moment. _____

6 When I finally succeeded, I **had been trying** to build a time machine for over a decade.
_____

2 **Choose the correct word to complete the dialogue.**

Anna: How are your computer coding lessons going?

Beth: Oh, great! I **(1) have / has** been working on something really interesting lately.

Anna: That's good. The last time we spoke you **(2) was / had** been getting a bit bored with computing.

Beth: Well, you know I **(3) were / was** thinking about giving it up. I'm definitely staying for this new project!

Anna: What is it?

Beth: We **(4) have / had** been building a new app for young inventors. It **(5) guides / guided** you through turning your ideas into reality, how to approach companies, that kind of thing.

Anna: That sounds really interesting. You know, I **(6) was / have** been thinking recently about inventing something myself. It must be great to come up with something new.

Beth: I've met some fantastic young inventors through it. Most of them **(7) have / were** been working on their ideas for months, and sometimes years. And now they **(8) is / are** getting the rewards for their efforts. Amazing, really.

Anna: Cool! Let me know when it's finished and I'll download it!

3 **Choose the best form of the verb to complete each gap.**

Japan's robot hotel

If you **(1)** ____ developments in the world of robotics recently, you'll know that Japan is a world leader in this field. No surprise, then, that someone in Japan has come up with the world's first hotel run entirely by robots!

You may **(2)** ____ how guests check in, check out and do all the things that normally require a human behind the desk at reception. First of all, guests who **(3)** ____ use a computer terminal with face recognition technology. A robot receptionist **(4)** ____ by to help in case of problems and there's even an English-speaking dinosaur robot! Next, a robot porter **(5)** ____ your bags to your room, where a personal assistant in the shape of a flower (called Tuly) **(6)** ____ to adjust the lights, tell you the time and give you the weather forecast. The room automatically adjusts the heating by detecting how hot you **(7)** ____ . And a room only costs £46 a night!

1 **A** have been following	**B** follow
C are following	
2 **A** wondering	**B** be wondering
C been wondering	
3 **A** checked in	**B** were checking in
C are checking in	
4 **A** was standing	**B** is standing
C has been standing	
5 **A** is taking	**B** takes
C has been taking	
6 **A** be waiting	**B** is waiting
C had been waiting	
7 **A** feeling	**B** have been feeling
C are feeling	

Words connected with *manufacturing* and *tools*

1 ◁)) 1.13 **Write a verb from the box in the correct form to complete each sentence. There may be more than one correct answer for some gaps. Listen and check.**

> create | develop | discover
> generate | invent | manufacture

1 Do you know who first _invented_ that magnetism and electricity are connected?

2 How much energy does a solar panel _generate_ ?

3 The bikes are _manufactured_ in a factory in Taiwan and then shipped to Europe.

4 We had a competition to see who could _create_ the best app.

5 It's a good idea, but you need to _develop_ the product further before you can sell it.

6 I'd love someone to _invent_ an app that did all your homework for you.

2 ◁)) 1.14 **Write a word or phrase from the box in the correct form to complete each sentence. Listen and check.**

> appliance | engine | machine
> motor | remote control | tool

1 The plane is powered by four enormous jet _engines_ .

2 The bikes used in the city's cycle hire scheme are powered by an electric _motor_ .

3 Oh no! My bottle of water is stuck inside the vending _machine_ .

4 Can you pass me the _remote control_ ? I want to change the channel.

5 The _tool_ box had a hammer, a screwdriver and a saw for doing jobs around the house.

6 The company manufactures a number of kitchen _appliances_ , including fridges and cookers.

Phrasal verbs

3 ◁)) 1.15 **Write a phrasal verb from the box in the correct form in each gap so that the second sentence has a similar meaning to the first. Use any other necessary words. Listen and check.**

> carry out | come on | come up with
> figure out | look into | plug in

1 I couldn't understand how the app worked at first, but now I've got it.
I wasn't able _to figure out_ how the app worked at first, but now I've got it.

2 The machine won't work without electricity!
The machine won't work if you don't _plug it in_ first!

3 The source of the radiation is being investigated by physicists.
Physicists _are looking into_ the source of the radiation.

4 The project's developing nicely – I'm very optimistic.
The project's _coming on_ nicely – I'm very optimistic.

5 They do a number of tests on the equipment to check that it's safe to use.
A number of tests _are being carried out_ on the equipment to check that it's safe to use.

6 Who had such a brilliant idea first?
Who _came up with_ such a brilliant idea first?

Collocations with *top* and *high*

4 ◁)) 1.16 **Write *top* or *high* in each gap to complete the sentences. If both words are possible, write *top/high*. Listen and check.**

1 Dan loves _____-tech equipment and is always buying the latest gadgets.

2 This information's _____ secret so don't tell anyone what you've seen.

3 The Nobel Prizes in physics and chemistry are two of the _____ *awards* in science.

4 The engine's very _____-powered, but extremely quiet.

5 The car has a _____ *speed* of about 200 km/h, but you can't drive at _____ *speed* on the roads round here!

6 My dad's company designs _____ -performance software for NASA's spacecraft.

7 I love watching movies on our new _____-definition TV.

8 It's _____ time I got my invention manufactured and sold – in fact, it's now a _____ priority.

1 Read the advert for a TV programme and ask and answer the questions.

ay April 14th, 2017

0	8:00	8:3
nel 2	**Invest in Me!** Series 3 – episode 4 Four more young entrepreneurs present their new inventions to the expert panel, hoping to attract an investment. **INVEST IN ME!**	**Co** In th find entre with for th char be v the g busi lead moc
nel 3	**Culture tonight** Myriam Cottley explores the impact of the Futurists.	

1 How do you think people convince the investors to invest in their inventions?
2 Why do you think some inventions might be more successful than others?

2 🔊 1.17 Listen to six people expressing their opinion. Decide whether each statement is T (True) or F (False).

1	Speaker 1 is uncertain what her own opinion is.	T / F
2	Speaker 2 is expressing surprise about a situation.	T / F
3	Speaker 3 says she doesn't like something.	T / F
4	Speaker 4 says that he sometimes changes his mind.	T / F
5	Speaker 5 is making a suggestion.	T / F
6	Speaker 6 admits he has problems coming up with ideas.	T / F

3 🔊 1.17 Listen again and complete the phrases.

1 I'm not _____ that …
2 I'd be _____ if …
3 I'm not particularly _____ on … / … it doesn't really _____ to me.
4 I _____ to think that …
5 I _____ if …
6 I can't _____ why …

4 Match expressions 1–8 that have the same meaning as phrases A–H in Exercise 5. Think of other ways to express the same ideas.

1 how simple it is to operate ____
2 you can carry it around easily ____
3 the product selection on offer can be developed ____
4 it's not expensive ____
5 you'll be able to buy it in different countries ____
6 it's an answer to several issues ____
7 people use top-class products to make it ____
8 how it looks ____

▼
OPTIMISE YOUR **EXAM**

Multiple matching
- Make sure you read the instructions carefully. For example, in Exercise 5, you have to choose what each speaker likes <u>most</u> from the list A–H.
- It's very possible that a speaker will like a number of things in the list. Listen carefully for them to say or suggest that they like one aspect more than the others.

▼
5 🔊 1.18 You will hear five people on a TV programme talking about an invention. Choose from A–H what each speaker likes most about it. There are three extra letters you do not need.

A how easy it is to use
B its appearance
C the quality of the materials used in its production
D how affordable it is
E the possibility of selling it abroad
F how it can expand into a wider range of products
G how it solves a number of problems
H that it's portable

Speaker 1: ☐
Speaker 2: ☐
Speaker 3: ☐
Speaker 4: ☐
Speaker 5: ☐

6 🔊 1.18 Listen again and check your answers to Exercise 5.

THINK | RESEARCH | CULTURE | LEARN | ME

In pairs, come up with an invention to present to the experts. What is it? Why is it a good invention? Who is it for?

Grammar in context

Look at these sentences from the audio in the listening lesson. Underline any comparatives and superlatives. Explain what is being compared in each case.

1 *I wonder if your product would be better if it was more portable.*

2 *Invest in Me! is a great programme to watch, but I'm not sure that it's the best way of finding businesses to invest in.*

1 Write a comparative or superlative form of the word given in each gap. Add any other words you need.

1 My new laptop seems to be _____ slower than _____ (**slow**) my old one.

2 I always try to keep up with ___ the latest ___ (**late**) developments in the world of technology.

3 What do you think is ___ the most useful ___ (**useful**) invention of the last ten years?

4 I decided to get ___ the least expensive ___ (**expensive**) tablet I could find in order to save money.

5 Kate figured out how to work the app easily. She thought it would be ___ more difficult ___ (**difficult**).

6 I think that's _____ (**bad**) idea I've ever heard of!

7 If you're in a hurry, you can travel a lot _____ (**far**) in a car than on a bike.

2 Complete the second sentence so it has a similar meaning to the first. Do not change the word given. Use two to five words, including the word given.

1 I've never heard such a good idea as that for helping people in developing countries! **EVER**

That's the ___ best idea that I've ever ___ heard for helping people in developing countries!

2 This is the coolest phone I've ever owned by far. **MUCH**

This phone ___ is much cooler than ___ all the others I've ever owned.

3 Nobody I know has Olivia's talent for programming computers. **THE**

Olivia is ___ the most talented ___ computer programmer I know.

4 Thomas Edison enjoyed more success than other inventors. **SUCCESSFUL**

Other inventors ___ enjoyed less successful than ___ Thomas Edison. were less

5 Jake works much faster than anyone else in the group. **AS**

Nobody in the group ___ works as fast as ___ Jake does.

3 Write a comparative or superlative form of a word in the box in each gap. Add any other words you need.

| healthy | late | long | poor |
| simple | small | well | wide |

THE SHOE THAT GROWS

When we think of technology, we tend to think of (**1**) ___ the latest ___ high-tech digital gadgets. However, in the developing world, much (**2**) _____ inventions are making a real difference to people's lives. One example is The Shoe That Grows. A common problem for children is that as their feet grow, they outgrow their shoes and need another pair. However, children in (**3**) _____ communities can't afford new shoes and so they often wear shoes that are (**4**) _____ their feet, causing a number of problems. That's where The Shoe That Grows comes in.

The design is basically a rubber and leather sandal with press studs. As the child's feet grow, the press studs can be adjusted to increase the length of the shoe. They can also make the shoe (**5**) _____ across the middle. In this way, the shoe can fit up to five sizes and last up to five years. That's much (**6**) _____ a traditional pair of shoes.

Not only that, but because a number of diseases can be passed on through not wearing shoes, The Shoe That Grows means that kids are (**7**) _____ . Simple but thoughtful inventions like these can help poor young people to live (**8**) _____ in many parts of the world.

It's far better than …

Flipped classroom

1 ⊳ Watch the *Talk2Me* video and answer the questions.

1 What gadgets do the people have at home? How often do they use them?

2 What advantages and disadvantages of technology and gadgets do they mention?

3 Tick the adjectives that are mentioned by the people on the video.

angry	annoyed	bored	excited
fed up	happy	lonely	stressed

2 ⊳ Watch the video again. Number the phrases in the *Phrase expert* box in the order you hear them.

PHRASE EXPERT

however | I think the people are feeling (excited) because … | It's as … as … | It's far better than … | It's (far) more/less than … | There aren't **as** (many people here) **as** … | (This) is better **than** / more stressful **than** … | whereas | while

---

3 In pairs or groups, answer the questions.

- What gadgets do you have at home?
- How much time do you spend on your mobile phone every day? What do you use it for?
- Do you stay up late chatting to your friends on social media?
- What are the advantages and disadvantages of using technology?

4 Write a word or short phrase from the *Phrase expert* box in each gap to complete the phrases.

1 It's _____ easier to type messages on my phone than on yours.

2 The Wi-Fi connection here isn't _____ fast _____ the connection at home.

3 I think the small headphones deliver a better sound _____ the bigger ones are cheaper.

4 I definitely spend _____ time playing videogames than I used to. I hardly ever use my games console now.

5 The silver smartwatch is _____ _____ expensive than the black one. I don't have the money for the black one.

5 In pairs, look at these two photographs which show people using different kinds of technology. Make notes to complete the chart.

A

B

	PHOTO A	PHOTO B
Briefly describe the photos you are about to compare	In the first photo …	In the second photo …
Are there any similarities between the photos?		
Are there any differences between the photos?		
How do you think the people might feel? Think of adjectives to describe feelings		

OPTIMISE YOUR EXAM

Photo task

- Remember, in an exam you need to compare the photos and not describe them in detail. Give a short description of what you can see and then find two or three similarities or differences between them.

- Make sure you answer the question with the photos. You may have to say how you think the people are feeling.

6 In pairs, take turns to compare the photos in Exercise 5 and say how you think the people in the photos might be feeling. Ask your partner to time you for one minute.

SAY IT RIGHT

Resource centre: Unit 3
Stress in comparatives

1 Look at the words in capitals in Exercise 2 and answer the questions.

Which of them …
1 have a noun form ending in *-ion*? _____
2 have a noun form that is a person? _____
3 have an adverb form? _____

OPTIMISE YOUR EXAM

Word formation

● If you need to form a noun, check whether it's countable or uncountable. If it's countable, decide whether you need the singular or plural form.

2 Write a form of the word in capitals in each gap to complete the text.

This week's weird and wonderful inventions

Here at *CrazyTech* magazine, we know there are (1) _____ everywhere who, after a hard day finding (2) _____ to serious problems, sit back and have some fun. For this reason, we never cease in our (3) _____ of the far corners of the internet, looking for their fabulous gadgets and weird inventions. This week, we bring you two of the latest inventions.

SCIENCE
SOLVE
EXPLORE

This first invention is a real (4) _____ : the Ping Pong Door, which comes from the hugely (5) _____ mind of designer Tobias Fränzel. It's a real door that opens and closes, but it also folds down to reveal a table tennis table. Innovative!

ACHIEVE
CREATE

We're not so sure about our second (6) _____ : plastic Pen Cap Eating Utensils. Designed for students and office workers who eat at their desks, there's a knife, a fork and a spoon pen cap. You (7) _____ put them on the end of a biro to create what you need to eat your meal. Is the inventor the saviour of working lunches? Sadly, and (8) _____ , we're not convinced.

DISCOVER

SIMPLE
FORTUNATE

3 Look at the gaps and options in Exercise 4. Which of them need phrasal verbs to get the right answer?

_____

OPTIMISE YOUR EXAM

Multiple-choice cloze

● Check the words after the gap carefully. If there is a preposition and the options are verbs, you may need to choose a phrasal verb or decide which option can be followed by that preposition.

4 Choose the correct word to fill each gap.

Daedalus and Icarus

The story of Daedalus and Icarus is very well known. Icarus thought he was invincible, but flew too close to the sun. His wings made of wax and feathers melted, and he crashed into the sea and drowned. He died because he'd been too (1) ____ and self-confident.

But it's important not to forget Icarus' father Daedalus, who was one of the greatest inventors in Greek mythology. It was Daedalus who (2) ____ up with the idea of making wings out of feathers. He was in a difficult (3) ____ with his son on Crete, and they had to escape from the island as a top (4) ____ . He (5) ____ out that the only way to leave the island was to fly. Daedalus was responsible for the (6) ____ of the wings, and although Icarus didn't survive the (7) ____ , it needs to be remembered that Daedalus did. He landed safely because he'd understood the physics, firmly (8) ____ Icarus from flying too high. Unfortunately, Icarus didn't listen.

1	**A** superior	**B** proud
	C high-powered	**D** extraordinary
2	**A** came	**B** made
	C went	**D** did
3	**A** complaint	**B** state
	C condition	**D** situation
4	**A** value	**B** importance
	C significance	**D** priority
5	**A** estimated	**B** calculated
	C figured	**D** computed
6	**A** production	**B** conclusion
	C cause	**D** fashion
7	**A** trial	**B** ordeal
	C test	**D** suffering
8	**A** excluding	**B** prohibiting
	C rejecting	**D** dismissing

1 In pairs or as a group, answer the questions.

1 When you buy something, such as a new gadget, how do you reach your decision? (*design, features, price*, etc.)

2 When you buy something new, how important to you are recommendations from family and friends?

2 Read this review and answer the questions in your own words.

THE ECLIPSE 2 SMARTWATCH:
THE NEXT GENERATION

I've had an Eclipse 2 Smartwatch for a few months now. I've tried out all the features and I'd like to share some of my thoughts and maybe help you decide whether to buy one or not. It's a fantastic gadget, although it's not all good news.

First of all, the advantages. It's faster than the Eclipse 1 and has an even more modern-looking design. You'll find the biggest upgrade, though, through the addition of the camera. It really is the best on the market. With the built-in HD camera, you can capture all the detail you need, even in low light. It's perfect for those all-important selfies!

There is a downside to this watch, though. It's slightly wider than other similar smartwatches. It might not seem like a big difference at first, but you'll notice it after you've been wearing it for a while.

On the whole, the Eclipse 2 is a very good smartwatch. It's particularly suitable for people interested in photography. I'm happy to recommend it, especially if you're one of those people who are snap happy.

1 What is the best feature of this watch, and why?

2 What is the worst feature of this watch, and why?

3 Who does the writer recommend the watch to?

3 Find words and phrases in the review that mean the same as these words and phrases.

1 ... there are some negative points.
(paragraph 1) _____

2 ... the positive points.
(paragraph 2) _____

3 There is one disadvantage ...
(paragraph 3) _____

4 Generally, ...
(paragraph 4) _____

5 It's ideal for ...
(paragraph 4) _____

4 Read these recommendations and decide what kind of device each one might be referring to. Then compare your answers with a partner.

1 I'm happy to recommend this device for people who need to work when they are travelling.
_____

2 I would recommend it for people who lead an active lifestyle. _____

3 This device is suitable for anyone who travels and likes reading. _____

4 People who are interested in music will find this device very interesting and easy to use.
_____

5 This device is ideal for drivers who like to know where they are at a glance. _____

5 Underline the expressions in Exercise 4 that you can use to make recommendations for any device.

OPTIMISE YOUR EXAM

A review

● When you are reviewing a product, you need to describe the key positive and negative features.

● The key features might include use, size and weight, technical details and other functions.

● Make a clear recommendation to the reader based on one or two key features.

6 Look at this writing task and make notes to answer the questions. Use your imagination if necessary.

You see this advert in an English-language magazine for young people.

> ### REVIEWS WANTED!
>
> The Latest Gadgets
>
> Our next issue is all about the latest gadgets and we want your reviews! Write a review of a device you've bought or used recently. Your review should include information about the device, its features, and other relevant information. Would you recommend this device to other people your age?
>
> We'll use the best reviews in our next issue!

Write your **review**.

- What device are you going to review?
  _____

- What is the single best feature of the device?
  _____

- Why is that a useful feature?
  _____

- What is the single worst feature of the device?
  _____

- Why is that a problem?
  _____

- Who would you recommend the device for?
  _____

7 Plan   Make a paragraph plan.

Part	Purpose	Useful phrases	My notes
Title	name the device and add a short phrase that summarises your opinion		
Paragraph 1	introduce the device, and describe your experience of it	*I've used this device for …*	
Paragraph 2	describe the best feature of the device, giving details, and saying why it's useful	*The big advantage of this device is …* *One of the positive features of this device is …*	
Paragraph 3	describe the worst feature of the device, giving details, and saying why it's a problem	*Unfortunately, one of the minuses is …* *On the downside, this device …*	
Paragraph 4	say if you recommend the device and who you recommend it for	*In conclusion,* *To conclude,* *To sum up,*	

8 Write   Write your review in an appropriate style. Write 140–190 words.

9 Check   Before you hand in your review, complete this checklist.

Checklist ✓

- ◯ I've given my review a title.
- ◯ I've written at least four paragraphs.
- ◯ I've described the key positive and negative points of the device.
- ◯ I've said who should and/or shouldn't use this device.
- ◯ I've checked my spelling and grammar.

4 Crime doesn't pay

READING | Questions with short answers | A news article

1 **In pairs or as a group, answer the questions.**

1 Is crime a problem in your area/country? If so, what kinds of crime exist?

2 What are the main ways of preventing crime?

2 **Read the article quickly. Choose the best summary for each paragraph.**

Paragraph 1:
an intriguing experiment / an impossible idea

Paragraph 2:
the reasons for bad behaviour / public versus private behaviour

Paragraph 3:
an improvement to a system / taking an expensive risk

Paragraph 4:
forms of social pressure / copying the insects

Paragraph 5:
more police in stores / not an isolated example

Paragraph 6:
moving the problem elsewhere / comparing this to other solutions

3 **Find and underline these words and phrases in the questions in Exercise 4. Choose two synonyms for each word or phrase.**

1 perceived
   a) seen   b) considered   c) expressed

2 exert control
   a) limit   b) regulate   c) approve

3 put off
   a) discourage   b) happen   c) deter

4 drop
   a) decrease   b) reduce   c) increase

5 rates
   a) solutions   b) levels   c) amounts

OPTIMISE YOUR EXAM

Questions with short answers

● Look for words and phrases in the text with a similar meaning to key words and phrases from the question. This will help you find the approximate location of the answer to the question.

● Then read that section in the text very carefully, thinking about the question. Write a short phrase that answers the question.

Has someone got their eye on you?

Can a simple poster help to prevent crime? **Michelle Moran** investigates.

CYCLE THIEVES
WE ARE WATCHING YOU

Newcastle University Estate
Security Service in partnership
with Northumbria Police   **OPERATION CRACKDOWN**

Does your behaviour change when you think other people are watching you? That's the question scientists expected to answer in a recent experiment that took place at Newcastle University in the north-east of England. The experiment involved scientists putting posters of eyes over bicycle racks to deter thieves from stealing the bikes. Some people were sceptical that such simple measures would make people change their behaviour. So why did the researchers think that a poster might prevent another crime wave where other crime prevention measures had failed?

People generally prefer to be seen as honest and trustworthy, even when they don't always behave that way. When other people are watching us, we tend to act in a certain way, otherwise people might judge us negatively. However, when we think we are unobserved, some of us may risk doing something that we wouldn't necessarily want other people to see us doing.

A good example of this is an honesty box. This is when a place such as a canteen provides drinks and snacks, together with a list of prices, but no-one is there to collect the money. They expect you to be honest and pay for whatever you take by putting money into a box. But what do you think happens when you put a picture of staring eyes above the box? Dr Melissa Bateson, a behavioural biologist, did just that in an experiment and found that people tended to put almost three times as much money in the box when there was a picture of eyes above it!

The basis of our reaction seems to be the fact that humans are social beings. Throughout history, people in communities have been regulated through the approval and disapproval of fellow members. When we are seen to go against the rules of society, we feel a sense of shame. This instinct is so powerful that it works on us even in the case of the honesty box and the eyes, when we know consciously that the eyes are merely a picture. Another possibility is that staring eyes remind us of the eyes of dangerous animals, and that this prevents us from breaking the rules. It's a strategy that a number of birds and insects use in the wild. The 'eyes' on some butterflies' wings, for instance, may mimic the eyes of a predator and so deter birds from eating the butterflies.

In the experiment with bicycle theft, the results seemed to confirm Dr Bateson's research. Those bicycle racks which had eye posters over them saw a 62% drop in incidents. This was without also having to take precautions such as the use of CCTV cameras or other measures to tackle crime. A similar principle is at work when supermarkets place a cardboard cut-out of a police officer in certain parts of the store or at the entrance to deter criminals. In those cases, there's a 75% reduction in shoplifting offences. As a consequence of the success of such approaches, it's possible that in the future we'll see pictures of eyes on, for example, speed camera warnings, which would encourage drivers to react more quickly.

However, before we start thinking that posters and cardboard cut-outs are going to prevent all crime, it's important to note something else that happened in the Newcastle University experiment. Other bicycle racks, without posters of eyes, were used for comparison. There, the crime rate increased by 63%, implying that the crime hadn't been prevented but had been relocated to other parts of the campus. Still, as part of a range of crime prevention measures, it is remarkable that something as simple as a poster can achieve such significant results. Perhaps next time you'll know what's going on when you see a poster of eyes staring down at you from a wall.

---

4 🔊 1.19 **For each question, write a short answer using a maximum of four words.**

1 How do people usually want to be perceived by others?

_____

2 How do groups of people often exert control over members of the group?

_____

3 What illusion may put birds off from eating some insects?

_____

4 What may drop by three quarters because of a fake human figure?

_____

5 What happened to rates of theft in other areas of the university?

_____

5 **Complete this summary with highlighted words or phrases from the article. You may need to change the form. Explain what each word or phrase means.**

At Newcastle University, an experiment was carried out to see if a poster with eyes on it would (1) _____ thieves from taking bicycles. It seemed to work, perhaps based on the way members of a (2) _____ control the behaviour of others. We have a strong (3) _____ to follow rules when we think we are being watched. Similarly, it's also possible that animals in the wild may feel that a (4) _____ is watching them. Results like this (5) _____ the results of other experiments, even though the scientists didn't (6) _____ _____ that might help, like using (7) _____ . It's not clear whether these posters affect the overall (8) _____ _____ .

Grammar in context

Look at these extracts from the article on page 37 and answer the questions.

However, before we start thinking that posters and cardboard cut-outs are going to prevent all crime …

1 Would it be correct to say *will* instead of *are going to*?

2 Would it be correct to say *are preventing* instead of *are going to prevent*?

Perhaps next time you'll know what's going on when you see a poster of eyes staring down at you from a wall.

3 Would it be correct to say *will see* instead of *see*?

✓ **REMEMBER**

● We use *will* for predictions based on knowledge/experience, decisions made at the moment of speaking, and to make offers, requests, promises and refusals (*won't*) – '*Will* you hide this for me?' 'No, I *won't!*'

● We use *shall* to make offers and suggestions and ask for advice in the question form – *Shall* I call the police?

● We use *be going to* for predictions based on evidence we can see – *Look! I think they're going to arrest him!*, and intentions – *I'm going to be a detective when I'm older.*

● We use present continuous for arrangements – *The police are coming round at 2 o'clock to interview the victim.*

● We use present simple for timetabled and scheduled events – *The workshop on crime prevention starts at 7 pm tomorrow evening.*

● After time words and phrases such as *as soon as*, *before, once, the moment that, unless, until, when,* we use present simple or present perfect.

▶ See Grammar reference, Unit 4, page 151

---

1 **If a tense in bold is correct, put a tick. If it's incorrect, write the correct tense and explain why.**

1 That documentary about the police **starts** at 8:30 pm, not 8 pm. _____

2 When I'm older, I**'m studying** forensic science. _____

3 Look! It looks like he **will steal** that woman's handbag any moment. _____

4 Let's do a project on crime prevention, **shall** we? _____

5 No, I **don't drive** faster. That's illegal round here. _____

6 **Will** I **check** that all the doors are locked properly? _____

---

2 **Rewrite the pair of sentences as one sentence, using the word or phrase given.**

We'll find the thief. Then we'll call you.

Example: when *We'll call you when we find the thief.*

1 once _____

2 the moment that _____

3 as soon as _____

4 until _____

✓ **REMEMBER**

● We use future continuous (*will/won't + be + -ing*) to talk about actions in progress at a point in the future – *What will you be doing this time next week?*

● We use future perfect simple (*will/won't + have + past participle*) to talk about actions completed some time between now and a point in the future. – *I'll have finished my project on famous unsolved crimes by the end of tomorrow.*

● We use future perfect continuous (*will/won't + have been + -ing*) to talk about actions happening up to a point in the future – *At the end of next month, Dad will have been working as a prison officer for exactly ten years.*

▶ See Grammar reference, Unit 4, page 151

---

3 **Put the verbs into the correct tense. There may be more than one correct answer for some gaps.**

My older brother, Jamie, is a huge fan of all the CSI TV series. It doesn't matter how old the episodes are, or how many times he's seen them. In fact, he reckons that by the end of this year, he (**1**)_____ (**see**) every episode at least twice.

This weekend, his best friend Luke (**2**)_____ (**come**) over for a 'CSI marathon session'. In other words, they (**3**)_____ (**watch**) episodes of CSI all weekend. By this time on Saturday, they (**4**)_____ (**already / finish**) at least one box set! I think they (**5**)_____ (**survive**) on pizzas and takeaway meals and I'm sure they (**6**)_____ (**do**) any homework all weekend. My dad knows all about Jamie's CSI obsession so he (**7**)_____ (**not / be**) too annoyed – as long as it doesn't happen every weekend! Basically, by the end of the weekend, Jamie and Luke (**8**)_____ (**watch**) CSI non-stop for about 36 hours!

Words connected with *law* and *order*

1 🔊 1.20 **Write a word from the box in each gap to complete the text. Listen and check.**

> accused | evidence | fine | guilty
> imprisonment | judge | jury
> justice | trial | verdict | victim

The (**1**)_____ system in the UK plays an important role in society. When the (**2**)_____ of a crime reports it to the police, they must then decide if there is enough (**3**)_____ to charge someone with that crime. If there is, then it may lead to a (**4**)_____ . In serious cases, a (**5**)_____ (which consists of 12 ordinary citizens) decides whether the (**6**)_____ is (**7**)_____ or not. Depending on this (**8**)_____ , a (**9**)_____ then either releases the defendant or sentences them. This could mean (**10**)_____ for a certain length of time, or a (**11**)_____ , or both.

Phrasal verbs

2 🔊 1.21 **If a word in bold is correct, put a tick. If it's incorrect, write the correct word. Listen and check.**

1 When her photo appeared on the internet, the thief decided to go to the police station and *turn* herself **in**. _____
2 Armed robbers *held* the bank **off** and stole thousands of pounds in cash. _____
3 Police are appealing for members of the public who have any information about the crime to *come* **forward**. _____
4 The guilty man was lucky to be *let* **up** with just a fine. _____
5 After escaping from prison, she *made* **for** the coast where she could hide. _____
6 'You'll never *get* **on** *with* this!' I shouted after the thief. _____
7 Police are looking for two men who *beat* **up** a young man and stole his phone. _____
8 The burglars obviously *broke* **up** through the window and then stole the car keys. _____

Collocations with *crime*

3 🔊 1.22 **Write a word from the box in each gap to complete each phrase. Listen and check.**

> hate | lab | organised | petty | prevention
> rate | scene | wave | youth

1 *crime* _____ : a place where forensic scientists analyse evidence
2 _____ *crime*: crime controlled by a powerful secret organisation
3 *crime* _____ : a sudden increase in the amount of crime in an area
4 _____ *crime*: an attack against a person because of their race, religion, etc.
5 *crime* _____ : the place where a crime has been committed
6 _____ *crime*: crime committed by young people
7 _____ *crime*: a crime that is not very serious
8 *crime* _____ : the amount of crime in an area
9 *crime* _____ : measures to deter criminal activity

4 **Write a phrase from Exercise 3 in each gap to complete each sentence.**

1 Send the evidence to the _____ and let me know the results immediately!
2 I believe that when there are no jobs for young people, _____ goes up.
3 The _____ is dropping, but people are still afraid because of reports in the media.
4 He had a history of _____ , such as vandalism and shoplifting.
5 CCTV cameras and bicycle locks are good _____ measures.
6 The recent _____ has seen a 30% increase in violent crime in just one year!
7 The police prevented people from entering the _____ while they collected evidence.
8 Groups such as the Mafia are well known for their involvement in _____ .
9 When the young disabled man was attacked, the police said it was a _____ .

THINK | RESEARCH | CULTURE | LEARN | ME

How much of a problem is youth crime in your area?
What do you think can be done about youth crime?

1 In pairs or as a group, ask and answer the questions.

1 What things can you see in the photos?

2 Do you enjoy watching crime and mystery programmes on TV and movies? Why do you think they are popular?

2 For each sentence, choose a second sentence that expresses the same idea.

1 *The idea has its origins in the classic detective fiction of the 1920s and 30s.*

   a) This first happened in the 1920s and 30s.

   b) The inspiration for this comes from crime stories.

2 *Finally, they are asked who they think is guilty of the crime.*

   a) They have to say who is responsible for something.

   b) They have to say who is a victim of something.

3 *We love to look for clues, test out our theories and try to be cleverer than the criminal.*

   a) We enjoy showing that we are more intelligent than someone else.

   b) We love learning about how clever criminals can be.

4 *Apart from that, we have a very deep desire to see justice done.*

   a) We secretly want to break the rules.

   b) We want very much to see that criminals get caught.

5 *Often, it's the crazy ideas that help you find the solution!*

   a) Unusual solutions can often be the right ones.

   b) The correct solution is usually quite ordinary.

6 *Events such as these give you the chance to get away to a time and place that seems simpler than today.*

   a) These events can help you forget about the problems of today.

   b) You usually have to travel to get to these events.

3 Read the statements in Exercise 4 and find synonyms for these words and phrases.

1 clever _____

2 crazy ideas _____

3 desire _____

4 detective fiction _____

5 everyday life _____

6 get satisfaction from _____

7 guilty of _____

8 opportunity _____

OPTIMISE YOUR EXAM

True/false

- Before you listen, read each statement carefully and underline the key words. Think about other ways to say the same ideas.

- When you listen, try to identify words and phrases that are similar to those in the statements.

4 ◁))) 1.23 Listen to an interview with someone who organises weekend events. Decide whether each statement is T (True) or F (False).

1 The events Serena puts on were first organised by writers of crime stories.	**T / F**
2 Once the crime has been committed, guests must stay in the hotel.	**T / F**
3 During the event, the guests try to figure out who is responsible for a crime.	**T / F**
4 The events offer a chance for families to develop their relationships.	**T / F**
5 Serena says we enjoy proving how intelligent we are.	**T / F**
6 An interest in crime stories is based on our secret wish to break the law.	**T / F**
7 People who can come up with unusual theories do well at this kind of event.	**T / F**
8 Serena believes that events like hers provide an escape from the real world.	**T / F**

5 ◁))) 1.23 Listen again and check your answers.

THINK | RESEARCH | CULTURE | LEARN | ME

Think about hosting your own mystery party. Who would the characters be? What would the theme be? What would the mystery be?

Grammar in context

Look at this sentence from the audio in the listening lesson and answer the questions.

If you work out the solution, you get a lot of satisfaction from it.

1 Is this an example of a zero conditional or a first conditional?

2 Is this talking about one specific occasion or a general truth?

3 How would the meaning change if it said this:
If you work out the solution, you'll get a lot of satisfaction from it.

✓ **REMEMBER**

- We use the zero conditional for general truths and scientific facts – *If you **go** to prison, you **lose** your freedom.*

- We use the first conditional for real, likely or possible situations, now, generally or in the future – *I'**ll be** so happy if the police **find** my bike.*

- We can also use other words and phrases in place of *if*:

  ○ *Unless* means 'if not' or 'except if' – *I won't call the police **unless** I hear another noise. = I won't call the police **if** I **don't** hear another noise.*

  ○ *As/so long as* and *provided (that)* mean 'if a certain condition is true or happens' – ***As long as / Provided (that)** you promise not to do it again, I'll let you off with a warning.*

  ○ Be careful with *in case*. It doesn't mean *if*. It means 'because the following might happen' – *Put your bag away **in case** someone tries to steal it.*

▶ **See Grammar reference, Unit 4,** page 152

---

1 **Choose the correct word or phrase to complete the text.**

FACT AND FICTION

You're not alone if you (**1**) **enjoy / will enjoy** watching programmes about crime on TV – many people do. There are two main types of programme: factual and drama. Factual programmes focus on real crimes, so it's not a good idea to watch them late at night (**2**) **unless / if** you get scared easily. They sometimes put a phone number or a website on the screen (**3**) **in case / as long as** people have information about the crime.

There are also a huge number of movies and series about crime-fighting and criminal investigation. If you've never watched one, (**4**) **you'll watch / watch** one today! Crime dramas are my favourite type of TV programme. If the new Sherlock series comes out this year, (**5**) **I watch / I'll watch** it immediately! Sometimes these programmes contain a lot of violence. In my view, it's OK to enjoy this as long as (**6**) **you'll / you** remember it's fiction, not real life.

2 **Rewrite each sentence using the words given.**

1 Do what I say and you won't get hurt!   **PROVIDED**

2 I'll let them go if you give me a helicopter and a million dollars.   **LONG**

3 We can't arrest him if we're not sure he did it.   **UNLESS**

4 I'll come with you because there might be trouble.   **CASE**

5 I'm not letting the President in unless we're certain it's safe.   **IF**

6 If you understand the danger involved, go ahead.   **SO**

3 **Write a short dialogue between a police officer and a criminal for a TV crime show. Try to include the words and phrases from Exercise 2.**

Start your dialogue like this:

Police officer (through megaphone):
If you don't come out with your hands up,
you might get hurt!

• **SAY IT RIGHT**

Resource centre: Unit 4
Intonation in conditionals

Talk2Me

To my mind ...

1 ▷ Watch the *Talk2Me* video and answer the questions.

1 What different crimes and punishments are mentioned?

2 How do the people suggest crime can be tackled?

2 ▷ Watch the video again. Write the name of the person who says the expressions in the *Phrase expert* box.

> **PHRASE EXPERT**
>
> As I see it ... | Do you agree? | Do you think ...? | I don't think it matters if ... | I'd say that ... | In my opinion, ... | I think / don't think ... | It's hard to say, but ... | Personally, I ... | To my mind, ... | What do you think about ...? | What's your opinion?

3 Look at photographs A and B. In pairs, discuss what the crimes are and appropriate punishments for them.

4 Note down your main opinion and any reasons or examples to justify your ideas about the crimes in Exercise 3.

5 Complete the dialogues with the words and phrases in the box.

> agree | as I | hard to | matters | my mind opinion | personally | think

1 **A**: What do you _____ about his idea?
  B: _____ , I don't think it will work.

2 **A**: What's your _____ on this case?
  B: To _____ , there's no doubt that she is guilty.

3 **A**: Do you think that the judge believes the defendant?
  B: I don't think it _____ if he does, because the jury will decide the result.

4 **A**: Do you _____ with the verdict?
  B: _____ see it, they committed a crime so they need to be punished.

5 **A**: Do you believe that he's innocent?
  B: It's _____ say, but there is a lot of evidence against him.

OPTIMISE YOUR EXAM

Discussion

● In a discussion, the examiner may ask you a question individually. Answer the question, giving your opinion and then try to bring your partner into the discussion.

● Ask your partner what they think or if they agree with you. Then continue the discussion with more ideas about the question.

6 In groups of three, discuss the following questions. Take turns to be the examiner and candidates. Ask your partner for their opinion and try to keep the discussion going.

● Why do you think some people commit crimes?

● What punishment would you give to students at school who did the following:
  — writing graffiti on classroom walls or in the playground
  — vandalism: breaking objects or furniture in the classroom
  — throwing litter and paper around the school

● How useful do you think community service is for people who commit petty crimes? What kinds of things should they do?

● What are effective crime prevention measures?

● What qualities might you need to be a good police officer?

● Is there crime in your local neighbourhood?

1 **Look at the words in capitals in Exercise 2 and answer the questions.**

Which of them …

1 could be a noun or a verb? What other words can you form from that word?

2 are verbs? What nouns can you form from those words?

3 can transform to words ending in -*th*? There are two of them.

▼ OPTIMISE YOUR **EXAM**

Word formation

- If you are not sure of an answer, try the next question. Then look at the whole text to see if the context and your other answers help you with the more difficult questions.

2 **Write a form of the word in capitals in each gap to complete the text.**

Preventing crime

Crime (**1**) _____ is part of the job of all police officers who patrol the streets, but there are some who try to increase the public's (**2**) _____ of crime risks and the causes of crime. This may include visiting people who have been the victims of (**3**) _____ to advise them on how to make their homes safe, or speaking to the owners of businesses that suffer from (**4**) _____ to explore ways in which the problem can be tackled.

    PREVENT

UNDERSTAND

    BURGLE

    VANDAL

It also involves visiting schools to speak to students about subjects such as (**5**) _____ crime. It is often forgotten that one of the most (**6**) _____ aspects of crime committed by young people is that it is young people themselves who are usually the victims. Tackling this (**7**) _____ problem by showing young people how to protect themselves is one of the most (**8**) _____ aspects of this job.

    YOUNG

    SHOCK

    GROW

    SATISFY

3 **Look at the sentences in Exercise 4 and answer the questions.**

1 Which transformations test the work you did on the grammar pages of this unit? ____ , ____ , ____

2 Which transformations test the work you did on the vocabulary page of this unit? ____ , ____

▼ OPTIMISE YOUR **EXAM**

Sentence transformation

- If the word you are given is a preposition or an adverb, e.g. *up*, *out* or *over*, you may need to use a phrasal verb in the second sentence. Try putting different verbs in front of the preposition or adverb to see if they make sense.

4 **Complete the second sentence so it has a similar meaning to the first. Do not change the word given. Use two to five words, including the word given.**

1 Privileges are given to prisoners if they behave well. **PROVIDED**
Prisoners _____ they behave well.

2 If the jury aren't convinced of his guilt, he won't go to prison.   **UNLESS**
He won't go to prison _____ that he's guilty.

3 I can't believe the only punishment he got was just a small fine!   **OFF**
I can't believe he _____ just a small fine!

4 If you promise not to be late again, I'll let you off this time.   **AS**
I'll let you off this time _____ you promise not to be late again.

5 The robbery was almost successful but the police finally got the criminals.   **AWAY**
The criminals almost _____ but the police finally caught them.

6 The staff at the crime lab will finish the tests and then send the results immediately.   **SOON**
The staff at the crime lab will send the results _____ the tests.

1 In pairs or as a group, answer the questions.

1. What do you think about graffiti? Is it art or vandalism, or can it be both?

2 Are there places in your local area where people are allowed to produce graffiti?

2 Read this letter and find extracts 1–4. Decide what the function of each one is.

Dear Editor,

I was interested to read the article in your last issue called 'Graffiti – vandalism or art?'. I agreed with many of the points made by the writer, and definitely agree it can be either vandalism or art depending on the situation.

In my opinion, people need to recognise that some graffiti artists are extremely talented. Graffiti is not just writing your name on a wall. It's possible to create wonderful designs and pictures with just a few cans of paint. It seems to me that if there are more places where people are allowed to do graffiti – in certain parts of town or in parks, for example, then some graffiti artists won't have to damage private property to produce their art.

Of course, even if we take these steps, some people will continue to vandalise the neighbourhood. As far as I'm concerned, they should be punished, because we can't allow people to suffer because of vandals.

To sum up, society needs to respect graffiti and graffiti artists, and graffiti artists need to respect their neighbours and their environment. This way, everybody wins.

Yours faithfully,

Alex Parker

1 Graffiti is not just writing your name on a wall. It's possible to create wonderful designs and pictures with just a few cans of paint.

   a) giving advice on how best to produce graffiti
   b) explaining in more detail why some graffiti artists are talented

2 … in certain parts of town or in parks …

   a) an example of places where graffiti is damaging
   b) an example of places where graffiti should be allowed

3 … then some graffiti artists won't have to damage private property …

   a) the reason why we need more places to practise graffiti
   b) an example of getting graffiti artists to change their behaviour

4 … we can't allow people to suffer because of vandals.

   a) the reason why vandals should be punished
   b) an example of why graffiti shouldn't be allowed

3 Rewrite the sentences using the words and phrases given.

We need places for graffiti. These might be certain walls at school or in parks.

1 for example

_____

2 for instance

_____

3 such as

_____

They should be punished. We can't allow them to make people suffer.

4 as

_____

5 since

_____

6 because

_____

7 Because of this,

_____

OPTIMISE YOUR EXAM

A letter / An email

● The style of a letter to an editor should be quite formal. If you are writing about a specific topic, the main part of the letter can be similar to an essay, e.g. you need to give your opinion about the topic and give reasons for it with examples.

● Remember to start and finish your letter in an appropriate way, and refer to the magazine article you read in the first paragraph.

4 **Look at this writing task. In pairs or groups, make notes and discuss the questions in the task.**

> You have recently read an article in a magazine for young people on the subject of ways to prevent crime at school. One of the suggestions in the article was to ban students from taking money or mobile phones to school.

Write a letter to the editor of the magazine giving your opinion on the suggestion made. Include your own suggestions for preventing crime at school.

1 What do you think about the suggestion?

2 What are the best ways to prevent crime at school?

5 **Plan** Make a paragraph plan.

Part	Purpose	Useful phrases	My notes
First line	address the reader in an appropriate style	*Dear Editor,*	
Paragraph 1	introduction	*I was interested to read the article in your last issue entitled …*	
Paragraph 2	your opinion about banning mobile phones and money in schools, giving reasons and examples	*It seems to me,* *In my view,* *To my mind,* *For example,*	
Paragraph 3	other effective ways to prevent crime at school, giving reasons and examples	*For instance,* *such as* *since* *as* *because* *Because of this,*	
Paragraph 4	conclusion	*To sum up,* *To conclude,* *In conclusion,*	
Closing phrase	politely and respectfully say goodbye	*Yours faithfully,* *Yours truly,* *Yours sincerely,*	
Your name	show who wrote the letter (first name + surname)		

6 **Write** Write your letter in an appropriate style. Write 140–190 words.

7 **Check** Before you hand in your letter, complete this checklist.

Checklist ✔

- ○ I've written a formal letter.
- ○ I've started and ended my letter in an appropriate way.
- ○ I've written at least four paragraphs.
- ○ I've expressed my opinions, giving reasons and examples.
- ○ I've discussed the idea of banning money and mobile phones.
- ○ I've suggested other effective ways to prevent crime at school.
- ○ I've checked my spelling and grammar.

UNITS 3–4

GRAMMAR AND VOCABULARY

1 Write a form of the word in capitals in each gap.

APPS TO FIGHT CRIME

Since the (**1**) _____ of the smartphone, it has been used for all kinds of purposes, from work to entertainment. Now, it has a (**2**) _____ role in fighting crime. A number of apps help with crime (**3**) _____ by providing safety information or sending an alert to friends and family. They also provide a (**4**) _____ to the problem of collecting information on a crime in progress. Using the phone's camera and microphone, apps collect (**5**) _____ that can be used in court. This could, for example, be a video of a (**6**) _____ entering a property. An app might send that footage to the police automatically, giving them what they need to catch the (**7**) _____ person. By using smartphones (**8**) _____ , app developers are doing their bit to help keep us all safe from crime.

INVENT
GROW
PREVENT

SOLVE
EVIDENT
BURGLE

GUILT
CREATE

___/8

2 Write the word in brackets in the correct form in each gap. Add any other words you need.

1 Is this _____ crime you have ever investigated, Sergeant? (**bad**)

2 Sadie won't win the science prize – her app design is _____ Nadia's. (**innovative**)

3 Charlie is one of _____ people I know – he knows the answer to everything. (**clever**)

4 I hated the restaurant and it was probably _____ meal I've ever had. (**enjoyable**)

5 In this game, the person who throws the ball _____ wins. (**far**)

___/5

3 Write one word in each gap.

1 The technicians have carried _____ a number of tests on the new gadgets.

2 Be careful because someone got beaten _____ in the park last night.

3 How did you _____ away with not doing your homework?

4 The police are _____ into the robbery and will let us know what they find.

5 Would you mind just plugging the printer _____ for me?

___/5

4 Put the verbs into the correct form to complete the sentences.

1 If you _____ anyone my secret, I'll be really annoyed. (**tell**)

2 Your text message arrived just as I _____ you a message! (**write**)

3 This time next week, we _____ on the beach! (**lie**)

4 Don't worry – I _____ enough money for our flights to Greece by July. (**save**)

5 You're late! What _____ all this time? (**do**)

6 Let me know as soon as your plane _____ on Friday. (**land**)

7 _____ anything interesting this weekend? (**do**)

8 By the time I take the exam, I _____ English for about seven years. (**study**)

9 What _____ if you find that your bike really has been stolen? (**do**)

10 Call me at six – I _____ work by then. (**finish**)

___/10

5 Choose the correct word to complete each sentence.

1 Our area suffers from a lot of ____ crime, such as shoplifting.   **a)** petty   **b)** little   **c)** small

2 Who ____ the fact that the Earth goes round the Sun?   **a)** discovered   **b)** invented   **c)** produced

3 The crime ____ has fallen recently but people are still worried.   **a)** count   **b)** amount   **c)** rate

4 The judge asked the ____ to consider their verdict very carefully.   **a)** committee   **b)** jury   **c)** crowd

5 Thieves broke into the builder's van and stole ____ and other equipment.   **a)** engines   **b)** tools   **c)** appliances

6 I've decided I have to make passing the exam my ____ priority.   **a)** top   **b)** high   **c)** best

7 A witness ____ forward to help police identify the guilty woman.   **a)** put   **b)** took   **c)** came

8 No-one was allowed to enter the crime ____ until the police had finished.   **a)** place   **b)** scene   **c)** area

9 My sister has just bought a new smartwatch. She loves ____ -tech gadgets.   **a)** top   **b)** high   **c)** best

10 This invention has the ____ to change the lives of millions of people.   **a)** potential   **b)** possibility   **c)** option

__/10

6 Complete the second sentence so it has a similar meaning to the first. Do not change the word given. Use two to five words, including the word given.

1 If we don't have photos, it'll be hard to prove who committed the crime.   **UNLESS**

It'll be hard to prove who committed the crime _____ photos.

2 I started working on this idea over six months ago.   **BEEN**

I _____ six months on this idea.

3 Have you ever seen such an expensive phone?   **ANY**

Is this phone _____ you've seen before?

4 Whose idea was it to use a picture of staring eyes to prevent crime?   **UP**

Who _____ the idea of using a picture of staring eyes to prevent crime?

5 The police finally managed to identify the robber.   **FIGURE**

The police finally managed to _____ the robber was.

6 People will try my invention and immediately love it!   **SOON**

People will love my invention _____ it!

__/12

Total score   __/50

▼

EXAM | SKILLS

Tick the statements that are true for you. Review the skills in the unit if you need more help.

I can …	Unit/page
☐ scan a science magazine article to find specific information	Unit 3 p26
☐ identify speakers' opinion and attitude in short extracts	Unit 3 p30
☐ compare photos in a photo task	Unit 3 p32
☐ create noun forms and collate verbs + prepositions accurately	Unit 3 p33
☐ use phrases for making recommendations in a review	Unit 3 p34
☐ identify synonyms in a news article	Unit 4 p36
☐ listen for synonyms in a conversation	Unit 4 p40
☐ compare photos in a photo task	Unit 4 p42
☐ use the context of a text to complete difficult questions and use prepositions and adverbs accurately	Unit 4 p43
☐ give reasons and examples in a formal letter or email	Unit 4 p44

5 You win some, you lose some

READING | Gapped text | An online article

1 **In pairs or groups, answer the questions.**

1 How often do you play video games? Which games are popular at the moment?

2 What type of real life skills do you think video games might teach you? e.g. *to be organised*

2 **Read the text quickly, ignoring the gaps. Match summaries A–G to paragraphs 1–7.**

A Some games teach players to develop very important qualities. ____

B Playing video games in the classroom can be positive if there is a time limit. ____

C Research suggests that video games may help young people with life skills. ____

D It's necessary to be informed about the dangers of playing video games. ____

E Making errors in a game may help players understand their consequences. ____

F We need to develop life skills every day at school and at work. ____

G One popular game teaches players to organise and think in an analytical way. ____

3 **Read the text again. Decide if each idea is mentioned in that paragraph. Write *Yes* or *No*.**

Paragraph 1: Some parents disapprove of the time spent playing video games. _____

Paragraph 2: Video games teach us how to socialise better from an early age. _____

Paragraph 3: Some games help players to become more determined and to master difficulties. _____

Paragraph 4: Players often make mistakes when selecting a character in a virtual world. _____

Paragraph 5: StarCraft helped Sylvia to get better marks at school. _____

Paragraph 6: Ian was banned from playing video games because he spent a lot of money. _____

Paragraph 7: Video games developers want schools to increase the hours that students play games in class. _____

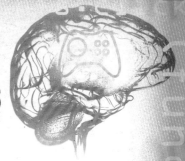

VIDEO GAMES and Life Skills

'You mustn't spend so long playing computer games! Stop staring at that screen!'

Does that sound familiar? Some parents still believe that playing video games is bad for you, however, in a recent survey over 80% of the people questioned agreed that some games could help teenagers develop valuable life skills.

Every day we face challenges at school, work or in our personal lives, and we need to develop the skills to deal with them. Computer skills, for example, are vital for most activities we carry out in our daily lives as well as helping you with studying. When we are young we are able to learn basic social skills but there are other important skills that can be more challenging to acquire. [1]

For example, there are many video games which can help us to develop problem-solving skills. Some games help develop patience and perseverance skills by continuing to increase the level of difficulty. [2] As a result of playing these games, players can develop confidence, as being able to overcome the obstacles gives you a real sense of achievement. Patience, perseverance and overcoming difficulties are three essential skills in everyday life.

As humans we often learn through mistakes, however some mistakes would be best avoided. Video games can expose you to making decisions in the virtual world by allowing you to choose your characters' actions and then showing you the results of these actions. [3]

In the game The Sims, players control every aspect of a Sim's life including making important decisions and learning how to budget, so that the Sim can successfully build a life in society. 14-year-old Sylvia is a big StarCraft fan. She says: 'To succeed in the world of StarCraft you have to plan ahead and think strategically. [4 E] I could use those same skills to plan my studies.'

However beneficial these games may be, there are things to remember. Too much screen time can isolate you from the real world and if you play multi-player games online, then you need to be sure who you are playing with. [5 C] It's also vital to make sure that you are not running up a huge bill in games that you pay for online. Ian, 16, said: 'I used my Dad's credit card and when the statement came, I wasn't allowed to play games online for six months! Now we have special internet awareness classes at school to educate and inform us better. I certainly learnt my lesson.'

Links between schools and video games developers have resulted in more games focused on developing life skills. The not-for-profit organisation, Makerspace, has developed an education programme based around games in conjunction with Minecraft. The programme claims that 30 minutes of video play in the classroom can improve planning skills, memory and motor skills. [6 F] So, play on and learn two valuable lessons at the same time.

`>VIDEO/GAMES<&>LIFE>SKILLS:|>>VIDEO/GAMES<&>LIFE>SKILLS:|>>VIDEO/GAMES<&>LIFE>SKILLS:|>>VIDEO/GAMES<&>LIFE>SK`

---

4 **Look at the seven sentences in Exercise 5. Match each sentence with an idea.**

1 Difficulties are found on the way until you resolve them. ____

2 Be careful because something might not be reliable. ____

3 You have to make practical and sensible decisions. ____

4 It's important to protect yourself. ____

5 A positive lesson could help you make better decisions in real life. ____

6 Video games help us become more skilful at something. ____

7 A combination of skills might be useful for the future. ____

OPTIMISE YOUR EXAM

Gapped text

- Read the whole of the main text quickly first to get a general idea. Try to make some short notes to summarise the main point of each paragraph.
- Then read the sentences which are missing from the main text and look for connections with the main ideas in each paragraph.

5 ◁))) 1.24 **Read the text again. Choose which sentence A–G fits each gap 1–6. There is one extra sentence you do not need. Listen and check.**

A This may help you to make more informed choices in the real world.

B This teaches you not to trust all characters in a virtual world.

C You shouldn't give out personal information about yourself to someone you don't know.

D Surprisingly, video games can often help us to master these.

E You need to decide what to build, how to use resources effectively and which strategies work.

F As well as developing life skills, having excellent computer skills could also help you with a future career.

G They constantly place obstacles in your path until you reach the solution.

6 **Find these words and phrases in the article. Work out what they mean from the context.**

> achievement (n) | acquire (v) | carry out (phr v)
> expose (v) | motor skills (n) | running up (phr v)
> staring (v)

Grammar in context

Look at these sentences from the text on page 49 and decide what each word or phrase in bold expresses.

1 *You **mustn't** spend so long playing computer games!*
   obligation / advice

2 *When we are young we **are able to** learn basic social skills ...*
   permission / ability

3 *I wasn't **allowed** to play games online for six months!*
   permission / obligation

 REMEMBER

We can use modals, semi-modals and other phrases such as *be able to* to express:

● ability – *can, could, be able to*

● permission – *can, could, may, be allowed to*

● advice/criticism – *should, ought to*

● obligation – *must, mustn't, have to, have got to, need to*

● lack of obligation – *don't have to, haven't got to, don't need to, needn't*

Modals are followed by the bare infinitive (*She could **swim** at an early age.*). We can also use the continuous infinitive (*You should **be wearing** trainers.*), the perfect infinitive (*I could **have played** all day.*) and the perfect continuous infinitive (*She shouldn't **have been playing** with that injury.*).

▶ **See Grammar reference, Unit 5,** page 153

1 **Complete the sentences using a word or phrase from the box and the verbs in brackets. Put the words, phrases and verbs into the correct form.**

| be able to | be allowed to | can | must |
| not have to | ought to | should not |

1 I'd love to _____ (**play**) hockey one day.

2 We were the stronger team so we really _____ (**lose**) yesterday.

3 Sarah _____ (**win**) the tennis tournament but she didn't train enough.

4 My cousin _____ (**watch**) wrestling but my parents won't let me.

5 Don't you think you _____ (**try**) and find a local football team to join?

6 Anyone wishing to enter the race _____ (**register**) by 10 o'clock at the latest.

7 I thought we'd have to rearrange the team in the second half, but in the end we _____ .

2 **Rewrite each sentence using the words given.**

1 It's not necessary to read aloud all the rules but you can if you want.   **HAVE**

_____

2 It wasn't necessary for you to bring a racket for me, but thanks anyway.   **NEEDN'T**

_____

3 I hope you can play next Saturday.   **WILL**

_____

4 It was a mistake for the referee to stop the game at that point.   **STOPPED**

_____

5 It's against the rules for a player to pick up and carry the ball.   **NOT**

_____

3 **Write one, two or three words in each gap to complete the text.**

Epic fails

One of my favourite kinds of video online is the 'epic fail' video. There are literally thousands of them, so you (**1**) _____ to spend a long time looking to find one. I personally (**2**) _____ get enough of them! If you haven't ever seen any, then you (**3**) _____ watch one as soon as you can. You won't regret it!

They often involve people doing things like skateboarding, often getting hurt when they needn't (**4**) _____ – if they'd just been a bit more careful. When I watch them I think, 'You really (**5**) _____ doing that – it'll end in tears.' And in epic fail videos, it always does.

I know we (**6**) _____ laugh at people failing, but in the videos, you just (**7**) _____ help it. They're just so funny!

So – thank you to all the silly people who do silly things which end in disaster. Carry on doing that so we'll all (**8**) _____ to enjoy epic fail videos for years to come.

THINK | RESEARCH | CULTURE | LEARN | ME

Why do you think epic fail videos are popular? Think of three reasons and compare with a partner.

Words connected with *sports*

1 🔊 1.25 **Match each sport with a place. Listen and check.**

1 football ____   a) course
2 boxing ____   b) court
3 golf ____   c) field/pitch
4 ice skating ____   d) ring
5 motor racing ____   e) rink
6 tennis ____   f) track

2 🔊 1.26 **Choose the correct word and explain what the other word means. Listen and check.**

1 A person who watches a sports match in a stadium: **spectator / viewer**
2 A person taking part in a race: **opponent / competitor**
3 A judge in a tennis or cricket match: **umpire / referee**
4 A piece of equipment used in squash: **racket / cue**
5 Hockey players play with this: **bat / stick**
6 This is used in fishing: **rod / ball**

3 🔊 1.27 **Write a verb from the box in the correct form in each gap. Listen and check.**

beat | draw | score | win

1 We've just got one more team to _____ and we're in the final!
2 Who _____ the final goal, do you know?
3 Both teams scored the same number of points, so they _____ the first game.
4 Two runners reached the line at the same time, so it was difficult to see who'd actually _____ .

Phrasal verbs

4 🔊 1.28 **Match each phrasal verb with a meaning from the box. Use each meaning twice. Listen and check.**

be visible | leave | look and see | pay attention

1 Dom really *stands out* in that team – he's far better than all the others. ____
2 We got through to the semi-final, but then we were *knocked out*. ____
3 Hey! *Check out* this new fitness app. It's brilliant! ____
4 *Mind out* – you're about to start walking on the golf course. ____
5 Caroline's had to *pull out* of the match on Saturday because of an injury. ____
6 He *stuck out* as the weak player in the team. ____
7 *Listen out* for the whistle – it's a sign that the match has finished. ____
8 I can't *make out* which horse is in the lead – can you? ____

Words + prepositions

5 🔊 1.29 **Write one preposition in each gap to complete the sentences. Use the words in italics to help you. Listen and check.**

1 A string of injuries *prevented* her _____ *participating* _____ the squash championship.
2 No, I've never *cheated* _____ pool or snooker!
3 I'm really *anxious* _____ the hockey game tomorrow as it's so important.
4 He was *banned* _____ professional cricket for 10 years after failing a drug test.
5 The sports kit *consists* _____ a yellow shirt, blue shorts and white socks.
6 What's the *difference* _____ tennis and badminton?
7 Our baseball coach *insists* _____ us staying in the night before a big match.
8 It's not always easy for new players to *adjust* _____ being in a professional team, and many of them *benefit* _____ getting financial and media advice.

• SAY IT RIGHT

Resource centre: Unit 5
Stress in phrasal verbs (2)

THINK | RESEARCH | CULTURE | LEARN | **ME**

What are the sports facilities like in your local area?

Where are the nearest facilities to you? (e.g. *The nearest ice rink is in a town 20 kilometres away.*)

1 In pairs or as a group, ask and answer the questions.

1 In most professional and Olympic sports, women and men don't compete against each other. Why do you think this is?

2 Why do you think it's a good (or bad) idea for girls and boys to do PE and sport together at school?

2 ◁))) 1.30 Listen to the beginning of a radio interview with a teenager called Adam, who's talking about his football team. Tick the ideas that are mentioned.

1 Adam's team is doing well this season. ____

2 Adam's a good role model for other teenagers. ____

3 Some remarkable changes have happened to Adam's team. ____

4 Adam and Rachel were in different football teams. ____

5 Adam and Rachel would often kick a ball around in their garden. ____

6 Adam and Rachel do PE together at school. ____

3 Look at questions 1 and 2 in Exercise 4. How many of the A/B/C options relate to the ideas you ticked in Exercise 2?

OPTIMISE YOUR **EXAM**

Multiple choice (single extract)

● Read the question and the options carefully so you know what you need to listen for.

● The first time you listen, make some short notes. Then look again at the options to see if any of your notes help you choose the correct answer when you listen for the second time.

---

4 ◁))) 1.31 Listen to the complete interview. For questions 1–7, choose the best answer (A, B or C).

1 Adam has been asked onto the programme mainly because
  A his team is very successful at the moment.
  B his team has been through an unusual experience.
  C he will be able to help and teach other teenagers.

2 Two years ago, where would Adam and Rachel usually play football together?
  A at home
  B at school
  C in their teams

3 What's the main difference between this year and last year?
  A There are more people playing for Eastbrook this year.
  B The girls are better players than they were last year.
  C There was no mixed team of boys and girls last year.

4 Who believed that the experiment might fail?
  A a few of Adam and Rachel's teammates
  B several older relatives of the players
  C Adam and Rachel themselves

5 What is mentioned about changing rooms?
  A There aren't usually separate rooms for boys and girls.
  B There aren't usually changing rooms for the players at all.
  C Most players prefer to get changed and shower at home.

6 What does Adam suggest about other mixed teams?
  A There may be new ones in the near future.
  B There are already plenty of them in existence.
  C He's not optimistic that others will be created.

7 Adam believes that next year's captain
  A definitely won't be a girl.
  B shouldn't be a girl.
  C might be a girl.

5 ◁))) 1.31 Listen again and check your answers.

THINK | RESEARCH | CULTURE | LEARN | ME

What do you think of Adam's team's experiment? Would the same experiment work in your school?

Grammar in context

Complete these sentences from the audio in the listening lesson so that they match the descriptions.

1 I'm sure there aren't many. = *There _____ be many.*

2 I'm sure it was an interesting time. = *It _____ _____ been an interesting time.*

 REMEMBER

We can use modals and semi-modals to express:

● possibility – *can, could, may, might*

● probability – *should, ought to*

● certainty (deductions) – *must, can't, couldn't*

Note:

must have to = I'm sure you have to – *You **must have to** train very often to be so fit.*

Modals can be followed by the bare infinitive (*He could **be** the referee, but I'm not sure.*), the continuous infinitive (*She might **be swimming** now.*), the perfect infinitive (*You must **have felt** fantastic after the match.*) and the perfect continuous infinitive (*I may **have been playing** when you tried to call me.*).

▶ See Grammar reference, Unit 5, page 153

1 Look at the photo and write sentences expressing possibility, probability or certainty using the key words.

Example: play it on your own

You probably can't play it on your own.

1 fun to play

2 too expensive

3 download the game

4 play without a mobile phone

2 Write a verb or verb phrase from the box in the correct form to complete each sentence.

> cheat | check the football scores
> like the game | save the final game
> train harder | work

1 Andy is reading something on his phone. He might _____ .

2 The brain-training app won't download at the moment. The Wi-Fi can't _____ .

3 They played the new racing videogame three times yesterday. They must _____ .

4 Our basketball team came last in the tournament again. We ought to _____ .

5 Oh no, my game progress has been lost! I can't _____ .

6 Abi's scorecard is looking suspiciously high. I suspect she may _____ .

3 Put each verb in the correct form with an appropriate modal or semi-modal to complete the text.

Unlucky player

No-one (**1**) ___*can be*___ (**be**) lucky or successful all the time, and that seems to be particularly true of people doing sport. When footballer Aigeas Plomariou walked onto the pitch for a match on the Greek island of Lesvos, he (**2**) _____ (**know**) how strange his day would turn out to be. At one point, he had the chance of a goal. As a striker with the chance of a goal in front of him, his heart (**3**) _____ (**start**) beating a little faster as he aimed. Would it go in? It (**4**) _____ (**do**) – but luck was not on his side. First, it hit the goalpost on the left. Then it hit the top bar. Then the bar on the right. Then back to the bar on the left. The goalkeeper (**5**) _____ (**get**) the ball at any point, but he didn't, which (**6**) _____ (**make**) it even worse for Plomariou. Finally, a defender on the opposing team kicked the ball away. Plomariou (**7**) _____ (**be**) devastated – but of course there's a chance that he (**8**) _____ (**enjoy**) becoming famous when the video went viral.

 THINK | RESEARCH | CULTURE | LEARN | ME

Think of a famous successful or unsuccessful sporting moment. Write sentences using modals to show how the people must or might have felt.

Talk**2**Me

They seem to be …

Flipped classroom

1 ▷ Watch the *Talk2Me* video and look at the photo. For each person, note down their responses to the questions.

- What is the person in the photo doing?
- What do you think has just happened?
- Why do you think the person has decided to do this?
- What do you think could happen next?

2 ▷ Watch the video again. Circle the words and phrases in the *Phrase expert* box that you hear on the video.

> **PHRASE EXPERT**
>
> It can't have been (easy to jump out because) … | It/He, They might, could, may (have/be) … because | It looks as if he … because … | He must have been (running) because he looks (tired) | They seem to be (nervous)

3 In pairs, look at the photo in Exercise 1. How might the person be feeling?

4 Choose the correct word in each sentence.

1 Mike **might** / **looks** be feeling upset because he didn't win the race.
2 They seem to be **talk** / **talking** about something important.
3 It **seem** / **looks** as if they are lost because they are looking at a map.
4 She could **have been** / **be** on holiday recently as she's carrying a suitcase.
5 The exam **can't** / **might** have been difficult because she looks very pleased.
6 It **must** / **may** have been raining because they are holding wet umbrellas.

5 Look at photos A and B and make notes about them in the table.

A

B

	PHOTO A	PHOTO B
What is this a photo of?		
Where was the photo taken?		
What could the people be doing?		
What could have just happened?		
What might they do next?		
How do you think the people might be feeling?		

OPTIMISE YOUR EXAM

Photo task

- When you are comparing the photos try to use modal verbs and some expressions to speculate about the people or situations.
- Remember to try to expand on your ideas and give reasons why.

6 In pairs or groups of three, describe the situations in the photos. What do you think might have happened to the people? Use your notes to help you.

▶ **Workbook Unit 5:** Speaking, pages 40–41, exercises 1, 2, 3

1 **Look at the words in capitals in Exercise 2 and answer the questions.**

1 Which of them can form a noun ending in -*ment*? ·

arguement

2 Which of them require changing a vowel between two consonants to form a noun?

_____

3 Which of them can form a noun where we have to double the final consonant?

_____

OPTIMISE YOUR EXAM

Word formation

● When you have completed the question look at the words again and check your spelling carefully. It must be correct to get full marks.

---

3 **Read the text in Exercise 4 quickly. Answer the questions.**

1 Which gaps can be filled with a verb or modal verb? _____

2 Which gaps can be filled with a preposition or particle? _____

---

2 **Write a form of the word in capitals in each gap to complete the text.**

in general take in plural

Competitive and non-competitive sports

Many sports can be competitive or non-competitive depending on how you do them. Professional (1) _____ , **SWIM** for example, take part in (2) _____ where the **COMPETE** fastest person in each race is crowned the (3) _____ , **WIN** and those not so fast are considered the losers. Many other people swim but don't compete – perhaps they just swim 50 or 100 (4) _____ for the exercise. **LONG**

There is a debate within the school system about encouraging competitive sport at school. Some people think that playing sport against an opponent and experiencing both success and (5) _____ in sport is an important life **FAIL** skill. Other people argue that competitive sports can cause (6) _____ , with teenagers obsessing and worrying **ANXIOUS** too much about winning. They believe that one way to avoid (7) _____ on school sports day is to focus on **ARGUE** non-competitive sports. This may help in the (8) _____ of ideas such as teamwork and the **DEVELOP** shared enjoyment of sport, rather than rivalry and the need to beat your opponent.

OPTIMISE YOUR EXAM

Open cloze

● Sometimes the missing word completes a set phrase or an idiom.

● Look carefully before and after the gap and at the meaning of the whole sentence to see if this helps you find the correct answer.

---

4 **Write one word in each gap to complete the text.**

Indoor wall climbing

Last week I went indoor wall climbing for the first time. When I stood at the bottom and looked up, I felt extremely anxious (1) _____ falling and hurting myself, but in fact I needn't (2) _____ worried. The instructors insist (3) _____ you wearing a harness connected with a rope which prevents you (4) _____ falling if you slip or lose your grip.

My instructor, Jez, (5) _____ have thought I was a complete coward when I started – I was terrified, and it took me five minutes just to take the first step. But I soon got the hang of it, and really benefited (6) _____ Jez's patience and advice. Looking (7) _____ now, I don't know why I made such a fuss. It's really not that difficult or scary. I guess it's always like that (8) _____ you do something you haven't done before.

It was a fantastic experience, and I really hope I'll be able to go back there soon to do it again.

THINK | RESEARCH | CULTURE | LEARN | ME

Which of the ideas expressed in the text in Exercise 2 do you agree with most? Which do you disagree with most?

▶ **Vocabulary reference,** page 164   ▶ **Workbook Unit 5:** Use of English, page 41, exercises 1, 2

1 **In pairs or as a group, answer the questions.**

1 Look at the photo. What is happening?
2 What would your ideal school Sports Day be like?
3 What sporting equipment does your school have?

2 **Read this email and answer the questions.**

To: Mr Parker
Subject: Sports Day

Dear Mr Parker,

I am writing in response to your request for suggestions for this year's Sports Day. I would like to put forward a few ideas for you to consider.

Firstly, I believe that there is nothing wrong with competitive sports, and prizes being given to the winners. I understand that some schools do not like to award prizes because they do not want some students to feel as if they are failures. However, I have spoken to a lot of my classmates and other students about this and the majority agree with me. In fact, I did not speak to a single student who felt that there should only be non-competitive sports.

Secondly, I would like to suggest that this year there is more variety of sports, such as three-legged races. A lot of students enjoy these novelty sports and it would be entertaining and fun.

My final suggestion is to propose that Sports Day is held at the weekend so that more parents will be able to attend.

Please let me know if you have any questions regarding my suggestions.

Yours sincerely,

Alison Redman, Year 11

1 Where does Mr Parker probably work?
_____
2 What had Mr Parker asked for?
_____
3 What three things does Alison suggest?
_____
4 What reason or reasons does she give for each suggestion?
_____

3 **Decide if the statements are T (True) or F (False).**

1 When Alison writes emails to her friends, she probably uses exactly the same style and formality as in this email. · T / F
2 Alison probably thought carefully about what language and style to use as she was writing this email. T / F
3 Each main suggestion is in its own paragraph. T / F
4 The first paragraph explains why she is writing. T / F
5 The final paragraph is a summary of her suggestions. T / F

4 **Alison uses some formal vocabulary. Write the word or phrase that Alison uses in the first paragraph that has a similar meaning to these words and phrases.**

1 I'm writing about _____
2 what you asked for _____
3 ideas about _____
4 I want to tell you _____
5 think about _____

OPTIMISE YOUR EXAM

A letter / An email

● If you're asked to write a formal letter or email, use an appropriate style.
● Try to use formal words and phrases where possible and don't use exclamation marks.
● You should use complete forms rather than contractions (e.g. *do not* rather than *don't*).
● Use set phrases for starting and finishing a formal letter.

5 Look at this writing task. In pairs or groups, discuss the questions.

You see this notice on your school noticeboard:

> I am pleased to be able to announce that a former student has donated some money for the school to purchase new sporting equipment.
>
> If any of you would like to suggest what particular pieces of equipment we should buy, please send me an email by next Friday giving reasons for your suggestions.
>
> *Mrs Barton* Headteacher

Write your **email**.

1 Should you only suggest sporting equipment for one sport, or is it better to suggest equipment for more than one sport?

2 Do you have to say how much each piece of equipment will cost?

3 Do you have to give reasons for your suggestions?

6 In groups, discuss the different sporting equipment the school could buy. Choose three pieces/types of equipment to suggest, and make notes regarding the reasons.

1 _____

2 _____

3 _____

7 Plan Make a paragraph plan.

Part	Purpose	Useful phrases	My notes
First line	address the recipient in an appropriate way	*Dear Mr/Mrs/Ms + surname,*	
Paragraph 1	reason for writing	*I am writing with regard to …* *I am writing in response to …* *I would like to …*	
Paragraphs 2–4	suggestions + reasons	*Firstly/Secondly/Thirdly,* *It seems to me …* *I would argue that …* *To my mind,* *I would like to suggest/propose …* *Because of this,* *For this reason,*	
Final paragraph or sentence	make clear you are happy to give further information if they need it	*Please let me know …* *… if you have any questions …* *I look forward to hearing from you.*	
Closing phrase	politely and respectfully say goodbye	*Yours sincerely,* *Best regards,* *Yours faithfully,*	
Your name	show who wrote the email (first name + surname, school year/class/grade)		

8 Write Write your email in an appropriate style. Write 140–190 words.

9 Check Before you hand in your email, complete this checklist.

Checklist ✓

◯ I've used formal language.

◯ I've started and ended my email in an appropriate way.

◯ I've presented each suggestion in a separate paragraph.

◯ I've given reasons for my suggestions.

◯ I've checked my spelling and grammar.

READING | True/false with explanation | An information leaflet

1 **In pairs or as a group, answer the questions.**

1 How common is it in your country for young people to follow the same career path as their parents? Would you like to do the same job as either of your parents?

2 If you had to name one job you would like to do in the future, what would it be? What has influenced you to consider that job?

2 **Read the leaflet quickly. Choose the best summary.**

a) Your choice of school subjects can be based on many things. The important thing is to have a strong character, because that will help you find a good job. Working hard to get high marks will keep other people happy and make you happy later in life.

b) When they are making important decisions, some people base their choices on the wrong things. This can lead to unhappiness. By knowing what you are good at, you can choose to do things that match your skills and your abilities.

3 **These words and phrases come from the statements in Exercise 4. For each one, choose the word or phrase that does <u>not</u> mean something similar.**

1 results
a) influences   b) outcomes   c) consequences

2 choices
a) decisions   b) effects   c) selections

3 strengths
a) talents   b) abilities   c) qualifications

4 appropriate
a) suitable   b) proper   c) challenging

5 handle
a) cope with   b) avoid   c) deal with

6 demonstrated
a) shown   b) affected   c) indicated

OPTIMISE YOUR EXAM

True/false with explanation

- True/false statements often include words or phrases that are similar to words or phrases in the text.

- Read the statements carefully first and check for key words. Then locate the part of the text which includes the relevant information. Look for any similar words and phrases and decide if they give you key information to answer the question.

you, your subjects and your future career

Sooner or later, we all have to face big decisions regarding our hopes and ambitions and our future roles in society. That might mean selecting school subjects that will lead to a fulfilling career. Or it might mean deciding what kind of job we think will suit us and that will bring us the kind of rewards we're looking for. It can be daunting as some of our choices may have long-lasting consequences. Unfortunately, not everyone uses the best criteria to base their choices on.

In the UK, students make some key decisions at ages 14 and 16. At 14, they select school subjects to study for two years, leading to qualifications known as GCSEs[1]. That choice may sometimes be the result of parental or peer pressure, or even a desire to do something that is seen as an 'easy' subject. Another common factor influencing the choice is having a good relationship with a teacher. These decisions influence the decisions taken later, at age 16.

We caught up with careers adviser Ali Moore, who summed up the options for 16 year olds: 'Luckily, students aren't restricted to a choice between academia and the workplace. There are options for everyone. You might decide to follow a vocational course, getting a qualification in catering or business, for example. Or you might consider doing an apprenticeship and work for an employer who will train you to do a specific job. Students who decide to stay in education will choose a narrower range of A level[2] subjects, which often lead on to university education.'

There's a real danger that people find themselves doing the wrong course or subject, or end up training for a job that isn't what they imagined it to be. They regret making the choices they've made and may drop out of the course or training. For example, take Adam Fenton, 16. 'I chose to do a GCSE in music just because I got on well with the teacher,' he says. 'Big mistake! I hated it after a few months and decided to switch to French. I had to do a lot of work to catch up with the other students!'

Mistakes like this are made when we forget to focus on our strengths. We all have talents and abilities, and we are often more aware of some than of others. You can get a sense of what academic areas you are stronger in, based on your success in assessments. Consistently high marks indicate a suitability for that area, even if you don't enjoy the subject at that particular moment. Perhaps you don't like the teacher, or perhaps the lessons seem to be challenging because they come at the end of the school day. All that can change.

Ali Moore's advice is to dig a little deeper to find out what combination of personality traits and skills are involved in your past success, and which can be applied to other areas. 'You may do well at subjects such as modern languages or drama,' she says. 'This doesn't necessarily mean you should aim to become a language teacher or an actor. It may imply that you have good interpersonal skills and would be good at dealing with the general public. Online personality tests which try to match you to a particular job may seem light-hearted, but their results can help you to focus on your interests and can give you a starting point for investigating a possible career path or plans for future studies.'

Consulting parents and other people as well as gathering information about different options are important elements in such decisions. However, an honest analysis of your abilities is an essential part of understanding who you want to become. Although it may be possible to change your mind about some decisions at a later stage, there's no doubt that life is easier if you get it right early on.

[1]GCSE = General Certificate of Secondary Education [2]A level = Advanced level

---

4 🔊 2.01 **Read the text. Choose T (True) or F (False) for each statement. Write the first four words of the sentence in the text which support each answer.**

1 The permanent results of our decisions can make us feel nervous or afraid.
   T / F _daunting our choices consequences_

2 Some people make choices that are influenced by their family's or friends' opinions.
   T / F _____

3 Students who stay at school beyond GCSEs do fewer individual subjects.
   T / F _students have decided narrower range of A level subjects_

4 People often have a very good idea of all the areas they have strengths in.
   T / F _We all have talents_

5 A subject you dislike may be appropriate once you ignore irrelevant factors.
   T / F _consistently high marks indicate_

6 It's easy to understand how your own character fits in with your future career.
   T / F _honest analysis essential_

7 Your ability to handle people may be demonstrated by the subjects you excel at.
   T / F _It may imply that_

8 You should avoid asking for advice on big decisions and make them yourself.
   T / F _Consulting parents and other_

5 **Find these words and phrases in the text. Work out what they mean from the context.**

consistently (adv)	criteria (n)
daunting (adj)	fulfilling (adj)
peer pressure (n)	(personality) traits (n)
suit (v)	the general public (n)

▶ **Workbook Unit 6:** Reading, pages 44–45, exercises 1, 2, 3, 4

Grammar in context

Look at these extracts from the article on page 59. Underline places where an infinitive or an -*ing* form follows a verb.

1 *That might mean selecting school subjects that will lead to a fulfilling career.*

2 *They regret making the choices they've made and may drop out of the course or training.*

3 *… perhaps the lessons seem to be challenging because they come at the end of the school day.*

4 *This doesn't necessarily mean you should aim to become a language teacher or an actor.*

✓ REMEMBER

● Some verbs can be followed by the full infinitive. – *seem* **to be**, *hope* **to become**

● Some verbs, including modal verbs, can be followed by the bare infinitive. – *make him* **work**, *let her* **leave**, *should* **apply**

● After some verbs and prepositions, we use the -*ing* form. – *bored with* **watching** *TV*

● Some verbs can be followed by either the full infinitive or the -*ing* form without a change in meaning. – *start* **working**, *start to* **work**

● With some verbs, the meaning changes. – *Do you remember* **going** *to school for the first time?*, *Did you remember* **to get** *some milk at the shop?*

▶ **See Grammar reference, Unit 6,** page 154

---

1 Categorise the verbs that are followed by infinitives and the verbs that are followed by -*ing*.

admit	afford	agree	attempt	begin
choose	consider	continue	deny
dislike	enjoy	fancy	hate	hope
imagine	intend	involve	like	love
manage	mean	offer	prefer	pretend
promise	regret	suggest	try	want

verbs followed by full/bare infinitive	verbs followed by -*ing*	verbs followed by infinitive and -*ing*
		*
		*

2 Choose the correct word or phrase to complete each sentence. In one case, both options are correct.

1 You don't seem ~~enjoying~~ / **to enjoy** your new course. What's the problem?

2 My parents suggested **getting** / ~~to get~~ a part-time job over the summer holidays.

3 I stopped **working** / ~~to work~~ at the supermarket because the pay was too low.

4 Noah forgot ~~setting~~ / **to set** his alarm and he was late on the first day of his new course.

5 Do you mind **creating** / ~~to create~~ a presentation about your work experience placement?

6 I began **preparing** / **to prepare** for the internship by reading about the company.

7 We regret ~~informing~~ / **to inform** you that your apprenticeship application was unsuccessful.

3 Complete the text using the verbs in brackets in the correct form.

PUPIL ON WORK EXPERIENCE DISCOVERS A PLANET

When students in the UK are in Year 10, aged 14–15, they often do work experience. This involves (**1**) _____ (**work**) somewhere for a short time to get an idea of what the world of work is like. As with most pupils who hope (**2**) _____ (**learn**) a little about the job they want to do, Tom Wagg, from Newcastle-under-Lyme, chose an area that he was considering (**3**) _____ (**work**) in: science. He got a work experience placement with Keele University that meant (**4**) _____ (**look**) at data from images of the night sky. Tom was 15 at the time, and his job was to attempt (**5**) _____ (**find**) small changes in the brightness of stars that might indicate that the star had a planet orbiting around it. After a while, he found what seemed (**6**) _____ (**be**) signs of exactly that. Had he discovered a new planet?

Over the course of the following two years, the university aimed (**7**) _____ (**prove**) whether Tom really had found a planet. They finally managed (**8**) _____ (**show**) that he had, and rang him with the good news. Tom, who is studying for his A levels, admits (**9**) _____ (**feel**) 'hugely excited' about discovering a planet, and he's going to continue (**10**) _____ (**study**) science at university.

Words connected with *the world of work*

1 🔊 2.02 **Write a word or phrase from the box in each gap. Listen and check.**

| resign | retire |

1 You do this when you formally state that you are leaving a job permanently. _resign_

2 You do this when you stop working because you are officially too old to work. _retire_

| bonus | salary | tip | wage |

3 This is the fixed amount of money you get paid monthly or yearly. _salary_

4 This is a small amount of money you get for providing good service. _bonus_?

5 This is an extra payment some companies make, for example, at Christmas. _____

6 This is the amount of money you get according to how many hours or days you work. _wage_

| off sick | on maternity/paternity leave |
| on strike | unemployed |

7 You are this when you stop working to protest about pay or conditions in the workplace.
_____

8 You are this when you don't have a job. _unemployed_

9 You are this when you are away from work after the birth of a child. _on maternity/paternity leave_

10 You are this when you don't go to work because you are ill. _off sick_

Phrasal verbs

2 🔊 2.03 **Write a phrasal verb from the box in the correct form to complete each sentence. There are two extra phrasal verbs you do not need. Listen and check.**

| burn out | copy in | fill in for | get ahead |
| key in | lay off | take on | work up |

1 The company is growing so they've decided to _____ an extra hundred workers.

2 I'm really ambitious and will do whatever it takes to _get ahead_ and be successful.

3 The receptionist _____ my name and waited for my booking to come up on the screen.

4 One of the other waiters asked me to _____ him while he made a call.

5 I joined the factory as an intern and _worked_ my way _up_ to being the team leader.

6 Don't work late so often – you don't want to _burn out_ before you're 30!

3 **Write a sentence for each of the extra phrasal verbs in the box in Exercise 2 showing how we use them.**

1 _____

2 _____

Collocations with *go* and *get*

4 🔊 2.04 **Write *go* or *get* to complete each phrase. Listen and check.**

1 ____ a placement		**7** ____ abroad
2 _go_ bankrupt		**8** ____ crazy
3 ____ fired		**9** _get_ lost
4 ____ missing		**10** ____ quiet
5 ____ ready		**11** ____ the impression
6 ____ the sack ✓		**12** ____ upset

5 🔊 2.05 **Use eight phrases in the correct form from Exercise 4 to complete the email. There may be more than one correct answer for some gaps. Listen and check.**

| To: | Lee | Subject: | First Day! |

Hi Lee,

Well, the first day of my work experience is over! I told you I (**1**) _____ in an office, and maybe from my description you (**2**) _____ that it was my dream work experience placement. Well, today was a nightmare!

I was so excited when I (**3**) _____ for work this morning. And guess what? I (**4**) _got lost_ on the way to the office! I ended up in completely the wrong building. I was late, and the manager (**5**) _____ with me because I'd missed my induction meeting with the whole department. And then an important file (**6**) _____ and it took me an hour to find it. After that, my head was all confused and I had so much to do that I thought I would (**7**) _go crazy_! I didn't manage to do it all, and the manager wasn't happy.

So, I almost (**8**) _____ on my first day! Imagine that – losing your job before you've even started! Let's hope the rest of my work experience is better!

Mel

● SAY IT **RIGHT**

Resource centre: Unit 6
Stress in phrasal verbs (3)

THINK | RESEARCH | CULTURE | LEARN | ME

What do you think an office job is like?

What skills do you need to work in an office?

1 In pairs or as a group, ask and answer the questions.

1 What kind of job might suit somebody who is good at maths?

2 What kind of job might suit somebody who is good at sport?

2 ◁))) 2.06 **Listen to a woman called Kerry Lipford talking about work. Decide whether each statement is T (True) or F (False).**

1 Kerry takes on young people to work for her.
T / F

2 In a SWOT analysis, S stands for 'strengths'.
T / F

3 In a SWOT analysis, W stands for 'work'.
T / F

4 In a SWOT analysis, O stands for 'occupations'.
T / F

5 In a SWOT analysis, T stands for 'threats'.
T / F

3 Look at these sentences which a student has completed after listening to Kerry's talk. If a sentence is correct, put a tick. Cross out any unnecessary words in the incorrect sentences.

1 Kerry works as *is a careers adviser* .

____

2 One example of a strength is *such as ability in maths*.

____

3 Kerry convinced one boy that *played a lot of video games* teach you skills.

____

4 If your list of weaknesses is *honest with yourself* , it can be useful.

____

5 Knowing someone who _____ *does a job* _____ can be a good opportunity.

____

6 When there are few *number of university places* available, it can create difficulties.

____

4 Look at the sentences in Exercise 5. If you think you remember any of the answers, make a note. Try to predict a word or short phrase that could go in each gap.

Sentence completion

● Write the exact word or phrase you hear in the recording – you don't need to rephrase anything.

● Check that the word(s) you write make sense grammatically in the sentence and are spelt correctly.

● You normally need to write one or two words, and a maximum of three words, so don't add any unnecessary information.

5 ◁))) 2.06 **Listen again. For questions 1–10, complete the sentences with a word or short phrase.**

1 Kerry helps young people make _____ when it comes to their careers.

2 SWOT analysis is a _____ Kerry uses with young people.

3 Interpersonal skills and _____ you are good at are possible strengths.

4 When you _____ , you may discover strengths you hadn't thought of.

5 One boy's free-time activity showed that he had a lot of _____ , as well as planning skills.

6 Kerry admits that _____ is the least enjoyable part of her job.

7 Being shy may prove to be a _____ in some occupations.

8 Opportunities show how you can _____ by using your strengths.

9 Kerry uses the example of working for a _____ to show what an opportunity is.

10 Working as a _____ may be difficult for people who don't have enough money.

THINK | RESEARCH | CULTURE | LEARN | **ME**

Make a list of your own strengths and weaknesses. Compare your list with a partner's. Which strengths might be most useful to you in the future?

Grammar in context

Look at these sentences from the audio in the listening lesson. In each sentence, underline the reason the speaker gives for doing (or not doing) something. What three different structures are used?

1 *I give them information about different occupations in order to help them make better choices.*

2 *One tool that I use with young people to guide them in this area is a SWOT analysis.*

3 *Sometimes I make myself busy with other work so as not to do it.*

✓ REMEMBER

● We use infinitives of purpose to show the reason why we do something. – *I rang her* **to tell** *her my news.*

● We can use *in order to* and *so as to* for the same thing. – *I rang her* **in order to** *tell her my news.*

● When the reason is negative and includes *not*, we don't usually use an infinitive on its own. We use *in order not to* or *so as not to*. – *I opened the door quietly* **so as not to** *disturb her work.*

▶ **See Grammar reference, Unit 6,** page 154

---

1 Complete the second sentence so it has a similar meaning to the first. Do not change the word given. Use two to five words, including the word given.

1 I didn't want to be late for my interview, which is why I set two alarms on my phone! **AS**

I set two alarms on my phone _____ late for my interview.

2 Taking on more young people was the company's aim so they offered the job to a recent graduate. **TO**

The company offered the job to a recent graduate _____ more young people.

3 I didn't want to forget about the meeting so I made a note on my phone. **NOT**

I made a note of the meeting on my phone _____ about it.

4 I checked the route to the office so that I wouldn't get lost on my way there. **IN**

I checked the route to the office _____ lost on my way there.

✓ REMEMBER

● After *prefer*, we can use a noun, a full infinitive or an *-ing* form. – *I prefer* **working** *part time.*

● When we are talking about preferring one thing to another, we can use *to* or *rather than*. – *I prefer working outdoors* **to** / **rather than** *working in an office.*

● After *would prefer*, we use a full infinitive. – *I would prefer not* **to answer** *that question.*

● After *would rather*, we use a bare infinitive or a past tense. – *I'd rather* **work** *in the media. I'd rather you* **didn't tell** *my boss about this.*

● After *had better*, we use a bare infinitive. – *You'd better* **call** *the supervisor!*

▶ **See Grammar reference, Unit 6,** page 154

---

2 Write one word in each gap to complete the dialogue. Do you think Ed does well in the job interview or not?

Manager: OK, Ed. So, why would you like to work for us here?

Ed: I need to get a weekend job (**1**) ____ order to make money, really.

Manager: Right ... before we talk about money, I'd (**2**) ____ discuss your skills first. Do you have any experience?

Ed: Not really. I (**3**) ____ playing video games rather (**4**) ____ working, to be honest, but my mum said I (**5**) ____ better apply for a job.

Manager: I see. Let's try a different approach. What (**6**) ____ you rather do, work in the kitchen or serve the public?

Ed: I'd prefer (**7**) ____ work in the kitchen, I think.

Manager: Ah, good. Now we're getting somewhere. Why is that?

Ed: So (**8**) ____ to be sure I always have snacks handy when I want one.

Manager: Right. Well, thanks, Ed. We'll let you know.

Weekend restaurant staff needed

Please apply inside ➔

THINK | RESEARCH | CULTURE | LEARN | ME

How should Ed have answered the manager's questions in Exercise 2? Write a dialogue between the manager and Ed which shows how to give a successful job interview.

Talk2Me

Shall we move on to ...?

Flipped classroom

1 ▷ **Watch the *Talk2Me* video and answer the questions.**

1 What are the most common part-time jobs for teenagers in the UK?

2 What jobs have the people had? Where are they working at the moment?

3 What advantages and disadvantages of working part time do they mention?

2 ▷ **Watch the video again. Underline the phrases in the *Phrase expert* box that you hear on the video.**

> **PHRASE EXPERT**
>
> How about …? | I'd suggest … | Let's think about … | My first suggestion is … | Shall I start? | Shall we move on to …? | Shall we start with this point first? | What about …? | Why don't we …

3 **In pairs or as a group, answer the questions.**

• Do you or any of your friends work? If so, what do you/they enjoy about it? If not, do you ever earn money in other ways?

• What jobs do people your age do in your country?

4 **In pairs, make some notes for each point about working part time when you are a student.**

1 learning to manage money
  you might be able to save money you have earned

2 meeting different people

3 becoming independent

4 learning new skills

5 organising your time better

5 **Write a word or short phrase from the box in each gap.**

> How | I'd suggest | Let's | Shall we
> What about | Why

1 _____ think about what you might learn about money.

2 _____ about learning to save money you've earned?

3 _____ we choose organising your time better.

4 _____ move on to the next point?

5 _____ discussing 'becoming independent'?

6 _____ don't we choose 'learning new skills'?

OPTIMISE YOUR EXAM

Collaborative task

● In an exam you need to try and talk about as many of the different points with your partner. Remember to talk together. Don't talk individually about each point!

● It's a good idea to ask for and make suggestions. This will give the discussion a structure and help you move on to different points.

6 **In pairs, talk for two minutes about whether it's a good idea for students to work part time. You can use the ideas below to help you.**

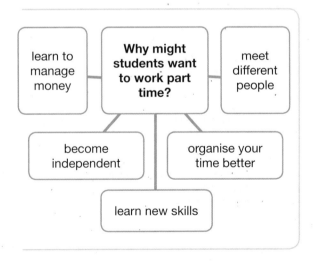

7 **In pairs, talk for a minute and decide which two things are most important for students to consider when they are thinking about getting a part-time job.**

1 **Look at the words in capitals in Exercise 2 and answer the questions.**

1 Which of the words are verbs? What abstract nouns can you form from those verbs? _____

2 What other words referring to people can you make from *employ*? _____

3 Which of the words can you add *-ly* to, without making any other changes, to make new words? _____

2 **Write a form of the word in capitals in each gap to complete the text.**

Working for nothing?

One of the main reasons young people find (**1**) _____ is to make money, and that's important. But have you ever considered doing (**2**) _____ work? You might think of it as 'working for nothing', but that's definitely not the case! Although you won't see any (**3**) _____ reward for your work, you'll get a lot of (**4**) _____ from doing something for other people and for your community.

EMPLOY

VOLUNTEER

FINANCE
SATISFY

Volunteers do a wide (**5**) _____ of work. They might help to clean up an area in their own (**6**) _____ , or go abroad and help people who live in (**7**) _____ in other countries. The skills they learn, the experience they get and the (**8**) _____ they form are all things that volunteers gain from giving their time to help other people.

VARY
NEIGHBOUR
POOR
FRIEND

3 **Read the text in Exercise 4 quickly. Answer the questions.**

1 Which two gaps are followed by prepositions or adverbs? ____ , ____

2 Which gap has a phrasal verb as the answer? ____

3 Which gaps test your knowledge of collocations with *go* or *get*? ____ , ____ , ____ , ____

4 Which gap is followed by an *-ing* form? ____

4 **Choose the correct word to fill each gap.**

Young actors' working lives

Many young people dream of (**1**) ____ a place in a stage production, and you might get the (**2**) ____ that being in a professional play or musical involves taking lots of time off school, but that's generally not the case. Because most of the performances are in the evening, young stars often do a full day at school, eat something at home and then make their way to the theatre to (**3**) ____ ready.

Theatre work often (**4**) ____ performing late into the evening and not getting to bed until nearly midnight. Not only that, but you may (**5**) ____ upset because you cannot fully enjoy your weekends because of rehearsals or extra homework. It can be very demanding, and you need to be able to (**6**) ____ with a lot of pressure at a young age. It's certainly not a job that (**7**) ____ everyone, and only those who are really determined will get (**8**) ____ .

1	**A** working	**B** making	**C** getting	**D** going
2	**A** impression	**B** feeling	**C** thought	**D** look
3	**A** be	**B** go	**C** become	**D** get
4	**A** takes	**B** manages	**C** means	**D** does
5	**A** get	**B** come	**C** go	**D** hang
6	**A** cope	**B** avoid	**C** handle	**D** succeed
7	**A** fits	**B** matches	**C** likes	**D** suits
8	**A** forward	**B** ahead	**C** front	**D** straight

1 **In pairs or as a group, answer the questions.**

1 What are the advantages and disadvantages of having a part-time job?

2 Look at the photos. What jobs are these?

2 **Read this letter and answer the questions in your own words.**

Hi Carlos,

It was great to hear from you! I'm really happy you're enjoying your new school. Your classmates sound like a lot of fun but we miss you!

You said you're thinking about getting a weekend job in order to earn some money. That's a great idea, as long as it doesn't affect your schoolwork. I reckon working teaches you a lot about handling money, and gives you a sense of independence.

In my country, some of my friends prefer to work as babysitters. It's popular because it's quite easy and you don't need any special training to do it. Another thing that they do is help out on local farms. There are quite a few farms around here, and they're always looking for someone to help feed the animals. It's not a bad way of earning a bit of money.

Why not try asking farmers in your area if they need any help? You mentioned that you like animals, so I think that kind of work would definitely suit you. I suggest giving it a go to see if you like it.

Hope that helps!

Love,

Scarlett

1 What are the main points the writer mentions in favour of getting a job?

in order to earn some money/handling money

2 What warning does the writer give about getting a job?

as long as it doesn't affect your homework

3 What job does the writer suggest her friend should consider and why?

farmer because she wants to be babysitters

Second to suggest to help feed the animals

because she like

3 **Find informal words and phrases in the letter which mean the same as these words and phrases.**

1 Dear Mr Williams, _____

2 I would like to thank you for your previous letter. _____

3 You mentioned your intention of finding part-time employment. _____

4 An additional source of employment for adolescents is the local agricultural industry. _____

5 I hope this information has been of use. _____

6 Yours sincerely, _____

4 **Rewrite the writer's suggestions using the words given.**

Why not try asking farmers in your area if they need any help?

1 how _____

2 what _____

3 suggest _____

4 should _You should ask farmers in your_ _____

I suggest giving it a go to see if you like it.

5 how _about giving it a go to see if you like it_

6 what _about giving it a go to see_

7 why _not giving it a go_

8 should _give it a go to_

A letter / An email

- When you write to a friend you can use informal language and punctuation, including exclamation marks.

- Remember to start and finish your letter with phrases such as *Hi/Dear Carlos, Love, Scarlett.*

- Start with a fixed phrase to show you know the reader, for example, *It was good/great to hear from you …*

5 **Look at this writing task and make notes to answer the questions. Use your imagination if necessary.**

You have received a letter from your English-speaking pen friend.

I need your help, if you don't mind! I'm thinking of getting a part-time job. I need the money, but I'm really not sure if I should or not. Do you think it's a good idea? What jobs do teenagers usually do in your country? Why? And do you have any suggestions for what jobs I should consider?

Thanks!
Ellie

1 What are the main advantages and disadvantages of getting a part-time job you would like to mention to your friend? Choose two or three of the options below or add your own idea.

- You become independent. ☐
- It can affect your schoolwork. ☐
- You learn about money. ☐
- You can get very tired. ☐
- You gain useful experience. ☐
- You don't make much money. ☐
- _____

2 Name two jobs it's possible for teenagers to do in your country. For each one, say why someone might choose this job.

- job: _____
  reason: _____
- job: _____
  reason: _____

3 What job would you suggest your friend should do? Why?
_____

6 **Plan** Make a paragraph plan.

Part	Purpose	Useful phrases	My notes
Greeting	say hello	*Hi …*	
Paragraph 1	start in a friendly way and refer to something your friend told you last time	*Great/Good to hear from you.* *Thanks for your letter.* *I was glad/sorry to hear about …*	
Paragraph 2	write about the advantages and disadvantages of working	*One plus of working is …* *There are some disadvantages, though, including …*	
Paragraph 3	write about a couple of jobs teenagers do and say why	*Teenagers here often work as …* *They might also be employed as …*	
Paragraph 4	suggest a job that your friend should do and why	*How about working …?* *You should …* *I suggest you …*	
Closing phrases	say goodbye	*Love,*	

7 **Write** Write your letter in an appropriate style. Write 140–190 words.

8 **Check** Before you hand in your letter, complete this checklist.

Checklist ✓

- ○ I've started and ended my letter in an appropriate way.
- ○ I've written at least four paragraphs.
- ○ I've covered all the points my friend mentioned in her letter.
- ○ I've checked my spelling and grammar.

GRAMMAR AND VOCABULARY

1 Write a form of the word in capitals in each gap.

PROFESSIONAL SPORTING EVENTS

Behind every successful sporting **(1)** _____ , such as an athletics event or a football match, there are many people who are working to make the event a success for both the athletes, the spectators in the stadium and the **(2)** _____ watching on TV at home.

COMPETE

VIEW

There are **(3)** _____ types of people involved. Some of them are professionals – paid to organise and run the event every week – and some are **(4)** _____ , giving their time for free with no **(5)** _____ reward.

VARY
VOLUNTARY
FINANCE

While the athletes may feel some **(6)** _____ about how they do – after all, there can always only be one **(7)** _____ in a race or match – the organisers have their own worries, and feel great **(8)** _____ and relief if the event goes off without a problem.

ANXIOUS
WIN
SATISFY

___/8

2 Write a form of *go* or *get* in each gap.

1 There's no need to _____ upset. I'm only joking!
2 We've been thinking about _____ abroad this summer.
3 Two employees _____ the sack yesterday for stealing from the company.
4 It's the first time a shop in the high street _____ bankrupt.
5 It took me an hour _____ ready to go out.

___/5

3 Write one word in each gap.

1 The team consists _____ eleven players and four substitutes.
2 He was banned _____ driving for three years.
3 What's the difference _____ basketball and netball?
4 It took me a while to adjust _____ the new rules.
5 Knee pads and a helmet help prevent you _____ hurting yourself when skateboarding.

___/5

4 Choose the correct word or phrase.

1 If I save enough money, I'll **be able to / can** get that smartphone I want.
2 You **mustn't / don't have to** come to the supermarket with me, but you can if you want to.
3 You **should / could** be wearing a jacket – we're going to get cold and wet today.
4 She **should / must** have had to sacrifice a lot to become so successful.
5 You **can't / mustn't** be hungry – you've just had lunch!

___/5

5 Write a word from the box in each gap.

check | make | mind | pull | stand

1 Can you _____ out what that sign says over there? I can't read it.
2 _____ out this new blog! It's really interesting.
3 Why did Becky _____ out of the race halfway through?
4 Two players this year _____ out as being exceptionally talented.
5 _____ out! That lorry's reversing.

___/5

6 Write each verb in the correct form (*-ing* form, full infinitive, bare infinitive) to complete the sentences.

1 Will your parents let you _____ (**stay**) at mine tonight?

2 Eddie seems _____ (**be**) upset about something.

3 The game involves _____ (**get**) your counter around the board first.

4 We regret _____ (**inform**) you that your application has not been successful.

5 Did you intend _____ (**buy**) an extra ticket, or was it a mistake?

6 I suggest _____ (**take**) the train tomorrow – it's quicker than the bus.

7 Oh no! I forgot _____ (**ask**) our neighbours to feed the cat.

8 Do you mind _____ (**help**) me take the rubbish out to the dustbin?

9 I don't know how you managed _____ (**write**) that essay so quickly.

10 Dad promised _____ (**drive**) us to the match on Saturday.

___/10

7 Complete the second sentence so it has a similar meaning to the first. Do not change the word given. Use two to five words, including the word given.

1 Megan's ill, so we'll need someone to replace her in the match on Saturday. **FILL**

Megan's ill, so we'll need to find someone to _____ in the match on Saturday.

2 Mum said we had to do the washing-up before we could go out. **US**

Mum insisted _____ the washing-up before we could go out.

3 It seems like Phil's upset about something. **IMPRESSION**

I _____ Phil's upset about something.

4 You knew it was a test, so why were you talking? **BEEN**

You knew it was a test so you _____ !

5 My parents don't let me use my tablet or phone when I'm in bed. **ALLOWED**

I _____ use my tablet or phone when I'm in bed.

6 Please don't interrupt me, Chris. **RATHER**

I _____ interrupt me, Chris.

___/12

Total score ___/50

▼
EXAM SKILLS

Tick the statements that are true for you. Review the skills in the unit if you need more help.

I can ...	Unit/page
☐ understand text logic in an online article	Unit 5 p48
☐ identify relevant information in an interview	Unit 5 p52
☐ speculate about a situation in a photo task	Unit 5 p54
☐ remember the importance of accurate spelling and use phrases and idioms accurately to complete activities	Unit 5 p55
☐ use formal language in a letter / an email	Unit 5 p56
☐ identify synonyms in an information leaflet	Unit 6 p58
☐ identify key information in a short talk	Unit 6 p62
☐ make suggestions in a collaborative task	Unit 6 p64
☐ create adjective forms and use particles and prepositions accurately	Unit 6 p65
☐ make suggestions to a friend in an informal letter/email	Unit 6 p66

7 Exploring art

READING | Gapped text | A news article

1 **In pairs or as a group, answer the questions.**

1 Look at the photos and title of the article. What do you think a street arts festival is like?

2 What kind of things might you see or do?

3 Why might it be important to have street art festivals?

2 **Read the article quickly (ignore the gapped sentences). Then answer questions 1–4.**

1 How can people interact with some of the exhibits during Lumiere London?

2 What opportunities does the festival create?

3 What kind of people does it attract?

4 What can you see or do at other Lumiere festivals around the world?

3 **Discuss your answers with a partner. Which of the exhibits described would you find most interesting and why?**

4 **Look at the sentences with gaps in the article and the sentences in Exercise 5. Answer the questions.**

1 Which sentences need a preposition after the last word before the gap? Which preposition? _____

2 Which sentence adds information? Which pronoun can replace a city, e.g. London? _____

3 Which sentence contrasts information? Think of a word which means 'don't have to pay for something'. _____

4 Which sentence has the word *audience*? Which pronoun can replace it? _____

5 What synonyms do you know for *rubbish* and *ocean*? _____ , _____

OPTIMISE YOUR EXAM

Gapped text

- To complete a gap with the ending of a sentence, you need to read the main part of the sentence in context first.

- Check the main sentence and the missing sentence ending for any grammar links. Look for reference words, such as pronouns (*she*, *it*), words with dependent prepositions, verb tenses and linking words (e.g. *and*, *but*, *because*).

LIGHTING UP *the city*

t's a cold January night and I'm standing in Oxford Circus, one of London's main shopping areas, but I'm not doing any window-shopping. Instead I'm gazing at a 3-D image sculpture called *1.8* which is hanging here between the buildings. This amazing sculpture was inspired [1]. And it's not just for admiring. I'm now downloading an app onto my smartphone which means I'll be able to actually interact with the sculpture. This is fun … there's a huge captive audience here and with just a phone [2]!

This is part of Lumiere London and it's one of the many exhibits that are lighting up central London for three days. I've been all over the city centre looking at some fabulous sights. I've seen fish in a telephone box, a neon dress which stands up by itself and lots of people enjoying themselves. Earlier on I was at the Kings Cross light graffiti installation where I bumped into a group of young French people. I asked 16-year-old Gaston for his impressions. 'We're students on a school exchange visiting London for the first time and [3]. I'm really impressed by everything. Light graffiti is incredible. You can use your smartphone torch to paint graffiti on any surface because the installation turns it into light and it looks like you're painting. Your phone becomes a sort of spray can … amazing! We're enjoying ourselves a lot.'

So, just what is Lumiere London? It's a free arts festival designed to temporarily transform the city. Organised by Artichoke, a company whose mission it is to use public spaces to show ambitious and different art forms, the festival has the backing of the London city council and aims [4]. It creates an opportunity to expose people to more art and anyone can get involved. The fact that so many of the exhibits are interactive means that the audience really get to have a hands-on experience.

Judging by the crowds of teenagers and young children with their parents, the festival is fulfilling its aim. In Trafalgar Square I discovered *Plastic Islands*, glowing plastic shapes made from thousands of bottles floating in the fountains which represent all the rubbish dumped in the North Pacific Ocean. No-one looking at this could ignore the fact that we need to be more aware [5].

While thinking about what to see next I talked to Darina, who was visiting from Odessa, Ukraine. 'What's fantastic is that it's all here for everyone. I don't have a lot of money to spend but [6]. I love London! But I've also visited Berlin to see the Festival of Lights there. They even have artists who walk around in costumes made of light. Incredible!'

This got me back on my smartphone to have a look for other light festivals from around the world. Vivid Sydney sounded worth a visit to see iconic buildings like the Opera House lit up with amazing designs. Or Kobe Lumiere in Japan, which stands as a symbol of hope after the 1995 Great Hanshin earthquake, and Amsterdam Light Festival, where you can take a trip along the canals to see all the illuminated artworks. What a night! I've had a great time and met people from all over the world who have come to London and found something different, educational and free for everyone to enjoy.

5 🔊 2.07 Read the text again. Choose which sentence ending A–G fits each gap 1–6. There is one extra sentence ending you do not need.

A we've discovered that it is full of light this week

B of the litter dumped in our seas and take more care of our environment

C on ideas the artist got when travelling in South East Asia

D all this is free and you make friends in the crowd

E to bring art to all kinds of people and age groups

F by fishing nets that the artist saw when travelling

G they are moving the light and patterns around on the sculpture itself

6 Find these words and phrases in the article. Work out what they mean from the context.

bumped into (phr v)	captive (audience) (adj)
fulfilling (v)	gazing at (v)
the backing of (phr)	worth a visit (adj phr)

THINK | **RESEARCH** | CULTURE | LEARN | ME

Go online and find out about another light festival from around the world. Write a short summary of it, including what people can see and do there. Include any photos you can find. Give a short presentation in groups to your classmates.

Grammar in context

Look at these sentences from the article on page 71. Choose the correct word. Then find these extracts in the article on page 71 and check your answers.

1 *We're enjoying* **themselves / ourselves** *a lot.*

2 *... anyone / anything can get involved.*

3 *... they / there 's a huge captive audience ...*

> ✓ **REMEMBER**
>
> ● *Myself, yourself, himself, herself, oneself, itself, ourselves, yourselves* and *themselves* are reflexive pronouns.
>
> ● We often use reflexive pronouns when the subject and object are the same: *We had to draw ourselves in art class today.*
>
> ● We can also use them for emphasis: *Did you take that photograph yourself?*

▶ **See Grammar reference, Unit 7,** page 155

1 **Write a reflexive pronoun in each gap.**

1 Did you all enjoy _____ at the art gallery?

2 I chose the subject matter _____ , but Dad helped me with the colours and style.

3 I'd love to invent a paintbrush that cleaned _____ after you'd used it.

4 All the artists should be pleased with _____ because the exhibition was a success.

5 We decided that we could paint Sean's room _____ .

2 **Decide which reflexive pronouns in Exercise 1 are essential and which just add emphasis.**

> ✓ **REMEMBER**
>
> ● We use *there + to be* to talk about something that exists: ***There's*** *a book about street art I really want for my birthday.*
>
> ● We use *it + to be* to refer to the weather and temperature (***it's*** *raining,* ***it was*** *cold*), distances (***it's*** *a long way*), situations (***it was*** *a great exhibition*) and in phrases such as ***It is*** *believed/thought/said that ...,* ***It has been*** *found that ...*
>
> ● We use *one* when we're not being specific (*These posters are great! I might buy* ***one***.), and *it* when we're being specific (*This poster is great! I might buy* ***it***.).
>
> ● We usually use *something, someone/somebody, somewhere* in positive statements and *anything, anyone/anybody* and *anywhere* in negative statements and questions.

▶ **See Grammar reference, Unit 7,** page 155

3 **If the word or phrase in bold is correct, put a tick. If it's incorrect, rewrite it correctly.**

1 **It's** fantastic now that we do sculpture for three hours a week. _____

2 **It** is a public space near here where you're allowed to do graffiti. _____

3 Do you know **anything** about using acrylic paints? _____

4 If these photographs were cheaper, I might get **it**. _____

5 Don't tell **someone** I've entered that screenwriting competition. _____

6 Are **they** any galleries round here that show local art? _____

7 There must be **anywhere** round here that sells art supplies. _____

4 **Write one word in each gap to complete the text.**

CAVE PAINTINGS

(**1**) _____ are many fantastic examples of early human art in caves in Spain and France. Because of this, scientists thought that the human ability to create art was (**2**) _____ that first originated in Europe around 37,300 years ago.

However, a recent discovery in Indonesia has changed that view. (**3**) _____ may seem incredible, but at least 40,000 years ago, artists on the island of Sulawesi were creating images of (**4**) _____ and their bodies by pressing their hands against a cave wall and blowing paint in the spaces, or painting full human figures and animals. But (**5**) _____ aren't just paintings there from so long ago. (**6**) _____ has been discovered that nearby are cave paintings which are around 27,000 years old. Scientists hadn't seen (**7**) _____ like this outside Europe before.

● **SAY IT RIGHT**

Resource centre: Unit 7
Stress in reflexive pronouns

THINK | RESEARCH | CULTURE | LEARN | ME

Have you visited any ancient artistic remains? What were they, how old were they and what were they like?

Words connected with *the arts*

1 ◁))) 2.08 **Write a word from the box in each gap. Listen and check.**

> abstract | illustration | masterpiece

1 A painting consisting of coloured lines, circles and squares: _____

2 A very famous and important painting, e.g. Da Vinci's *Mona Lisa*, Van Gogh's *Sunflowers*: _____

3 A picture in a children's book: _____

> set | stage | studio

4 The temporary construction where a film or TV show is made: _____

5 The part of the theatre where actors perform in front of an audience: _____

6 Where artists create their work: _____

> auction | exhibition | installation

7 Pieces of art that have been arranged in a specific way to produce a particular effect: _____

8 An event when items are sold to people who offer the most money: _____

9 A public show where works of art and other things are displayed so people can go and see them: _____

> choreographer | conductor | producer

10 This person directs the musicians in an orchestra: _____

11 This person plans the movements performed by dancers: _____

12 This person plans and coordinates film projects: _____

Phrasal verbs

2 ◁))) 2.09 **Choose the correct word to complete each sentence. Listen and check.**

1 I wasn't happy with the drawing, so I *tore* it **up / away** and started again.

2 The director said that we had to *edit* **up / out** the music from the scene because she didn't like it.

3 I didn't use to enjoy ballet at all, but it*'s grown* **on / over** me recently.

4 I always *sketch* **off / out** a rough outline of the picture before I start the painting itself.

5 The local council*'s drawing* **down / up** plans to build a new art gallery in the town centre.

6 As he was painting, you couldn't see what it was – then he turned it upside down and it *turned* **up / out** to be a self-portrait!

Collocations from the art world

3 ◁))) 2.10 **The words and phrases in bold are in the wrong sentences. Write each one next to the correct sentence. Listen and check.**

1 Writing a novel, play or song is difficult because you basically start with a blank **part**. _____

2 Our hotel seems quiet and organised to guests, but it's often very hectic behind the **centre stage**. _____

3 When we go out, Sam always tries to take **scenes**. She loves being the centre of attention! _____

4 Performing on stage and doing schoolwork is a very difficult **canvas** for young actors. _____

5 Mrs Parker was a wonderful headteacher, so she'll be a difficult **balancing act** to follow. I'm going to do my best, though. _____

6 Everyone in class played an important **act** in raising money for charity. _____

THINK | RESEARCH | CULTURE | LEARN | ME

> Look at the metaphorical words and phrases in Exercise 3. Which ones are similar to your first language?

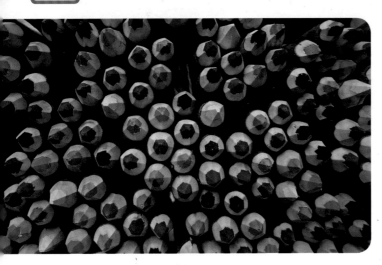

1 **In pairs or as a group, ask and answer the questions.**

1 In what different places and situations do people discuss things related to art and the arts, e.g. *art gallery, theatre, …*?

2 Why do you think people enjoy going to art exhibitions?

2 ◁))) 2.11 **Listen to some extracts from different conversations. For each extract, say what the speaker is doing.**

1 asking for help / making a suggestion / giving advice

2 expressing surprise / making a suggestion / describing a problem

3 giving advice / complaining about something / asking for help

4 expressing surprise / giving advice / describing a problem

5 making a suggestion / complaining about something / describing a problem

6 asking for help / giving advice / making a suggestion

3 **Look at Exercise 4. Which questions ask about the speaker's purpose?**

OPTIMISE YOUR EXAM

Multiple choice

- Some exam questions ask you what the speaker is doing, for example, explaining, describing or comparing something.

- Look carefully at the verbs in the options and think about what the speaker might say. For example, describing: you may hear details about what an object, person or place looks like or how/why something happened; or comparing: listen for comparative words like *bigger, more interesting, not as easy as.*

- If the verb is the same in all three options, e.g. question 2, you need to listen carefully to exactly what is explained.

4 ◁))) 2.12 **You will hear people talking in eight different situations. For questions 1–8, choose the best answer (A, B or C).**

1 You hear two people talking in an art class.
  What does Joel advise Chloe to do?
  A Ignore the mistake she has made.
  B Try to alter what she's done.
  C Go and get another piece of paper.

2 You hear a woman talking about an auction she went to.
  What is she doing?
  A Explaining why Matt wasn't keen to be there.
  B Explaining why she made a particular decision.
  C Explaining why the auction was so full.

3 You hear two people talking about a work of art.
  What do they agree about?
  A that the man isn't a fan of modern art
  B that there's a chance the man might appreciate the piece
  C that the piece is both powerful and beautiful

4 You hear a conversation in a shop.
  What persuades the customer to buy the product?
  A It's cheaper than he expected.
  B It has a lot of variety within it.
  C It's for a number of different interests.

5 You hear part of a documentary on TV about a famous painting.
  When did the artist take the painting to Paris?
  A after public disapproval
  B after critics first praised it
  C after coming out of prison

6 You hear a conversation at a concert.
  Why don't the couple decide to move seats?
  A because one of them still wouldn't be able to see
  B because moving will annoy other people
  C because they might not be allowed to stay there

7 You hear part of an interview with an artist.
  What is she doing?
  A explaining the basic techniques of sculpture
  B comparing her work to another sculptor
  C describing her entry into the world of art

8 You hear two friends talking about a project for school.
  Why do they dismiss their initial idea?
  A because their teacher wouldn't like it
  B because it's a difficult subject to describe
  C because of the difficulty in finding pictures

5 ◁))) 2.12 **Listen again and check your answers.**

THINK | RESEARCH | CULTURE | LEARN | ME

Imagine you could do a project on any aspect of art or the arts you like. Which would you choose, and why?

Grammar in context

Look at these extracts from the audio in the listening lesson and write a word in each gap.

enough	so	such	too

1 … it's got _____ dark that it's practically black …

2 You're _____ old-fashioned to understand modern art …

3 I didn't have _____ money on me to bid for much …

4 … the person sitting two rows in front of me has got _____ a big hat on I can't see anything at all!

✓ REMEMBER

- We use *so* + adjective/adverb: *The auction was **so exciting** (that) I bought several things.*

- We use *such* (+ article) + adjective + noun: *It was **such a brilliant film** (that) I bought the soundtrack.*

- *Too* means 'so much/many that it's negative', and isn't followed by a *that* clause. We use *too* + adjective/adverb (+ for someone/something) (+ full infinitive): *There are **too many** exhibits in the Louvre (for someone) to see them all in one day.*

- We use *much/far* before *too* + adjective/adverb to add extra emphasis and indicate that something is extremely negative: *You did that **much / far too quickly** – you can't have done it right!*

- *Enough* isn't followed by a *that* clause. We use (*not*) adjective/adverb + *enough* (+ for someone/ something) (+ full infinitive), or (*not*) enough + noun: *I think you're **talented enough** to become a professional dancer. / I haven't got **enough patience** to be a painter.*

▶ **See Grammar reference, Unit 7,** page 155

1 Choose the correct word or phrase.

1 These scissors are **so / such** blunt that they can't even cut a piece of paper.

2 'I'm worried she's working **so / too** quickly to produce a quality piece of work,' said the judge.

3 Working for a theatre company must be **such an / a too** interesting job.

4 There aren't **visitors enough / enough visitors** coming to the museum to keep it open.

5 I'm not **knowledgeable enough / enough knowledgeable** to be an art critic.

6 I'm **much too / too much** impatient to be a sculptor.

7 Opera singers have **so / such** incredible voices.

8 You've put **much too much / far too many** paint on that brush.

✓ REMEMBER

- *Although*, *even though* and *though* separate two different clauses. They go at the beginning of a sentence, or in the middle: ***Even though** it was tricky at first, I managed to paint a great picture!*

- *In spite of* and *despite* are followed by a noun, an *-ing* form, or the phrase *the fact (that)* + clause. They go at the beginning of a sentence, or in the middle: ***Despite** hav**ing** two auditions, Coleen failed to get a place at drama school.*

- With *however*, the things being contrasted are in separate sentences. It can go at the beginning of a sentence, in the middle, or at the end. *The modern art area was empty. **However**, the sculpture exhibition was packed.*

▶ **See Grammar reference, Unit 7,** page 155

2 Rewrite the sentence in different ways using the words given.

I got a new camera last month but I haven't taken any photos recently.

1 even _____

2 spite _____

3 however _____

4 although _____

5 despite _____

3 Write one word in each gap.

Tiger and Turtle – Magic Mountain

(1) _____ though when many people think of modern art they think of abstract paintings hanging on a wall, some modern art isn't inside at all. Take *Tiger and Turtle – Magic Mountain* in Duisburg, Germany, for example.

From a distance, it looks like a rollercoaster. (2) _____ , it is a piece of art – a sculpture, in fact! And despite (3) _____ a sculpture, it's interactive, and visitors can walk and climb on it.

You can't, (4) _____ , walk all the way from one end to another along the 'track' because of the loop in the middle. It's (5) _____ steep to climb all the way up. On a rollercoaster, the cars are going fast (6) _____ to get round the complete loop without falling off.

The piece was created by artists Heike Mutter and Ulrich Genth, who entered the design in an international competition. The judges were so impressed with it (7) _____ it was chosen as the winner.

It is (8) _____ an unusual work of art it's appeared in lots of newspapers and magazines, and on many websites.

Talk 2 Me

If I had to choose ...

Flipped classroom

1 ▷ **Watch the *Talk2Me* video and answer the questions.**

1 How many of the people prefer listening to live music to listening to music at home?

2 What types of music are mentioned?

3 What type of concert is the most popular: indoor concerts or outdoor festivals?

2 ▷ **Watch the video again. Write the names of the people who use these phrases and what opinion they give.**

> **PHRASE EXPERT**
>
> Although (intimate concerts are good), I'd rather (listen with a crowd of people) | I'd go for … because | If I had to choose, I'd prefer … because | I'm not really very interested in (live music) so … | I think I'd prefer to be … as | I wouldn't mind (going to a festival) because … | One of the reasons why I'd prefer this is …

3 **In pairs or as a group, discuss the following questions.**

• Would you prefer to listen to music at home or go to a live concert? Explain why.

• How often do you listen to music?

• What genres of music do you like listening to?

4 **Look at the underlined words and phrases. Substitute them with appropriate alternatives from the box. Not all of the alternatives will be used.**

> because | I'd rather | if I had to choose
> I'm not really very interested in | that's
> the reason why

> I love listening to music at home with my friends and I love going to concerts and <u>so</u> I'd like to be in both situations, but <u>if I could only do one</u>, <u>I'd prefer to</u> go to a live concert <u>as</u> it's incredible to experience something so creative happening in front of your eyes.

5 **Look at photographs A and B. Make notes to complete the chart.**

A

B

	PHOTO A	PHOTO B
Describe what you can see briefly	In this photo I can see …	Whereas in the second one …
Similarities and differences		
What might the people enjoy about being in these places?		

OPTIMISE YOUR EXAM

Photo task

● In an exam, after one of you has compared the photos, the other will be asked a short question about them. You have about 30 seconds to talk.

● You may be asked about what situation you prefer. Look again at the photos and make a quick decision. Say which you prefer and give reasons or an example to explain your preference.

6 **In pairs, take turns to talk on your own for about a minute. Compare the two photographs in Exercise 5 and say what the people might enjoy about being in these different places.**

7 **Take turns to answer this question:** *Which place would you prefer to be in and why?* **You have about 30 seconds to talk. Ask your partner to time you.**

1 Look at the words in capitals in Exercise 2 and answer the questions.

Which of them …

1 needs a change other than just adding a suffix to form an adverb? ____
2 forms an adverb ending in -*fully*? ____
3 forms a noun ending in -*ment*? ____

Word formation

● If there is a gap after a verb, you may need to form an adverb.
● Be careful with the spelling of adverbs – some adverbs are spelt with a double *ll*, e.g. *hopefully, carefully*.

2 Write a form of the word in capitals in each gap to complete the text.

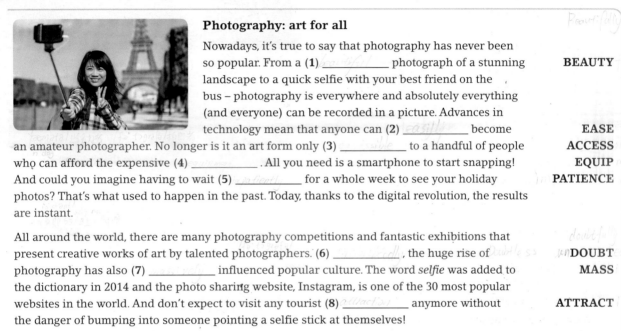

Photography: art for all

Nowadays, it's true to say that photography has never been so popular. From a **(1)** _____ photograph of a stunning landscape to a quick selfie with your best friend on the bus – photography is everywhere and absolutely everything (and everyone) can be recorded in a picture. Advances in technology mean that anyone can **(2)** _____ become an amateur photographer. No longer is it an art form only **(3)** _____ to a handful of people who can afford the expensive **(4)** _____ . All you need is a smartphone to start snapping! And could you imagine having to wait **(5)** _____ for a whole week to see your holiday photos? That's what used to happen in the past. Today, thanks to the digital revolution, the results are instant.

BEAUTY

EASE
ACCESS
EQUIP
PATIENCE

All around the world, there are many photography competitions and fantastic exhibitions that present creative works of art by talented photographers. **(6)** _____ , the huge rise of photography has also **(7)** _____ influenced popular culture. The word *selfie* was added to the dictionary in 2014 and the photo sharing website, Instagram, is one of the 30 most popular websites in the world. And don't expect to visit any tourist **(8)** _____ anymore without the danger of bumping into someone pointing a selfie stick at themselves!

DOUBT
MASS

ATTRACT

3 Look at the sentences in Exercise 4 and answer the questions.

Which of them …

1 will need a reflexive pronoun?
_____
2 relies on knowing the difference between *so* and *such*?
_____
3 will need a phrasal verb?
_____

Sentence transformation

● Read both sentences carefully, then decide what part of speech the word given is. Think about what structure it could be used with.
● Look at the words before and after the gap to see what kind of structure might fit the gap and the word given.

4 Complete the second sentence so it has a similar meaning to the first. Do not change the word given. Use two to five words, including the word given.

1 There were so many people at the exhibition that we ran out of programmes. **SUCH**
There were _____ people at the exhibition that we ran out of programmes.

2 Although the craft fair was great, we didn't buy anything. **SPITE**
We didn't buy anything at the craft fair _____ great.

3 The knives are really sharp so be very careful, won't you? **CUT**
The knives are really sharp so _____ , will you?

4 You're too young to decide that you're going to art college. **OLD**
You're _____ to decide that you're going to art college.

5 We haven't got any clay so we'll have to use Plasticine instead. **DO**
We'll have to _____ Plasticine as we haven't got any clay.

6 Some people say that art is food for the soul. **BEEN**
It _____ that art is food for the soul.

1 **In pairs or as a group, answer the questions.**

1 Look at the photo. Why do you think the object is protected?

2 In what other ways do you think galleries and museums protect their famous works of art?

2 **Read this story and make notes.**

One last time

Mickey was sure that they had thought of everything. He and his long-term partner in crime, Lou, were sitting in the reception of the Hotel de Chic. They had been working and planning this moment for a very long time, and its success or failure would decide how they spent the rest of their lives.

But they weren't looking at the rich and famous hotel guests. They were looking at the national gallery opposite and in particular a side door. Mickey had paid a security guard 500 euros to leave it unlocked. And if everything went according to plan, it wouldn't be long before they were walking out of that door with The Pharaoh's Gift, a vase worth 15 million euros!

As the clock struck 8 pm, Mickey's heart began beating faster. The time had come. The gallery had closed for the day two hours ago, and now the staff were leaving. The two friends looked at each other, took a deep breath and opened the door.

Suddenly, a voice shouted behind them – 'Stop! Put your hands up in the air!'

Title	Do you like it? Is it appropriate?
Main characters	Who are they? Are they believable? Are they interesting?
Setting	Where is the story set? Is this successful?
Plot	What happens in the story? Is it interesting?
Suspense	Does the writer manage to create any suspense? If so, how?
Emotions	What emotions do the characters feel?
Ending	Is this successful?
Tenses	What different tenses has the writer used? Why?
Language	How formal is it? Is there any direct speech? Are there any other interesting elements?

3 **In pairs or groups, compare your notes and discuss the questions in Exercise 2.**

OPTIMISE YOUR EXAM

A story

- Make the plot interesting but easy to follow.
- Try to get the reader's attention from the start by setting the scene or including a dramatic beginning.
- You can create suspense by writing short sentences.
- Remember to describe how the characters feel. Use a variety of adjectives to bring the people to life! Try to use different tenses including the past continuous and past perfect continuous.

4 **Look at this writing task and make notes to answer the questions.**

You have seen this announcement in an international magazine for teenagers.

Stories wanted

Write a story for our magazine. Your story must begin with this sentence:
Alex quickly opened the old sketchpad, and started looking at the drawings.
Your story must include:
- a surprising discovery
- a purchase

Write your **story**.

- Who is Alex and where is he?
  _____

- Who drew the pictures in the sketchpad?
  _____

- What are they pictures of?
  _____

- How does Alex feel about them?
  _____

- Who makes a surprising discovery? What is it?
  _____

- Who makes a purchase? What do they buy?
  _____

- What happens at the end of the story?
  _____

- What would be an appropriate title for the story?
  _____

5 **Plan** Make a paragraph plan.

Part	Purpose	My notes
Title	include a short, concise title and make us want to read it!	
Paragraph 1	copy the first sentence and set the scene and create suspense – where is Alex? what is he doing?	
Middle paragraphs	continue the story – what happened next? what was the surprising discovery? what did Alex buy?	
Final paragraph	bring the story to an end – how did Alex feel? did anything surprising happen afterwards?	

6 **Write** Write your story in an appropriate style. Write 140–190 words.

7 **Check** Before you hand in your story, complete this checklist.

Checklist ✓

- ◯ I've given my story a title.
- ◯ I've copied the first sentence of the story correctly.
- ◯ I've written at least three paragraphs.
- ◯ I've mentioned a surprising discovery and a purchase.

- ◯ I've interested the reader by creating some suspense.
- ◯ I've used a variety of appropriate tenses.
- ◯ I've used some direct speech.
- ◯ I've checked my spelling and grammar.

8 The world around us

READING | Multiple matching | A nature article

1 **In pairs or as a group, answer the questions.**

1 Which areas of your country are known for their natural beauty?

2 What can people visiting those areas expect to experience?

2 **Read the article quickly. Match each person with an overall opinion of the park. There is one extra sentence you do not need.**

A Aiden King: ____

B Chloe Morton: ____

C Nakaaya Kikwete: ____

D Manuel Garcia: ____

1) It faces challenges from different threats and its amazing natural wealth needs to be protected.

2) It doesn't deserve the reputation it has for outstanding beauty and amazing wildlife.

3) It impressed me with its natural beauty, but it also made me think about what is important.

4) It was interesting, but it didn't mean as much to me as it could have done with more information.

5) It helped me to connect with other people and what their lives were like in the past.

3 **Find phrases in the article for expressing attitude and opinion that mean the same as phrases 1–5.**

1 I thought it was …

_____

2 As you might expect, …

_____

3 In my opinion, …

_____ , _____

4 … my personal opinion is …

_____

5 … I am certain that …

_____

OPTIMISE YOUR **EXAM**

Multiple matching

- In this task, the writer's attitudes and opinions are often important. Look for key phrases that show this, e.g. *To my mind …*, *My own view is …*

- Also look for adjectives and descriptive phrases that show attitude and opinion, e.g. *it was (…) that really stuck with me, breathtaking, stunning.*
  incredible

NATIONAL PARKS

Four young people tell us about visiting a national park in their country.

A Mammoth Cave National Park, Kentucky, USA

Aiden King

The Mammoth Cave National Park is an extensive underground system of caves of which about 400 miles have been explored. I found it really impressive, and some of the rock formations are incredible. If I'd known more about the history before going, I'd have got more out of it. Not surprisingly, rocks get a little tedious after a while without a context, and unlike other national parks, there isn't a great deal of wildlife. It all seemed rather laid on for visitors, so it was a relief to go on a 'wild' tour, which takes you to some of the less-developed parts of the cave system. Crawling in small spaces in mud you can get a real sense of what it must have been like for the early explorers. Local legends say that wanted criminals used to hide in the caves!

Nakaaya Kikwete

The Serengeti National Park is world famous for the fact that one and a half million wildebeest migrate 600 miles every year in search of fresh grass and water. For me, it was an epic sight, and the struggle of the wildebeest to survive in dangerous conditions (the rivers are full of crocodiles!) reminded me

C Serengeti National Park, Tanzania

of the daily struggle to survive that many people in my country face. To my mind, national parks are there not only for the conservation of wildlife, but to inspire us to lead better lives. If you visited my country, you would see fantastic scenery and great natural beauty alongside difficult living conditions. It's vital that we explore ways in which our society can develop at the same time as preserving the spectacular natural resources we have. We can't encourage one at the expense of the other.

B Great Barrier Reef Marine Park, Australia

Chloe Morton

The Great Barrier Reef has become one of the global symbols of just how fragile nature can be. There's no doubt that the reef is something we have to preserve very carefully for future generations. The diversity of life in the area is breathtaking! I had an exciting opportunity to help out with a team of marine scientists to see what effect human activity is having on the reef. The area is divided up into zones and there are limits on different activities within each zone. This minimises the impact of some activities, such as diving, while still allowing people to enjoy the stunning natural beauty of the reef. If we had done something like that years ago, the reef would be in a much better state now! Unfortunately, past mistakes and a changing climate mean that parts of the reef are struggling to recover. Let's hope we can improve its cultivation for the future.

Manuel Garcia

Tikal is an amazing place with over 3,000 buildings from the Mayan civilisation! From about 900 BC to 900 AD, a major city of 100,000 people developed and you can still visit the ruins. The park is also home to jaguars and other animals. I visited with my class, and it was awesome to think we were walking in the footsteps of people from so long ago! The temples were very striking, but it was the courts for ball games that really stuck with me. It gave us some insight into

D Tikal National Park, Guatemala

what their lives were like. It's fascinating to think that they played sport just like us! We often look at constructions and monuments and think they represent what a culture was like, but my own view is that it's the ordinary aspects of everyday life that tell us a lot more.

---

4 2.13 **For each question, choose from the people A–D. The people may be chosen more than once.**

Which person

thinks that parks have a function beyond the preservation of animals and monuments? `1 ☐`

visited a place that is seen as a good example of problems faced by nature? `2 ☐`

found a connection with the past through everyday experiences? `3 ☐`

thinks they should have found out more before visiting? `4 ☐`

was impressed by the range of different creatures in the park? `5 ☐`

visited a place that preserves both wild creatures and a way of life? `6 ☐`

preferred to see a side of the place that most tourists don't see? `7 ☐`

thinks that important buildings don't tell the complete story of people's lives? `8 ☐`

thinks we should have done things differently in the past? `9 ☐`

draws a parallel between the natural world and human society? `10 ☐`

---

5 **Find these words and phrases in the article. Work out what they mean from the context.**

> fragile (adj) | insight (n) | inspire (v)
> laid on (phr v) | minimise (v) | preserve (v)
> striking (adj) | tedious (adj)

THINK | RESEARCH | CULTURE | LEARN | ME

Think about a national park in your country. How does it compare to those in the text? Tell the class about it.

Grammar in context

Look at these sentences from the article on page 81. Are they talking about hypothetical events or events that have happened?

If you visited my country, you would see great natural beauty alongside difficult living conditions.

If I'd known more about the history before going, I'd have got more out of it.

If we had done something like that years ago, the reef would be in a much better state now!

✓ REMEMBER

- The second conditional refers to the hypothetical present result of an unlikely or impossible present condition, e.g. *If I were you, I would visit the incredible caves.*

- The third conditional refers to the hypothetical past result of a past condition, e.g. *If I hadn't spoken to Annie, I wouldn't have known about her trip.*

- One type of mixed conditional refers to the hypothetical present result of a past condition, e.g. *If I had taken any photos, I would show them to you.* Another type refers to the hypothetical past result of a present condition, e.g. *If I were in better shape, I would have gone on the trek.*

- Instead of *if*, we can use an inversion. This is more formal, e.g. **Had I not** gone on the trip, I wouldn't have seen the amazing natural park.

▶ See Grammar reference, Unit 8, page 156

---

1 Choose the correct word or phrase to complete each sentence.

1 If you went on safari, do you think you ____ it?
   a) enjoyed   **b)** would enjoy

2 If I had visited the caves, I ____ it very interesting.
   a) would have found   **b)** would find

3 What ____ if we built a new recycling plant?
   a) happened   **b)** would happen

4 If you were in charge, ____ dropping litter illegal?
   a) did you make   **b)** would you make

5 If humans hadn't destroyed their natural habitats, Bengal tigers ____ endangered.
   a) would have been   **b)** wouldn't be

6 My sister ____ a zookeeper if our parents hadn't encouraged her.
   a) wouldn't become   **b)** wouldn't have become

2 Complete the questions using the prompts. Add any words you need and make any necessary changes.

1 If you knew your favourite animal was in danger of extinction, _____ ?
   (you / do)

2 Had you not come here today, _____ _____ ?
   (you / do / instead)

3 If you had been born in another country, _____ _____ ?
   (your life / be different)

4 If you could travel back in time, _____ _____ ?
   (you / like / see)

5 Had you known about the effects of climate change, _____ ?
   (you / start recycling / years ago)

6 If you could be any animal, _____ _____ ?
   (you / be)

3 Write the correct form of the verb or verb phrase from the box in each gap.

| be (× 2) | be aware | bring | have |
| learn | not save | see | survive | want |

EXTINCTION CAUSED BY HUMANS

If you (1) _____ to see a dodo today, you would search in vain of course. The dodo was discovered by Europeans on the island of Mauritius in 1598 and was extinct by 1680. If it hadn't been flightless, perhaps it (2) _____ . However, it was unable to escape sailors, who hunted and ate the bird. Apparently it wasn't particularly tasty, so the dodo population might have recovered from hunting, if the sailors (3) _____ rats, cats and dogs to the island. Perhaps the dodo (4) _____ here today if those animals hadn't eaten the birds and their eggs.

Sadly, the dodo's story is not uncommon. But perhaps if humans (5) _____ of the effects of climate change, hunting and even tourism on many species, there (6) _____ so many critically endangered species. However, there are some stories that bring hope to animals close to extinction. If you (7) _____ the news 15 years ago, you (8) _____ that the Iberian lynx was in danger of becoming extinct. Today, thanks to the efforts made through conservation initiatives, the population has slowly increased to a healthier level. (9) _____ conservationists not made such an effort, the species (10) _____ .

Words connected with *environmental issues*

1 ◁))) 2.14 **Write a word from the box in each gap to make phrases. Listen and check.**

> change | development | effect | energy
> footprint | layer | toxic | warming

1 global _____
2 climate _____
3 greenhouse _____
4 _____ waste
5 carbon _____
6 renewable _____
7 sustainable _____
8 ozone _____

2 **Write a phrase from Exercise 1 in each gap. There may be more than one correct answer.**

1 To measure _____ , you need to look at weather patterns over many years.
2 A person's _____ is a measure of the amount of carbon dioxide that is produced by their actions and its effect on the environment.
3 We need _____ so that our economy can grow without damaging the environment.
4 One of the harmful products produced by industrial processes is _____ .
5 Some countries may face serious problems if _____ is more than 2°C.
6 Wind power and wave power are excellent sources of _____ .
7 The _____ in the atmosphere protects us from dangerous ultraviolet light.
8 The _____ is when the warmth from the sun is trapped in the atmosphere.

Phrasal verbs

3 ◁))) 2.15 **Write a phrasal verb from the box in the correct form to replace the words in brackets in each sentence. Listen and check.**

> call for | chop down | clean up
> die out | do away with | run out
> throw away | wipe out

1 Some animal species _____ (became extinct) due to human activities.
2 People _____ (are demanding) urgent action on climate change.
3 Will we just keep using oil until it all _____ (finishes)?
4 We all have a responsibility to help _____ (tidy) our beaches.
5 If we're not careful, our actions are going to _____ (completely destroy) the wild elephant.
6 I think we should _____ (abolish) cars that produce lots of pollution in city centres to protect the environment.
7 When we _____ (destroy) trees, we remove the natural habitat of a number of species.
8 Don't just _____ (put in the rubbish) your old bottles. Recycle them!

Words + prepositions

4 ◁))) 2.16 **Choose the correct preposition to complete each sentence. Use the words in italics to help you. Listen and check.**

1 Water pollution can be *harmful at / to* fish and animals that live along the river.
2 The Sumatran rhino is *threatened from / by* hunters.
3 Without the ozone layer, we would be *exposed by / to* UV rays that can cause cancer.
4 Do you think we do enough to *protect* animals *by / from* illegal activity?
5 Which countries will be most *affected by / with* climate change?
6 Using drinking water to water the garden is a *waste from / of* natural resources!

THINK | RESEARCH | CULTURE | LEARN | ME

Choose one of the phrases in Exercise 1 and find out more about it. Tell the class what you discover.

1 **In pairs or as a group, ask and answer the questions.**

1 Look at the photos. What are these things? What are they used for? How do they help us?

2 What different kinds of renewable energy can you think of?

2 **Look at Exercise 4 and read the statements A–H. Match the statements to sentences 1–4.**

1 'The people there were really friendly and looked after me. I was grateful for that.'

Statement _____

2 'People in the area were worried about the effects and so was I.'

Statement _____

3 'They were looking for experts on energy, and they gave us a test to see what we knew.'

Statement _____

4 'People didn't seem to know very much about the problem so we need to tell them.'

Statement _____

3 **Look at the four statements in Exercise 4 you didn't use in Exercise 2. For each one, predict what the speaker might say. Use your own words.**

1 Statement _____

_____

2 Statement _____

_____

3 Statement _____

_____

4 Statement _____

_____

OPTIMISE YOUR EXAM

Multiple matching

● Read the statements carefully before you listen and try to predict what someone might say for each one.

● The first time you listen, make a note of any words or phrases that might match a statement and listen for any ideas that are similar to your predictions.

● The second time you listen, check the statement matches exactly what the speaker says.

4 🔊 2.17 **You will hear five extracts about different projects. Choose from A–H what each speaker says about their project. There are three extra letters you do not need.**

A I enjoyed seeing my ideas in practice.

B I was happy I did something I found difficult.

C I was worried we might not make a difference.

D I shared the concerns of local people.

E I discovered I could do more than I thought.

F I had to show that I knew a lot about energy.

G I was thankful for the way I was treated.

H I thought people needed to be educated.

Speaker 1: ☐

Speaker 2: ☐

Speaker 3: ☐

Speaker 4: ☐

Speaker 5: ☐

5 🔊 2.17 **Listen again and check your answers.**

THINK | RESEARCH | CULTURE | LEARN | ME

Do you think developing renewable energy sources is important? Why do you think developing renewable energy sources is considered important for the future?

Grammar in context

Look at these sentences from the audio in the listening lesson. For each one, decide whether the clause in bold refers to the present or the past.

1 *It's time **we did something about it**.*
present / past

2 *I wish **more people knew about geothermal energy**.*
present / past

3 *I wish **I had got involved sooner**.*
present / past

✓ **REMEMBER**

● After some phrases and in some types of sentence, we use past tenses to refer to the present, a general situation or the future. This includes:

  ○ *It's (high) time …*, e.g. *It's high time we **lived** a greener life.*
  ○ *Suppose …, Imagine …* and *What if …?*, e.g. *Imagine there **were** no elephants.*
  ○ *would rather + you/he/she/it/we/they*, e.g. *I'd rather we **didn't** waste so much food.*
  ○ second conditional sentences, e.g. *We'd help the planet if we **recycled** more.*
  ○ *wish* and *if only*, e.g. *I wish people **cared** more about the environment.*
  ○ we can use *would* with *wish* to express criticism, e.g. *I wish you **wouldn't** do that!*
  ○ we can use *could* with *wish* to express hypothetical ability, e.g. *I wish I **could** go camping this weekend, but I can't.*
  ○ for wishes about the past (regrets), we use past perfect, e.g. *I wish people **had thought** about climate change years ago.*

▶ **See Grammar reference, Unit 8,** page 157

1 Complete the sentences using the verbs in brackets in the correct form.

1 It's time we _____ (**stop**) polluting our streams and rivers.

2 Don't you wish you _____ (**have**) a lower carbon footprint?

3 We'd produce less toxic waste if we _____ (**burn**) less fossil fuel.

4 Don't you wish you _____ (**know**) the benefits of living a green life years ago?

5 If only there _____ (**be**) some way of reducing the effects of global warming.

6 Suppose you _____ (**try**) to live a low-carbon life. Would you enjoy it?

2 Rewrite the sentences in different ways using the words given.

1 Please don't throw your litter on the ground.   **RATHER**

_____

2 I shouldn't have bought such a large motorbike.   **WISH**

_____

3 We should manufacture more electric cars in order to help the environment.   **HIGH**

_____

4 I want to wave a magic wand and solve climate change, but I can't.   **COULD**

_____

5 People should realise that we have to use more renewable energy.   **TIME**

_____

6 Do you want people to take the threat to the environment more seriously?   **WOULD**

_____

3 Write a verb from the box in the correct form in each gap. Add any other words you need.

| can | face | get | go | have |
| provide | start | think | | |

Extreme green!

What if your family (**1**) _____ rid of the car, the air-conditioning unit, the tumble dryer, the fridge and almost everything else that uses energy in the home? Suppose you never (**2**) _____ on holiday or you (**3**) _____ to wear extra clothes in bed to keep warm because you had no heating. Those are just a few of the things that people who live an extreme green life have done to try to keep their carbon footprint as low as possible, and many of them wish they (**4**) _____ earlier.

Of course, we all wish we (**5**) _____ use less energy, and for many of us it's high time we (**6**) _____ of ways to cut down on our energy use. However, few of us are prepared to deliberately keep our house cold in the winter and grow all our own food. We'd much rather supermarkets (**7**) _____ us with everything we need, but the food in shops has often travelled a long way to get there. These 'food miles' increase your carbon footprint. Perhaps it's about time we (**8**) _____ up to reality and thought more carefully about the effect our everyday actions have on the environment.

THINK | RESEARCH | CULTURE | LEARN | ME

Could you live an extreme green life? What would you find most difficult?

In what ways could you make your life greener than it is now?

Talk**2**Me

The reason I say this ...

1 ▷ **Watch the *Talk2Me* video. Make notes about each person's replies to the following questions.**

1 How do you think these environmental problems could be prevented?

2 Who is responsible for improving environmental problems?

3 What can we do to help environmental problems in other countries?

4 What do you do to try to help prevent these environmental problems?

2 ▷ **Watch the video again. Tick the phrases in the *Phrase expert* box that you hear on the video.**

> **PHRASE EXPERT**
>
> And there's another thing … | Apart from that … | As well as … | Having said that … | In addition … | More importantly … | One of the most important … is … | Personally, I … | That said, … | The good/bad thing about … is … | The reason I say this is because … | This is why …

3 **In pairs or groups, answer the questions.**

- What are the environmental problems in your country?
- What can people do to help protect the natural world?

4 **Complete the sentences to introduce contrasting opinions with the correct words from the box.**

> addition | having | importantly
> said | well | why

1 In _____ , there are important social issues that need more attention.

2 _____ said that, I believe everyone can make a difference.

3 As _____ as zoos, there are wildlife centres that protect endangered animals.

4 More _____ , not all countries have the same resources.

5 That _____ , environmental issues should be taught at school.

6 That is _____ I think recycling is vitally important.

5 **In pairs, discuss the questions in Exercise 1. Use phrases from the *Phrase expert* box.**

OPTIMISE YOUR **EXAM**

Discussion

- In a discussion, listen carefully to the questions. Remember to give your opinion but try to develop your ideas by giving reasons or examples.
- Pay attention to what your partner says and try to add any new ideas to the discussion.

6 **In groups of three, discuss the following questions. Take turns to be the examiner and candidates.**

- What are the most serious environmental problems in your country?
- What can people do to help protect the environment?
- How could students learn about environmental issues at school?
- How can we encourage more people to take environmental issues seriously?
- How can zoos protect endangered animals?
- Why shouldn't people be allowed to keep wild animals as pets?

• **SAY IT RIGHT**

Resource centre: Unit 8
Stress in opinion phrases

1 **Look at the words in capitals in Exercise 2 and answer the questions.**

Which of them …

1 can form an adjective ending in -*al*? _____

2 can be made into another word by adding just one letter at the beginning or the end? _____

OPTIMISE YOUR EXAM

Word formation

● Think carefully about any small spelling changes you need to make, e.g. when adding a prefix or suffix (nature → natural) or in the middle of a word (strong → strength).

---

2 **Write a form of the word in capitals in each gap to complete the text.**

Shipping container homes

When Michael McLean, owner of a trucking business in the USA, invented the shipping container in 1956, he thought it would be cheaper than (**1**) _____ methods of moving cargo by ship. He had no idea that one day people would build (**2**) _____ places to live using the containers. But the containers are cheap, readily available and can keep you dry in (**3**) _____ weather.

TRADITION
ORDINARY

STORM

More and more people are realising that these (**4**) _____ boxes can be put to good use as homes, offices and sheds. And they have some (**5**) _____ advantages over other buildings. They are easy to move and to put up, and using them can be (**6**) _____ for the environment. With a little (**7**) _____, you can turn an old shipping container into a very comfortable (**8**) _____ space that uses fewer natural resources.

INDUSTRY
SIGNIFY
BENEFIT
ORIGIN
LIVE

---

3 **Read the text in Exercise 4 quickly. Answer the questions.**

1 Which gaps can be filled with part of a phrasal verb?

_____ , _____

2 Which gap is followed by a past tense that refers to the present?

_____

3 Which gaps can be filled by prepositions that are a part of word patterns?

_____ , _____

4 Which gaps can be filled by a modal verb?

_____ , _____

OPTIMISE YOUR EXAM

Open cloze

● Sometimes the word you need to fill a gap may be a preposition.

● Try different prepositions in the gap before you make a final decision.

---

4 **Write one word in each gap to complete the text.**

One day to heal the world

If we didn't understand any of the serious environmental problems facing us today, we (**1**) _____ not be able to do anything about them. Did you know that the United Nations organises a day to help make people more aware of these issues. It takes place on 5th June every year, and it's called World Environment Day (WED).

Last year, people from across the world got involved. In Korea, there were events organised to promote sustainable development and to encourage people to reduce their (**2**) _____ footprint. In Bosnia and Herzegovina, people called (**3**) _____ more protection for areas that had been exposed (**4**) _____ pollution in the past as well as places currently threatened (**5**) _____ destruction, and in South Africa they organised a campaign to encourage people to throw (**6**) _____ less food.

For people who wish they (**7**) _____ do more to help the environment, WED is a great way to get involved. Have a look at their website and see what you could do. After all, it's high (**8**) *time* _____ we all did something before it's too late.

---

1 **In pairs or as a group, answer the questions.**

1 What is happening in the photo?
2 What things could young children do to help protect the environment?

2 **Read this article and answer the questions in your own words.**

Teaching the next generation

If you're anything like me, you love nature. Perhaps you also worry about problems like climate change and the greenhouse effect. One important question is how can we teach students about those problems from an early age?

The first thing we should consider is making sure that schools all go green. For example, we're encouraged to recycle paper at our school. This is important due to the fact that schools generally use a lot of paper. Young students would be able to see the difference their behaviour makes in a practical way.

Another great way to teach very young children is to get them involved in a local environmental project. This includes cleaning up a local river, or picking up litter that people have thrown away. This can be very educational as the students are shown how their local environment is affected by different issues.

So, I would encourage everyone to make sure that future generations understand more about the way nature is threatened by some of our actions. We need them to grow up caring for the environment.

1 How does the writer try to make a personal connection with the reader?
_____

2 How many points does the writer mention? How is each point introduced?
_____

3 How does the writer summarise and conclude the article?
_____

3 **Find two ways in which the writer introduces examples. What other phrases for introducing examples do you know?**

1 _____
2 _____
Other phrases: _____

4 **Find two ways in which the writer introduces reasons. What other phrases for introducing reasons do you know?**

1 _____
2 _____
Other phrases: _____

OPTIMISE YOUR EXAM

An article

- When you write an article, you should try to make a connection with the reader.
- You can refer to your own experience using phrases such as *If you are like me, …*, *Have you ever noticed that …?* or *In my experience, …*
- Remember to give specific reasons and examples in your article to make it more interesting for the reader.

5 Look at this writing task and make notes to answer the questions. Use your imagination if necessary.

You see this advert in an English-language magazine for young people.

> ### ARTICLES WANTED
> Many ordinary people don't care for the environment as much as they could. We want to change that! Send us your articles explaining the two most important things ordinary people can do to help the environment. The best articles will appear in a special issue and win a prize!

Write your **article**.

1. What is one thing ordinary people can do to help the environment? (e.g. produce less waste)

   _____

   Is there a good example you can use? (e.g. Buy products with less packaging.)

   _____

   Give a reason why this helps. (e.g. It means less waste to burn or bury.)

   _____

2. What is another thing they can do?

   _____

   Is there a good example you can use?

   _____

   Give a reason why this helps.

   _____

6 Plan Make a paragraph plan.

Part	Purpose	Useful phrases	My notes
Title	show clearly what you are writing about		
Paragraph 1	make a connection with the reader	If you're anything like me … In my experience … Have you ever noticed that …	
Paragraph 2	make your first point – give specific reasons and examples	The first thing we should consider …	
Paragraph 3	make a second point – support your point with examples	Another great way to …	
Paragraph 4	summarise your article to encourage action from your reader	So, I would encourage everyone to … To summarise …	

7 Write Write your article in an appropriate style. Write 140–190 words.

8 Check Before you hand in your article, complete this checklist.

Checklist ✓

- ○ I've given my article a title.
- ○ I've written at least four paragraphs.
- ○ I've given examples and reasons for each main point I've made.
- ○ I've checked my spelling and grammar.
- ○ I've made a connection with the reader.
- ○ I've encouraged action from my reader.

GRAMMAR AND VOCABULARY

1 **Write a form of the word in capitals in each gap.**

PHOTO SAFARIS

The safari was (**1**) _____ a hunting expedition, and even today some people
still travel to Africa to hunt. However, most people now join photo safaris. On these
trips, you get to see the (**2**) _____ range of wildlife that Africa has to offer,
while at the same time improving your photography. Before you go, the instructors
will advise you on the best (**3**) _____ to take, and while on the safari, the
guides will show you the best locations to 'shoot' animals. But it's important to
remember that not all of the areas are (**4**) _____ to tourists, and you also
might need a lot of time and (**5**) _____ to see some of the rarer animals.

But whatever you see, going on a trip like this can (**6**) _____ improve your
photography. And it's not just animals. A photo safari can also be a great opportunity
to get to know some of the local people and experience (**7**) _____ activities
such as dancing or cooking. And if your photos are good enough, you may even be
able to show them in an (**8**) _____ when you get home!

ORIGIN

ORDINARY

EQUIP

ACCESS
PATIENT

SIGNIFY

TRADITION

EXHIBIT

__/8

2 **Put the verbs into the correct form to complete the sentences.**

1 I wish you _____ me that you were going to be late last night! (**tell**)
2 What would you do if you _____ an injured animal by the side of the road? (**find**)
3 I'd rather you _____ the dog for a walk before you play games. (**take**)
4 What would happen if we _____ something to take carbon dioxide from the air? (**invent**)
5 What do you think would _____ if you hadn't stopped the car in time? (**happen**)
6 If you hadn't trained as an artist, what job would you _____ now? (**do**)
7 If only you _____ to me when I advised you not to do it! (**listen**)
8 I think Esme would _____ the exam if she'd worked a bit harder. (**pass**)
9 It's time people _____ killing rhinos for their horns. (**stop**)
10 I'd never go hunting, even if you _____ me a million pounds! (**pay**)

__/10

3 **Choose the correct word or phrase.**

1 The scientist started to sketch her ideas **off** / **out** / **up** on a paper napkin.
2 Do you think our supply of clean water will ever run **away** / **out** / **over**?
3 Sophie tore the letter **down** / **through** / **up** and threw it onto the floor.
4 Isn't it time we did **away** / **back** / **off** with power stations that run on coal?
5 There won't be any trees left if we continue to chop them **away** / **down** / **off** like this!
6 You probably won't like this show at first, but it'll grow **from** / **in** / **on** you.
7 I'm going to volunteer to help clean **away** / **over** / **up** the local beaches.
8 Some animals will be wiped **back** / **off** / **out** if we don't act now!
9 The audience called **for** / **in** / **on** the actors to return to the stage.
10 The government have drawn **away** / **off** / **up** a proposal to protect endangered species.

__/10

4 **If a sentence is correct, tick it. If a sentence is incorrect, underline the mistake and correct it.**

1 Even it was tough, I finally managed to climb to the top of the mountain. _____

2 I can't wait until I'm enough old to ride a motorbike. _____

3 There really isn't somewhere I'd rather be than right here, right now. _____

4 It wouldn't have been such a bad picnic if it hadn't rained for hours. _____

5 Don't you sometimes wish that you don't have to do all this homework? _____

6 The producer was very pleased with herself because the film was a success. _____

7 Van Gogh didn't sell many paintings during his life, although he was very talented. _____

8 The interviewer asked me where I saw me in five years' time. _____

9 Are you really such upset you can't accept Damien's apology? _____

10 Jen and Will really enjoyed himself at the art exhibition. _____

___/10

5 **Complete the second sentence so it has a similar meaning to the first. Do not change the word given. Use two to five words, including the word given.**

1 Was the extinction of the dinosaurs a result of climate change?   **OUT**

Did the dinosaurs _____ climate change?

2 Mum regrets letting Dad learn to play the trombone!   **LET**

Mum wishes _____ Dad learn to play the trombone!

3 We all wanted to go to the beach because it was so hot.   **SUCH**

It was _____ we all decided to go to the beach.

4 Can humans be harmed by air pollution?   **TO**

Is air pollution _____ humans?

5 We missed the auction because you arrived so late!   **IF**

We wouldn't have missed the auction _____ so late!

6 Finally, it became clear that the man sitting next to me was the choreographer.   **OUT**

The man sitting next to me _____ the choreographer.

___/12

Total score   ___/50

▼

EXAM SKILLS

Tick the statements that are true for you. Review the skills in the unit if you need more help.

I can ...	Unit/page
☐ understand implication in a news article	Unit 7 p70
☐ understand the speaker's purpose in conversations	Unit 7 p74
☐ express my preferences and give reasons in a photo task	Unit 7 p76
☐ create adverb forms and use different grammatical structures accurately	Unit 7 p77
☐ create an engaging narrative in a story	Unit 7 p78
☐ understand the writer's attitude and opinion in a nature article	Unit 8 p80
☐ predict and anticipate a speaker's opinion in short extracts	Unit 8 p84
☐ qualify my opinion in a discussion	Unit 8 p86
☐ identify spelling changes when working with prefixes and suffixes and use prepositions accurately	Unit 8 p87
☐ give reasons and examples in an article	Unit 8 p88

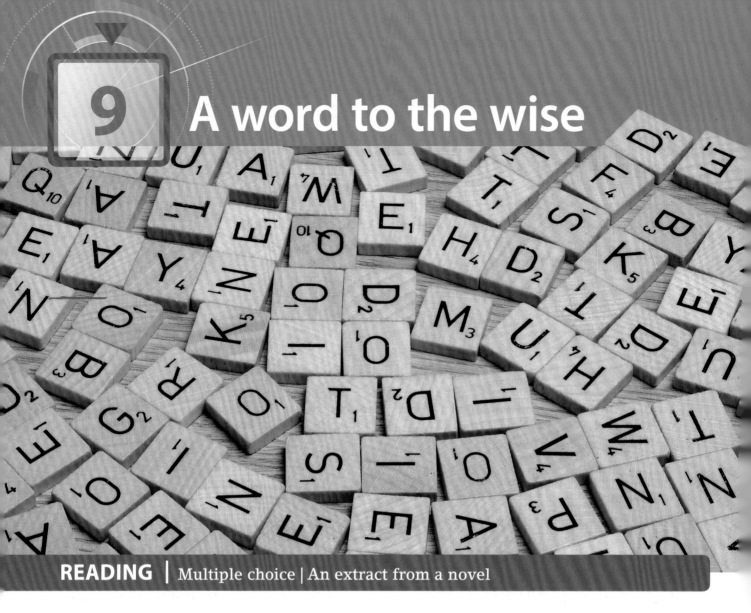

9 A word to the wise

READING | Multiple choice | An extract from a novel

1 **In pairs or as a group, answer the questions.**

1 What kind of books do you like reading? Do you have a favourite author or literature genre (e.g. suspense, fantasy)?

2 What are some of the advantages and disadvantages of (**a**) reading books electronically (**b**) reading books on paper?

2 🔊 2.18 **Listen to a summary of *Vanity Fair*. Complete the sentences using information from the plot summary.**

1 *Vanity Fair* is a novel set in the _____ and it includes _____ and _____ .

2 Amelia is kind but is also an _____ person. Her family is _____ but Becky's family is _____ Becky is a _____ person.

3 Becky goes to _____ and take care of Sir Pitt Crawley's daughters. She secretly marries Captain Rawdon Crawley who is Sir Pitt's _____ .

4 George Osborne is a family friend of the _____ family and he likes _____ .

5 The Sedleys lose all their _____ .

6 George's friend Dobbin encourages him to _____ Amelia, but because she is now poor, George's father leaves him no _____ after his death.

3 **Find these sentences quickly in the extract and read the sentences around them. For each one, decide what is suggested.**

1 'Dobbin's a strange fellow, Becky.'

Dobbin **doesn't like to associate with many people / isn't an easy person to comprehend**.

2 Everything had been bought on credit.

Things had been bought **with borrowed money / because they were needed**.

3 Miss Crawley was still refusing to see her nephew.

Miss Crawley **wouldn't have contact with her nephew / was planning to see her nephew**.

4 'Will she be very upset?'

Will she feel **uninterested / unhappy**?

OPTIMISE YOUR EXAM

Multiple choice

● Some questions ask about what the writer suggests. The text won't say exactly what is stated in the options so you need to 'read between the lines'.

● Carefully read the relevant part of the text and check the meaning carefully before choosing an option.

Extract from* Vanity Fair *by William Makepeace Thackeray
This extract begins when the Sedleys have lost their money and George's father forbids him to marry Amelia.

About a month later, there was a sale at a house in Russell Square. Everything in the house was being sold by auction. The furniture, wine and silverware had already been bought when the auctioneer held up a painting.

'Portrait of a large gentleman on an elephant!' he cried. 'Who will pay twenty guineas? Fifteen guineas? Five?'

'Five shillings!' called a tall army officer, who was standing beside a young lady with light-red hair and green eyes. Everyone laughed _line 11_ and the officer bought the picture. The same officer also tried to buy a little piano, but this time he was unsuccessful.

'Oh, look,' the lady said, pointing to a tall, thin man who was standing on the other side of the room. 'That's Captain Dobbin! He's bought Amelia's piano, Rawdon. What can he want with a piano? He can't play.'

'Dobbin's a strange fellow, Becky. I never could understand him,' her husband said. 'Well, it doesn't matter. We don't need another piano. Let's take the painting and go.'

Captain and Mrs Crawley were now living in a little house that Rawdon had rented. He had filled the house with pretty things for his wife. Everything had been bought on credit. Miss Crawley was still refusing to see her nephew, but he had not given up hope. One day she would forgive him, he was sure. _line 31_

Rawdon and Becky had gone to Russell Square to visit Amelia. They were very surprised to learn that the Sedleys had left the house and now everything in it was for sale. Mr Sedley had bought a great deal of stock on the French stock market. _line 35_ Then Napoleon returned from Elba and the stockbroker lost all his money. All his things were being auctioned.

'Mr Sedley was a kind old man,' Becky said, as they went home. 'I feel sorry for him.'

'I suppose Osborne won't be marrying your friend Amelia now,' Rawdon said. 'Will she be very upset?'

'Yes, but she'll forget about George Osborne one day,' Becky replied.

But Amelia Sedley was extremely unhappy. She had a gentle heart and that heart was broken. George's father wrote her a cruel letter, saying that the friendship between the two families was finished. Mr Sedley told his daughter to send back all of George Osborne's gifts and letters. Amelia sent back the gifts, but she kept the letters. She read them over and over again in her room in the little house in Fulham Road. The only thing that she could enjoy was her piano. It had been sent to her after the auction in Russell Square. There was no letter with the piano, but Amelia knew that George Osborne had bought it for her.

---

 4 ◁))) 2.19 **For questions 1–6, choose the answer (A, B, C or D) which you think fits best according to the text.**

1 Why does the writer say *everyone laughed* in line 11?
 A Because people thought the painting was funny.
 B Because no-one wanted to buy the painting.
 C Because the officer paid much less than the auction price.
 D Because people were happy everything had finally been sold.

2 What does the writer suggest about Captain Dobbin's purchase?
 A Dobbin really wanted to buy the painting and not the piano.
 B Dobbin didn't want Becky to buy the piano.
 C Dobbin should have paid more for the piano.
 D Dobbin isn't musical, so it's very odd.

3 What does the writer suggest about Captain and Mrs Crawley's finances?
 A They had bought everything they needed.
 B They were hoping to buy their own property soon.
 C They often bought expensive things at auctions.
 D They didn't have much money.

4 What does *forgive* mean in line 31?
 A reject someone
 B excuse someone
 C punish someone
 D apologise to someone

5 What do we learn about Mr Sedley in line 35?
 A His investments had been affected badly during the war.
 B He had bought shares at the right time in France.
 C He benefited from Napoleon's return from Elba.
 D His decision to auction things was surprising.

6 What do we know about Amelia by the end of the extract?
 A Amelia was so sad she couldn't play her piano anymore.
 B Amelia would never see George Osborne again.
 C Amelia felt sure that George Osborne was still interested in her.
 D Amelia's father would stop George Osborne contacting her.

5 **Find words and expressions in the extract that are similar in meaning to the ones in the box.**

> a considerable amount (phr)
> enormously (adv) | good-natured (adj)
> heartless (adj) | presents (n)
> sad (adj) | savings (n) | shouted (v)
> sweet (adj)

Grammar in context

Look at these extracts from the text on page 93 and write a word in each gap.

been	bought	sold

1 *Everything in the house was being _____ by auction.*

2 *The furniture, wine and silverware had already been _____ ...*

3 *Everything had _____ bought on credit.*

✓ REMEMBER

- We form the passive with *be* + past participle (+ *by/with/of/from/as/to*).

- If you're not sure what tense *be* should be in, try to imagine the active form of the sentence. Active: *Our teacher **hasn't marked** the essays yet.* The verb is *mark*, the tense is present perfect, so we need to use the present perfect of the verb *be* (i.e. *haven't been*) in the passive sentence: *The essays **haven't been marked** (by our teacher) yet.*

- We usually use *by* to show who or what does the action of the main verb. Sometimes we use other prepositions in passive sentences, such as *with*, *as*, etc., depending on the meaning, e.g. *A free dictionary was given **to** every student.*, *It's been described **as** the easiest language to learn.*

- Instead of saying *People say (that) ...*, *Scientists have estimated (that) ...*, we can use the passive with *It* as the subject: *It is said (that) ...*, *It has been estimated (by scientists) (that) ...*

▶ **See Grammar reference, Unit 9,** page 157

1 Write one word in each gap to complete the sentences.

1 'Be careful! The roads are covered _____ snow!' said Mel.

2 'What is this box made _____ ?' asked Ben.

3 'He's been described _____ the father of modern poetry,' stated the tour guide.

4 'This brilliant book was given _____ me by my best friend,' said Bex.

5 'It's often said _____ Shakespeare is the greatest playwright of all time,' said the actor proudly.

2 Each word or phrase in bold is incorrect. Rewrite it correctly.

1 Many English words were first **using** by Shakespeare in his plays. _____

2 Did *Vanity Fair* **written** by J.K. Rowling? _____

3 The new book **hasn't translated** into English yet. _____

4 It is **saying** that students don't study poetry at school anymore. _____

3 Put the verbs into the passive to complete the text.

Teen poetry slams

Do you think that poetry is boring? Think again! Poetry slams (spoken word poetry performances) (**1**) _____ first _____ (**perform**) in the USA, in the 1980s. Since then, slams have become an increasingly popular form of artistic expression all over the world. Slams (**2**) _____ (**organise**) in cafés, bars, bookshops, libraries, theatres, virtually anywhere that can hold an audience! They (**3**) _____ (**perform**) by anyone who wants to recite an original poem in public and the poets (**4**) _____ (**judge**) by a panel of people who (**5**) _____ (**choose**) from the audience. The slams can be fast paced and very competitive. No topic (**6**) _____ (**prohibit**) and they are usually events where slamming poets share their true identity and personal opinions and feelings with the general public.

Poetry slamming has appeared in all corners of society and it (**7**) _____ (**take up**) by teens across the world. It (**8**) _____ (**think**) that projects such as Urban Word NYC in New York have made it possible for over 25,000 teens to (**9**) _____ (**expose**) to the art of spoken word poetry. Additionally, centre-provided scholarships of over $1,000,000 (**10**) _____ (**award**) each year to students who want to study at colleges and universities. Lots of videos (**11**) _____ (**upload**) online so make sure you check some out!

THINK | RESEARCH | CULTURE | LEARN | ME

What do you think of these poetry events? Would you like to participate in a poetry slam event? What do you think you would perform?

Words connected with *literature*

1 🔊 2.20 **Put each of the following words into the correct column. Listen and check.**

crime fiction | critic | editor | fantasy
graphic novel | historical fiction | legend
novelist | playwright | romantic novel
science fiction | tragedy

Literary genres	Literary jobs

2 **Match a word from Exercise 1 to each definition.**

1 Someone who writes and publishes their opinions about a book, film or play: _____

2 A story which is told through a series of illustrations: _____

3 Someone who writes stories that later become published books: _____

4 A popular, historical story that is passed down through generations: _____

5 Books that are about breaking the law and the justice system: _____

6 A story which often features unbelievable and imaginary characters and situations: _____

3 **In pairs, add more literary genres and literary jobs to the lists in Exercise 1.**

Phrasal verbs

4 🔊 2.21 **Write a word from the box in each gap. Listen and check.**

across | forward | on
out | through (× 2) | up (× 2)

1 It's helpful if you *read* _____ *about* the play before you go and see it.

2 We will *bring* _____ the subject of reading in the education forum next week.

3 I've *flicked* _____ the magazine briefly but I haven't read the articles in detail yet.

4 It's not always easy to *get* your point _____ clearly in a different language.

5 It's good to *talk* _____ problems with a close friend.

6 If anyone has any suggestions, please *put* them _____ now.

7 Max is nice but he *goes* _____ a lot. He can't be quiet!

8 If you don't understand the instruction, let me *spell* it _____ to you.

Collocations with *say*, *speak* and *tell*

5 🔊 2.22 **Complete the phrases with *say*, *speak* or *tell*. Listen and check.**

1 _____ a lie / the truth

2 _____ sorry

3 _____ for yourself

4 _____ a joke

5 _____ your mind

6 _____ a story

7 _____ against or in favour of something

8 _____ well/highly of someone

9 _____ the difference between things

10 _____ hello/goodbye/goodnight

11 _____ the time

12 _____ someone a secret

THINK | RESEARCH | CULTURE | LEARN | ME

Look at the collocations in Exercise 5. When did you last do some of these things? Example: *I think I last said sorry to someone yesterday. I bumped into them in the corridor …*

1 **In pairs or as a group, answer the questions.**

1 Look at the photo. What language is it? Where is it from? Who speaks it?

2 Do you know any books or films that have invented languages? What are they?

2 **Read this short text and decide whether each statement is false (F) or not stated (NS).**

Invented languages

One of the most famous writers with a passion for inventing languages in his books was the author of *The Lord of the Rings*, J.R.R. Tolkien. As a child, he learnt Latin, French and German, and later on he taught himself Welsh and Finnish, as well as the ancient, dead languages Old Norse and Old English. These languages influenced Tolkien when he came to invent the Middle-Earth languages High and Common Elvish, Dwarvish, Black Speech and Entish, which became such an important part of his *The Lord of the Rings* trilogy. But why did he go to so much trouble to create so many different languages? Well, as an academic who taught students the history of languages, Tolkien knew better than most people that languages made communities, and were integral to preserving a history and keeping a culture alive.

1 Tolkien learned Welsh and Finnish
  a) at school. ____
  b) while living in those countries. ____

2 Old Norse and Old English
  a) are still spoken today. ____
  b) are very similar to the Middle-Earth languages High and Common Elvish. ____

3 Tolkien believed
  a) everyone should learn a foreign language. ____
  b) communities didn't need their own language.
  ____

3 **As a group, discuss your answers to Exercise 2. What makes some answers 'false' and some 'not stated'?**

4 ◁)) 2.23 **Listen to a radio interview about invented languages. Decide if each statement is true (T), false (F) or not stated (NS).**

1 Marcia believes that authors invent languages to make their worlds more realistic. ____

2 The majority of invented languages are in science-fiction books and films. ____

3 You can learn Dothraki online. ____

4 The Klingon language was created for the first Star Trek film in 1979. ____

5 For a later film, about 1,500 Klingon words were invented. ____

6 Fewer than a hundred people speak Klingon. ____

7 Newspeak sounds very different to English. ____

8 We don't use many of Shakespeare's words in modern English. ____

5 ◁)) 2.23 **Listen again and check your answers.**

THINK | RESEARCH | CULTURE | LEARN | ME

Why do you think people learn invented languages?

How do you think people invent languages?

Grammar in context

Look at these extracts from the audio in the listening lesson and choose the correct word.

1 ... they **had / did** a language created for the film ...

2 ... Okrand had a Klingon dictionary **published / publish**.

3 ... English has had many new words added to it **by / for** writers.

REMEMBER

- The causative form is *have/get* + object + past participle.

- We use the causative for situations when someone else performs an action or service for us, such as when *you **get your hair cut** by a hairdresser*.

- We also use it to talk about things that happen to us, such as things being stolen, broken. We don't usually use *get* with this meaning: *James says he **had his essay eaten** by his rabbit*.

- As with the passive, we can use *by* to show who or what does the action and may also use other prepositions depending on the meaning.

▶ See Grammar reference, Unit 9, page 158

---

1 Put the verbs into the causative form. Add *by* or other prepositions where necessary.

Ghostwriters

Many famous people – celebrities, sports personalities and politicians – dream of (1) _____ (**a book / publish**) that tells their story in their own words. But writing an autobiography is time-consuming and difficult. Even writers of bestsellers have to (2) _____ (**their work / edit**) an editor before it's ready to go to print. But what if you're not very talented or confident, or don't have enough time? This is where ghostwriters come in. Some famous people actually (3) _____ (**their autobiography / write**) someone else – a professional writer whose identity stays hidden or secret. There are several advantages to (4) _____ (**the job / do**) a professional. They (5) _____ (**all the facts / give**) by the celebrity, but then write the story in a way that makes the book a great read. Many celebs feel it's worth paying a lot of money in order to (6) _____ (**their story / tell**) in the best way possible. So, next time you read an autobiography, ask yourself: '(7) _____ (**the author / actually / this book / ghostwrite**) someone else?'

REMEMBER

- Some verbs can be followed by two objects: *Our teacher* (subject) *played* (verb) *us* (object 1) *a song* (object 2).

- We can also say this with the objects in the opposite order, but we need to use a preposition (usually *to* or *for*): *Our teacher played a song **to** us.*

- In the passive, there are often two ways of expressing this: *We were played a song by our teacher* and *A song was played to us by our teacher.*

▶ See Grammar reference, Unit 9, page 158

---

2 Rewrite the sentences in different ways **without** using the words in bold or adding any new words. There is one sentence you can't rewrite.

1 Dad read a bedtime story **to** the kids.

_____

2 Allie ordered a book **for** her brother online.

_____

3 Phil told a stupid joke **to** everyone.

_____

4 I'd like you to describe the two photos **for** me.

_____

5 The answers weren't given **to** the students beforehand.

_____

3 Look at the sentence in Exercise 2 which you couldn't rewrite. What makes it different to the others?

● SAY IT **RIGHT**

Resource centre: Unit 9
Sentence stress in the passive

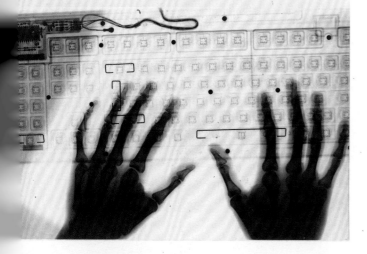

Talk**2**Me

Looking back now ...

Flipped classroom

1 ▷ **Watch the *Talk2Me* video and for each person, note down their responses.**

1 Have you ever met a famous novelist?

2 Have you ever enjoyed reading a book, but not enjoyed watching the film adaptation or vice versa?

3 Have you been to a book signing?

2 ▷ **Watch the video again. Circle the words in the *Phrase expert* box that you hear on the video.**

PHRASE EXPERT

I couldn't believe … | I felt (nervous/excited) because … | I was really (surprised) because … | Looking back now, | Sadly not, however, I have … | Unfortunately, I haven't ever …, but I have … | Well, it happened when …

---

3 **In pairs or groups, look at the photo. What is happening? What type of event do you think this is?**

4 **Match 1–5 to a)–e) to make sentences.**

1 Well, it happened when ____

2 Unfortunately, I haven't ever been to a film festival, ____

3 I felt really nervous ____

4 Sadly ____

5 Looking back now, ____

a) before meeting my favourite film star.

b) we went on a school trip to the theatre.

c) not, but I'd love to go one day.

d) it's my clearest memory from school.

e) but I have done something similar.

5 **Make notes to answer the questions. If your answer to a question is *no*, use your imagination to answer the question or try to think of a similar situation to talk about.**

Have you ever been to a poetry event or live book reading?

When/What/Where?_____

Describe the event._____

How did it make you feel?_____

Was it a positive/negative experience?_____

Have you ever been to the theatre to see a play?

When/What/Where?_____

Describe the event._____

How did it make you feel?_____

Was it a positive/negative experience?_____

Have you watched a film in a foreign language?

When/What/Where?_____

Which language?_____

How did it make you feel?_____

Was it a positive/negative experience?_____

OPTIMISE YOUR EXAM

Interview

● When you talk about personal experiences, try to give some details, such as where/when it happened, who you were with, how you felt, etc.

● Remember to use past tenses, such as the past simple, past continuous and past perfect.

● Say how you felt about the experience. Was it positive or negative?

6 **In pairs, ask and answer the questions in Exercise 5.**

1 **Look at the words in capitals in Exercise 2 and answer the questions.**

1 Which of them are not verbs? What are they? _____

2 Which nouns can you make from the verbs? Include negative forms. _____

3 Which adjectives can you make from the verbs? Include negative forms. _____

Word formation

● When you change the form of some words, the spelling may change in the root form of the word. For example, in questions 4, 5 and 7 in Exercise 2 which letters change when you make the new word?

2 **Write a form of the word in capitals in each gap to complete the text.**

Conversational Koko

Ask any cat or dog owner if they can communicate with their pet, and the answer will be yes. Cats and dogs certainly have the (1) _____ to understand different sounds, and tones of voice, and can make their needs and feelings known in (2) _____ different ways. But we wouldn't say they have a (3) _____ of human language.

ABLE
VARY
KNOW

However, Koko the gorilla (4) _____ does. Now in her 40s, Koko has been learning a form of sign language since she was one. According to her teacher, Dr Francine Patterson, Koko has learnt more than 1,000 words, and understands about 2,000 words of (5) _____ English.

APPEAR

SPEAK

Dr Patterson claims that not only is Koko able to talk about her immediate (6) _____ and possessions, she's also able to express her (7) _____ on more abstract concepts, such as love, grief, shame, (8) _____ , and other issues related to life and death.

SURROUND
THINK
LONELY

3 **Read the text in Exercise 4 quickly. Answer the questions.**

1 Which question is testing your knowledge of phrasal verbs?
_____

2 Which question is testing you know which verb collocates with *story*?
_____

3 Which ones are testing your knowledge of grammar structures?
_____

4 Which one is testing literary genres?
_____

Multiple-choice cloze

● Read the title and whole text first for general understanding.

● Try to think of what kind of word might fit in the gap before you look at the different options, e.g. is it a verb, preposition, noun …

4 **Choose the correct word to fill each gap.**

A teen novelist

You only have to flick (1) _____ a few pages of *The Catalyst* to see that it has been written (2) _____ an extraordinary talent. Many people dream of becoming published novelists and for London-born teenager Helena Coggan, that dream became a reality when she was just 15. Her debut novel, a (3) _____ story set in a world divided into magical and non-magical people, has received outstanding reviews from online (4) _____ and interviews with Helena have been featured in many newspapers and news programmes. This book (5) _____ the story of Rose, the main character, who has a terrifying secret that she can't tell anyone – a secret that could destroy her life and the lives of the people she loves. It's definitely worth a read – I was certainly impressed by the way this young writer was able to get her ideas (6) _____ so well.

The literary world is (7) _____ very highly of this young writer and it's been said (8) _____ she has an exciting future ahead of her. I'll definitely be recommending this book and its sequel, *The Reaction*, to all my friends.

1 **A** across	**B** through	**C** out	**D** on
2 **A** for	**B** as	**C** by	**D** to
3 **A** fantasy	**B** legend	**C** tragedy	**D** crime
4 **A** editors	**B** novelists	**C** playwrights	**D** critics
5 **A** speaks	**B** says	**C** expresses	**D** tells
6 **A** around	**B** across	**C** forward	**D** above
7 **A** saying	**B** speaking	**C** telling	**D** talking
8 **A** by	**B** for	**C** that	**D** than

1 In pairs or as a group, answer the questions.

1 How would you feel if you were in the place in the photo?

2 Where does the path lead to?

2 Read the story. In pairs or groups, answer the questions.

Lost in the dark

By now, the camp was miles away and Max was totally lost. He had no idea where he was or where he was going. His dirty map was covered in mud and the light was rapidly fading from his heavy torch. He knew he'd taken the wrong turn around an hour ago but it was too late to go back now. The sky was getting darker and the temperature was getting colder. He felt the first few drops of cool rain fall down his pale cheeks.

'What am I going to do?' he thought nervously to himself. 'I have no food, no water, no shelter and soon I won't have any light!'

Amy, the camp leader, had warned everyone about wandering too far but Max hadn't listened. She said the forest was extremely dangerous at night. Max thought she was being too strict but now, he was alone and he was scared.

Then suddenly, he heard a loud noise behind him.

CRRRRRACK!

He jumped out of his skin and started running quickly. He was terrified. But then, in the distance, could he see light and smoke?

1 Find and underline three different narrative tenses that are used in the story. How are they used? What is the difference between them?

2 Circle all the descriptive language in the first paragraph. What type of words are they? What do they add to the story?

3 Why do you think the author ends the story with a question mark? How does it make you feel?

4 How would you feel in Max's situation? Why?

OPTIMISE YOUR EXAM

A story

● Focus on one or two key characters in your story. Good descriptions make a story vivid and help the reader get a clear picture of what's happening.

● Use a variety of adjectives to show how someone feels or looks (*surprised, terrified* …), or adverbs (*wildly, enthusiastically* …), to bring the story and characters to life.

● Include some direct speech to bring the characters to life but make sure you use correct punctuation.

3 Look at this writing task and make notes to answer the questions.

You have seen this announcement in an international magazine for teenagers.

Stories wanted!

We're looking for stories for our new English-language magazine for young people.
Your story must begin with this sentence:

As Jane stared at the road ahead of her, she realised she had to make a choice.

Your story must include:

- **a decision**
- **a meeting**

Write your **story**.

- Who is Jane?
- Where was she?
- What was the situation?
- How did she feel?
- What did she do?
- What happened next?
- What decision does she have to make in the story?
- How does a meeting fit into the story?
- What other things are you planning to include in the story?

4 Plan **Make a paragraph plan.**

Part	Purpose	My notes
Title	briefly describe what the story is about – and create some suspense!	
Paragraph 1	copy the first sentence and set the scene – where was Jane?	
Middle paragraphs	continue the story – what happened next? how was she feeling? what did she do? who did she meet?	
Final paragraph	bring the story to an end – what happened in the end?	

5 Write **Write your story in an appropriate style. Write 140–190 words.**

6 Check **Before you hand in your story, complete this checklist.**

Checklist

- I've given my story an appropriate title.
- I've copied the first sentence of the story correctly.
- I've followed my paragraph plan.
- I've written at least four paragraphs.
- I've included some descriptive language in my story.
- I've checked my spelling and grammar.

▶ **Writing reference,** page 173 ▶ **Workbook Unit 9:** Writing, page 74, exercises 1, 2, 3, 4 and Progress check 9, page 75

10 Spending power

READING | Multiple choice | An online article

1 In pairs or as a group, answer the questions.

1 What proportion of the money you spend each week/month is on things you choose (e.g. clothes, music) and on things you don't choose (e.g. travel to school)?

2 What things or people influence the spending decisions you make?

2 Read the article quickly and number these points in the order they are mentioned (1–5).

a) Saving is a good way of avoiding some peer pressure. ____

b) Some teens are paid to persuade other people to buy things. ____

c) Various kinds of peer pressure influence spending decisions. ____

d) Teenagers influence the spending decisions of their parents. ____

e) The internet affects what pressure young people are under. ____

3 Look at the questions in Exercise 4 and read the text. Answer questions 1–6.

1 Which two questions ask you <u>why</u> the writer writes something? ____ , ____

2 In the first paragraph, the writer gives some statistics. Are these surprisingly high or surprisingly low?

_____

3 Why does the writer mention these statistics?

_____

4 In the fifth paragraph, the writer uses the word 'strategy'. What is a strategy?

_____

5 What strategies does the writer mention?

_____

6 Why does the writer mention these strategies?

_____

OPTIMISE YOUR **EXAM**

Multiple choice

● Some questions ask about the writer's purpose, e.g. question 1. All texts are written for a specific purpose or reason, e.g. to persuade, to describe, to advise, to warn, to encourage.

● Underline the words in the options that show purpose, e.g. *persuade*, *warn*.

● Read the relevant part of the text carefully, and decide which option best matches the writer's purpose.

SPENDING DECISIONS

We all make spending decisions, whether it's what snack to buy on the way to school or what our next holiday destination is going to be. And teenagers today have more buying power than ever. In the USA, for example, where there are around 25.6 million teens, the total spending on products which are bought by and for teens is about $210 billion a year. Teen income from allowances and employment, which comes to over $90 billion, is only part of the story. In fact, young people are influencing where the family budget goes more and more. Parents these days consult teens on spending decisions, including restaurants, weekly groceries and electronic devices. It seems there's no area of household spending that teenagers don't exert an influence over. But what influences young people themselves when it comes to making those spending decisions?

One of the main factors affecting the spending decisions that teens make is peer pressure. Many teenagers say that they often feel under pressure to fall into line with the opinions and expectations of their friends. This can take a number of different forms. Friends might be a source of positive and negative information about a product. They might also react positively or negatively to a new purchase you have made. When a classmate brings a new gadget to school and people remark on how 'cool' it is (or not!), it reinforces (or questions) their membership of a group. It can also be seen as an easy way to gain status within the group, particularly for younger teens. If you acquire cool products, you must also be cool, or so the thinking goes.

And it seems that peer pressure, which has no doubt always been around, may be taking new forms with the development of social media. Suddenly, rather than a dozen friends at school dictating what the latest trend is, there's a whole world of teenagers online telling you what you should or shouldn't be buying. This often adds to a feeling of FOMO ('fear of missing out'), which is when you worry that exciting things are happening that you are not a part of. Peer pressure is not just about friends' opinions, but about the things you think they may be doing and the lives you think they may be living.

On top of that, many of the teens on YouTube, Twitter, Instagram and other services are being paid by brands to promote their products.

Businesses know that the most powerful influence over teenagers is other teenagers, so any young person who has millions of followers online is in a very powerful position. And rather than traditional advertisements, which are clearly trying to sell a product, promotion from social media celebrities is made to appear genuine. We watch a young person who we admire talking about going to a certain cinema chain with her friends. That weekend, we go to the same cinema chain in our own town, without thinking about the fact that she might have been paid to talk about that particular brand.

So how can you enjoy your spending choices while at the same time resisting at least some peer pressure? One strategy is to focus on a long-term goal which you need to save for. If your money is put away for a great holiday next summer, you shouldn't spend it on something you don't really need or want right now. You might also think about putting together a weekly or monthly budget. That way, you have a fixed amount of money to spend on things which you can't go above. This will help you to save. It's also important to think carefully about how brands try to influence you through advertisements and through social media, and to realise that when that cool girl on Vimeo tells you about her life, all might not be as it seems.

4 🔊 3.01 Read the article again. For questions 1–6, choose the answer (A, B, C or D) which you think fits best according to the text.

1 What is the writer's purpose in paragraph 1?
A to give the reader an idea of the size of the issue
B to persuade people that they should spend less
C to warn teens about the dangers of their spending decisions
D to encourage parents to make their own spending decisions

2 What does 'fall into line with' in paragraph 2 mean?
A try to argue against
B defend from criticism
C keep secret and not reveal
D agree with and not contradict

3 What does the writer say about social media?
A It helps people arrange events for lots of people.
B It lets you ask people's advice on your spending decisions.
C It creates more pressure because more people are involved.
D It means you get fewer invitations to exciting events.

4 How does promotion on social media differ from traditional advertising?
A We may not recognise that it actually is promotion.
B It's better at telling us about the features of things like restaurants.
C It takes young people and their interests more seriously.
D The products advertised on social media are better.

5 What point is the writer making about 'that cool girl on Vimeo' in paragraph 5?
A She probably isn't actually cool in real life.
B Businesses might be paying her to say certain things.
C She might not be as influential as you think.
D Her followers probably don't really like her.

6 What is the writer's purpose in paragraph 5?
A to advise teenagers against listening to their friends
B to encourage young people to think about travelling more
C to present ways of lessening the effect of peer pressure
D to argue that paying for promotion on social media is wrong

5 Find these words and phrases in the article. Work out what they mean from the context.

consult (v)	dictating (v)	genuine (adj)
membership (n)	reinforces (v)	
status (n)	trend (n)	

▶ Workbook Unit 10: Reading, pages 76–77, exercises 1, 2, 3

Grammar in context

Look at these sentences from the article on page 103. Answer the questions.

a) *And it seems that peer pressure, **which has no doubt always been around**, may be taking new forms with the development of social media.*

b) *We watch a young person **who we admire** talking about going to a certain cinema chain with her friends.*

1 Which sentence has a relative clause which just gives us extra information about something the writer is talking about? ____

2 Which sentence has a relative clause which identifies the particular thing the writer is talking about? ____

3 In which sentence can we omit the relative pronoun? ____

✓ REMEMBER

- Relative clauses often start with a relative pronoun, such as *who*, *which*, *when*, *where*, *why* and *whose*.

- There are two kinds of relative clause. Defining relative clauses (without commas) identify the particular thing we are talking about, e.g. *The girl **who is on screen right now** is an Instagram star.*

- Non-defining relative clauses (with commas) give us more information about something we are talking about, e.g. *Vimeo, **where people share videos**, was launched in November 2004.*

- We can use *that* as a relative pronoun in defining relative clauses, but not in non-defining relative clauses, e.g. *The boy **that** is speaking to the viewers right now is a famous vlogger.*

- When the relative pronoun is the object of a defining relative clause, we can often leave it out, e.g. *I bought the trainers **I saw the other day**.* (without *which* or *that*)

▶ **See Grammar reference, Unit 10,** page 158

---

1 **Choose the correct sentence in each pair.**

1 a) The photos that she uploads are so cool!

 b) The photos, that she uploads, are so cool!

2 a) Social media which includes sites like Facebook is a popular way to communicate.

 b) Social media, which includes sites like Facebook, is a popular way to communicate.

3 a) Do you really need all the things you buy?

 b) Do you really need all the things, which you buy?

4 a) Do people who are on social media always tell the truth about products?

 b) Do people, who are on social media, always tell the truth about products?

---

2 **Find four sentences in the text that are incorrect and rewrite them correctly.**

Paid to promote to her fans

Essena O'Neill who is from Australia, was a social media star. At the age of 18, she had 612,000 followers on Instagram, where she shared photos of her everyday life. She also talked about products which she was being paid to promote. However, the people, who followed her, didn't know she was being paid. Essena, who said it was easy to make a lot of money for each post, finally quit Instagram and left it all behind.

She described how the photos who she put online were heavily edited. She also says that she became overwhelmed by social media. 'This was the reason why I quit social media: for me, personally, it consumed me. I wasn't living in a 3-D world.' She deleted over 2,000 photos that had appeared on her Instagram account. She decided to focus instead on her new website, where she can talk about things that really matter to her.

1 _____

2 _____

3 _____

4 _____

3 **Look at the text in Exercise 2 again. Underline any relative pronouns which can be omitted.**

• SAY IT **RIGHT**

Resource centre: Unit 10
Intonation in relative clauses

THINK | RESEARCH | CULTURE | LEARN | ME

What do you think about using social media to promote products? Have you ever seen someone on social media promote a product? Do you think they were paid to promote it or not?

Words connected with *spending money*

1 🔊 3.02 **Write a word from the box in each gap to complete the dialogue. Listen and check.**

> bill | cash | cashpoint | change
> credit card | discount | PIN
> receipt | refund | till

Assistant: Could you come to the other (**1**) _____ , please? Now, the total (**2**) _____ comes to £15, and that's with a 10% (**3**) _____ . How would you like to pay?

Customer: By (**4**) _____ . Oh, wait. It's a new one and I've forgotten the (**5**) _____ . I'll have to pay in (**6**) _____ . Luckily, I've just been to the (**7**) _____ , so I've got enough.

Assistant: That's fine, thank you. And here's your (**8**) _____ – £5 – and your (**9**) _____ . Keep it, because it's also your guarantee. If anything goes wrong with the headphones, just bring them back and we'll exchange them or give you a (**10**) _____ .

Customer: Thank you.

Phrasal verbs

2 🔊 3.03 **Match each phrasal verb with a meaning from the box. Use each meaning twice. Listen and check.**

> continue | start working
> think about | treat badly

1 If we *carry on* like this, we'll have no money left! _____

2 You need to *switch* the computer *on* and then enter your password. _____

3 Did you *decide on* the restaurant you want to eat at? _____

4 Why do you always *pick on* me when I haven't done anything? _____

5 I haven't *put* the heating *on* because we're trying to save money. _____

6 Don't *start on* me just because I forgot to bring any cash. _____

7 Let's just *press on* until we get the job done. _____

8 Let me *sleep on* the problem and I'll get back to you tomorrow. _____

3 **Write a phrasal verb from Exercise 2 in the correct form in each gap. There may be more than one correct answer for some gaps.**

1 I can't _____ the laptop I want so could you give me some advice?

2 You can't _____ spending money the way you are doing at the moment.

3 Every time you _____ the light it costs money.

4 _____ people is one of his worst characteristics.

5 How can I find ways of saving more for my holiday? I'm going to _____ it and hope I find a solution.

6 My parents _____ despite the difficulties and finally their business succeeded.

Collocations with *do, get, go* and *make*

4 🔊 3.04 **Choose the correct word to complete the collocation. Listen and check.**

1 I think she *does / gets / makes* a living from the weekly vlogs on her YouTube channel.

2 They're a good company to *do / have / make* business with.

3 If a company *gets / goes / makes* bankrupt, it has to stop trading.

4 Jake *did / made / went* a fortune when he sold his vintage comics at the auction.

5 Whenever you *do / make / take* a purchase online, be careful of the risk of internet fraud.

6 These trainers were in the sale and I really *did / got / made* a bargain.

7 Nina sold some old DVDs online but *did / had / made* a loss as she got less than what she paid for them.

8 They announced that the bookshop *did / made / took* a profit last year!

THINK | RESEARCH | CULTURE | LEARN | ME

Think of other phrasal verbs with *on*. Do any of them have similar meanings to the phrasal verbs in Exercise 2?

1 In pairs or as a group, ask and answer the questions.

1 Some people say money can't buy happiness. Why do you think some people say this?

2 What problems do you think having a lot of money can bring?

2 Read each dialogue and answer the questions.

> And did Eric find the hammer?
>
> Not to begin with.

1 Did the man find the hammer?

_____

> So, Eric and the farmer didn't receive anything for finding it?
>
> Far from it.

2 Did the men receive anything?

_____

> And this time everyone was sure it was real?
>
> Without a doubt.

3 Did everyone think it was real?

_____

3 What do you think the person in the photo is doing? Why?

Multiple choice

- When you listen to a longer extract, the questions will be in the order the speakers talk about things.
- You won't hear exactly the same words that are in the options, so listen for words and phrases that have similar meanings.
- When you listen the second time make sure the options you <u>don't</u> choose are not possible answers.

4 🔊 3.05 Listen to an interview with an online blogger. For questions 1–7, choose the best answer (A, B or C).

1 What does Simon say the blog entry is about?
 A becoming rich
 B what happens to people who experience luck
 C how to find valuable items

2 Peter Whatling
 A lost a hammer in a field.
 B wanted to find treasure in his friend's field.
 C discovered some treasure in a friend's field.

3 Who did the treasure belong to?
 A the landowners
 B the council
 C the country

4 Teri Horton
 A was looking for a painting.
 B bought a painting because she thought it was beautiful.
 C wanted to buy a present for her friend.

5 Teri kept the painting because
 A her friend didn't like it.
 B she knew it was valuable.
 C she really liked it.

6 Art experts
 A believed the painting was real after they saw the fingerprint.
 B believe the painting may be a fake.
 C are convinced that the painting is worth a lot of money.

7 The man bought the golden egg because
 A he knew what it was.
 B he liked it very much.
 C he thought he could sell it for more than he paid for it.

5 🔊 3.05 Listen again and check your answers.

THINK | **RESEARCH** | CULTURE | LEARN | ME

Go online and find a story of someone who has found or bought something that turned out to be very valuable.

Grammar in context

Look at these sentences. Delete two words from each one to make sentences you heard in the audio in the listening lesson.

1 *By thinking that it was funny, she decided to buy it there and then for $5.*

2 *… but having bought it and then taken it home, her friend wasn't keen …*

 REMEMBER

- Participle clauses can be formed using present participles (ending in *-ing*), past participles (usually ending in *-ed*, although there are many irregular forms) and perfect participles (*having* + past participle).

- Present participles and past participles can form clauses like relative clauses, e.g. *A brand **seen as cool amongst teens** can sell a lot.* = *A brand **which is seen as cool amongst teens** can sell a lot.*

- Adverbial participle clauses can be used to express:

  ○ conditions, e.g. ***Used occasionally**, product placement is effective.* (= *If it is used occasionally, …*)

  ○ reasons and results, e.g. ***Having experienced it myself**, I know what I'm talking about.* (= *Because I have experienced it myself, …*)

  ○ time relations: ***Having spent all my money**, I left the shopping centre.* (= *After I had spent all my money, …*)

▶ See Grammar reference, Unit 10, page 159

1 **Rewrite each sentence using participle clauses to replace the underlined clauses.**

1 Someone who is buying a product has often been influenced by advertising which is shown on TV.

_____

_____

2 Because I had read about product placement, I wasn't surprised to see an iPhone which was used by a character in the movie.

_____

_____

3 After I saw the film, I decided to go out and buy the same jacket which was worn by the star.

_____

_____

4 Some people are worried, since they see how easily teens who are exposed to product placement respond to that kind of marketing.

_____

_____

2 **Read the sentences. Underline any clauses that can be replaced by a participle clause and write an appropriate participle clause.**

Product placement

1 While you are watching TV today, you may well see your favourite character using a product you recognise.

_____

2 Shows that are watched by millions of people use product placement as a way of replacing traditional advertising.

_____

3 Because we are exposed to traditional ads all day, we stop noticing them and ignore their messages.

_____

4 The idea with product placement is that after you have seen the character use a product, you will go out and buy that product yourself.

_____

5 If it is used in moderation, product placement seems to be a powerful marketing tool for all ages.

_____

6 However, because they know teens in particular want to copy characters they admire, businesses pay a lot of money to get their products into films and TV shows which are aimed at young people.

_____

_____

THINK | RESEARCH | CULTURE | LEARN | ME

What are the biggest brands from your country? How do they market their products at teenagers?

Why do you think product placement is effective?

Talk 2 Me
To sum up ...

1 ▶ Watch the *Talk2Me* video and answer the questions.

1 How many people try to raise money for good causes?
2 What activities to raise money are mentioned?
3 What's the most popular way to raise money?

2 ▶ Watch the video again. Complete the sentences with one word to make phrases for making decisions.

1 I think we _____ choose the second option.
2 So, we _____ to decide what to do.
3 Let's _____ for …
4 _____ we make a decision?
5 To _____ up, we have chosen to …
6 _____ decide which option to choose.

PHRASE EXPERT

I think we should choose … | Let's decide which … | Let's go for … | Shall we make a decision? | So, we have to choose/decide … | To sum up …

OPTIMISE YOUR EXAM

Collaborative task

- In the second part of this exam task you have about one minute to make a decision about something together. You often need to choose two different options and say why you would choose them.
- Remember there are no right or wrong answers and it doesn't matter if you don't agree with your partner!

3 Match definitions 1–5 with the fundraising activities in the box.

a cake sale | a non-uniform day
a sponsored run | a student art exhibition
a talent show

This is when …

1 students pay some money to come to school in their own clothes. _____

2 people agree to pay you an amount of money for each kilometre you complete. _____

3 people pay to look at creative work that students have produced.
_____

4 people come to buy food that students have made.
_____

5 people pay to watch students perform, etc.
_____

5 In pairs, talk together for two minutes. Follow the instructions.

Here are some ways in which a school might raise money for a good cause. Talk to each other about the advantages and disadvantages of these ways of raising money.

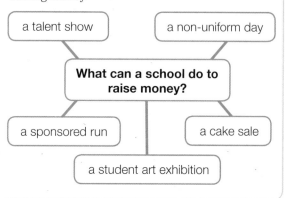

a talent show   a non-uniform day

What can a school do to raise money?

a sponsored run   a cake sale

a student art exhibition

6 Decide together which two ways of raising money in Exercise 5 are most effective and would interest the biggest number of people. You have one minute to make your decision.

4 Write one advantage and one disadvantage for each fundraising activity in the table.

fundraising activity	advantage	disadvantage
a cake sale		
a non-uniform day		
a sponsored run		
a student art exhibition		
a talent show		

▶ **Workbook Unit 10:** Speaking, pages 80–81, exercises 1, 2, 3

1 Look at the words in capitals in Exercise 2 and answer the questions.

1 Which of them can form a noun ending in -th? ____

2 What other nouns can you form? _____

3 Which of them can form verbs ending in -ise? ____

OPTIMISE YOUR EXAM

Word formation

- If you have to form a verb, make sure that the ending is correct.
- Common endings for verbs include -ate (e.g. *activate*), -ify (e.g. *classify*) and -ise (e.g. *advertise*).

2 Write a form of the word in capitals in each gap to complete the text.

The Bristol Pound

With its thriving arts scene, nightlife and some great cafés and restaurants, Bristol is often described as one of the most (1) _____ places to live in the UK.

DESIRE

But in the last decade, as more and more (2) _____ and international businesses moved into the city, some people began to feel that the increasing globalisation of the city was damaging the local economy. So in 2012, a group of people decided to (3) _____ Bristol's economy and created the Bristol Pound, a local currency that could only be used in the city.

NATION

REVOLUTION

Anyone in the city can use Bristol Pounds to pay for things in local shops, cafés and restaurants and experts believe it will (4) _____ the local community. Those shops and restaurants can then only use them to pay local (5) _____ , who can use them to pay local farmers and producers. This is called the Local Multiplier Effect, and it makes (6) _____ sense, ensuring that more money stays in an area, which can help to (7) _____ local employment. It also means that products travel fewer kilometres to get to consumers, promoting sustainable (8) _____ .

STRONG

SUPPLY

ECONOMY

STIMULATING

GROW

3 Read the text in Exercise 4 quickly. Answer the questions.

1 Which gaps can be filled with part of a phrasal verb? ____ , ____

2 Which gaps appear in relative clauses? ____ , ____

3 Which gap appears in a participle clause? ____

4 Which gaps are part of collocations? ____ , ____ , ____

OPTIMISE YOUR EXAM

Open cloze

- The missing word may be part of a collocation in a set phrase, e.g. *do a deal*, *go bankrupt*.
- The missing words are often relative pronouns, so look for sentences with relative clauses.
- If the answer is a verb, make sure that the ending is correct.

4 Write one word in each gap to complete the text.

Online fraud

The internet is a place (1) _____ you have to be careful. Every time you switch your computer (2) _____ and do any online shopping, you are leaving yourself open to fraud. Some criminals (3) _____ their living stealing passwords and internet banking details. They may use those details themselves to steal from your account, or (4) _____ a fortune by selling them on to other criminals (5) _____ can then access your accounts, like iTunes or Amazon. Online fraud costs the global economy over $100 billion a year. So, what should you do if you think you might be the victim of online fraud?

The first thing to do is to change your passwords. If you carry (6) _____ using the same ones, you will leave yourself vulnerable to more fraud. (7) _____ changed them, check your online bank statements. Have any suspicious purchases been (8) _____ ? If so, contact your bank immediately

1 **In pairs or as a group, answer the questions.**

1 In what ways do parents limit teenagers' spending habits?

2 How do teenagers in your country earn their own money?

2 **Read this essay. In your own words, write one or two sentences to summarise the writer's argument. Compare your summary with a partner.**

'Teenagers should be given complete freedom to spend their own money and to make their own spending decisions.' Is this a good thing or a bad thing?

The question of whether teens should be given complete freedom to spend their own money is a difficult one. I would argue that teenagers need to be allowed to make their own spending decisions, even if they sometimes make mistakes.

Parents who try to restrict their children's spending may not trust them to make sensible decisions. However, I don't see how teenagers can learn to make good decisions unless they are given the freedom to choose. Given that freedom, I believe that most teenagers would make sensible spending decisions.

Having said that, we cannot expect teenagers to be perfect. Like everyone, they are certain to make bad choices with money. For instance, they may waste money that they should have saved for a particular purpose. These mistakes give parents the opportunity to teach their teenage children about financial responsibility.

In conclusion, I would like to emphasise that lessons are learnt through experience. People have to know how to handle money responsibly throughout their lives, and the process of learning how to do so should start in their teenage years.

The writer argues that _____

_____

_____

3 **Find formal words and phrases in the essay which mean the same as these words and phrases.**

1 I want to say that … _I would argue that_

2 If you give teenagers that freedom, … _Given that freedom_

3 In spite of what I just said, … _Having said that,_

4 I'm sure they'll make … _they are certain to make_

5 To finish, … _In conclusion_

6 I want to stress that … _I would like to emphasise_

4 **Look at the first paragraph of the essay in Exercise 2. Find three phrases you could use in any essay, whatever the topic.**

I would argue

question of whether

is a difficult one

5 **Decide whether each of these phrases would probably appear in an introductory paragraph (I) or a concluding paragraph (C).**

1 C To conclude, I firmly believe that … ____

2 I To begin with, it's important to remember … ____

3 C Taking all this into account, it is clear that … ____

4 I There are two sides to this question, and … ____

5 I Nowadays, it seems that … ____

6 C Therefore, I have come to the conclusion that … ____

An essay

- In an essay, it's important to have a strong introduction and conclusion. This gives structure to your writing.
- Introduce the topic in the first paragraph and make a general statement about the main content.
- In the final paragraph summarise your ideas but use different words from the introduction or arguments in the main part of the essay.

6 Look at this writing task and make notes to answer the questions. Use your imagination if necessary.

In your English class you have been discussing how some teenagers do housework in order to get their allowance. Your English teacher has asked you to write an essay for homework.

> **Some parents make their teenage children do housework in order to get their allowance. Is this a good or bad thing for teenagers?**
>
> **Notes**
> Write about:
>
> **1** learning about money
> **2** sharing responsibility
> **3** .... (your own idea)

- Do you personally think this is a good or bad thing for teenagers?

  _____

- What is the main point you want to make about learning about money?

  _____

- What reasons / examples / supporting points do you want to mention?

  _____

- What is the main point you want to make about sharing responsibility?

  _____

- What reasons / examples / supporting points do you want to mention?

  _____

- What other idea are you going to talk about?

  _____

- What reasons / examples / supporting points do you want to mention?

  _____

7 **Plan** Make a paragraph plan.

Part	Purpose	Useful phrases	My notes
Paragraph 1	introduction – do you think it's a good thing or a bad thing? what's your opinion?	_The question of …_ _It seems to me that …_ _I would argue that …_	
Paragraph 2	your main point about learning about money – what are your reasons? give examples to support your reasons		
Paragraph 3	your main point about sharing responsibility – what are your reasons? give examples to support your reasons		
Paragraph 4	your own idea and conclusion	_In conclusion,_ _To conclude,_ _To sum up,_	

8 **Write** Write your essay in an appropriate style. Write 140–190 words.

9 **Check** Before you hand in your essay, complete this checklist.

Checklist ✓

- ○ I've introduced the essay in an appropriate way.
- ○ I've written at least four paragraphs.
- ○ I've included all the required information from the notes.
- ○ I've concluded the essay in an appropriate way.
- ○ I've checked my spelling and grammar.

UNITS 9–10

GRAMMAR AND VOCABULARY

1 **Write a form of the word in capitals in each gap.**

EUROPEAN CAPITALS OF CULTURE

Every year, the European Union holds an **(1)** _____ competition to choose cities from across Europe to organise cultural events, celebrate the arts and **(2)** _____ ties between European countries.

NATION
STRONG

Preparing a city to become a European Capital of Culture takes a lot of **(3)** _____ and effort. Cities need to organise a huge **(4)** _____ of events, exhibitions, performances and concerts. But for many cities, it is also an opportunity to encourage more tourists to visit and more companies to invest, which can help to stimulate local **(5)** _____ development. When Pecs in Hungary was the capital in 2010, there was a 27% **(6)** _____ in overnight visitors, and over 600 million euros was invested in projects in Marseille when it was the capital in 2013.

THINK
VARY

ECONOMY
GROW

Critics of the European Capital of Culture argue that money is often wasted on temporary buildings and exhibitions, leaving cities **(7)** _____ to pay for things they really need, like schools and hospitals. Having said that, with many cities competing to be the European capital of culture every year, it is still seen as a **(8)** _____ title to have.

ABLE

DESIRE

___/8

2 **Complete each gap with the correct form of a verb from the box.**

| carry | decide | flick | get | go | press | put | sleep |

1 I haven't read the magazine but I _____ through it quickly on the bus this morning.
2 We'd better _____ on if we are going to finish this job before dinner.
3 It was a very confusing play. I don't think the writer really _____ across what he wanted to say.
4 It's important that you _____ on a location for your film before you start making it.
5 Let's _____ on the problem. It's too late to make a decision tonight.
6 If the neighbours _____ on playing such loud music, I'm going to call the police.
7 Can everyone _____ forward their ideas for the new exhibition as soon as possible?
8 I wish Ellie would stop _____ on about her new boyfriend all the time. It's so boring.

___/8

3 **Choose the correct word.**

1 Please **tell / make / say** the truth. It's important that we are honest with each other.
2 The new restaurant didn't **make / tell / get** a profit in the first year.
3 Sean doesn't need me to tell you this. He can **do / say /speak** for himself.
4 The comedian **did / told / said** lots of jokes about his family. It was really funny.
5 Francesca never **does / makes / tells** business with people she doesn't know.
6 Do you know that the manager **tells / speaks / says** really highly of you? You should ask for more money!
7 Dan's new trainers only cost 30 euros. I think he **made / did / got** a real bargain there.

___/7

4 **Match to make sentences.**

1 Having lived in Paris for many years, ___
2 Thinking it could make a fortune, ___
3 I think that's the man who's ___
4 She's the kind of person whose ___
5 Books written by celebrities ___
6 The romantic novel, which was set in Italy, ___
7 Used every day, ___
8 This is the place where ___

a) only desire in life is to make money.
b) Alison started a website selling cakes.
c) this toothpaste will whiten your teeth.
d) was about a soldier and a musician.
e) Jamie and Petra got married.
f) Marta spoke French very well.
g) going out with your sister.
h) usually sell very well.

___/8

5 If a sentence is correct, tick it. If a sentence is incorrect, underline the mistake and correct it.

1 The playwright was asked to write a tragedy by her fans. _____

2 The actors were had their photos taken outside the cinema before the premiere. _had their photos taken_

3 It is estimate that this science fiction novel has been downloaded over a million times. _____

4 The gallery has had many paintings donated to it by artists this year. _____

5 A correct PIN must entered when using the card. _must be entered_

6 It's been described as one of the most heart-breaking novels of all time. _____

7 A refund was be given to all the customers who had the receipt for their damaged phones. _was given_

___/7

6 Complete the second sentence so it has a similar meaning to the first. Do not change the word given. Use two to five words, including the word given.

1 The manager gave me some money off the T-shirt because it was dirty.   **DISCOUNT**
I was _given a discount_ the manager because the T-shirt was dirty.

2 It is easy for new businesses to lose money in their first year.   **MAKE**
It isn't easy for new businesses _to make a profit_ in their first year.

3 Did you ask your friend to translate the poem?   **GET**
Did you _get the poem translated by_ your friend?

4 They didn't publish the book until the editor had checked it.   **WAS**
The _book wasn't published until_ it had been checked by the editor.

5 If you take the dress back to the shop, you might be able to get your money back.   **GIVE**
They might _give you your money back_ if you take the dress back to the shop.

6 Not enough people in politics say what they really think in important meetings.   **MIND**
More politicians should _speak their mind_ in important meetings.

___/12

Total score ___/50

▼

EXAM SKILLS

Tick the statements that are true for you. Review the skills in the unit if you need more help.

I can ...	Unit/page
☐ understand references in an extract from a novel	Unit 9 p92
☐ recognise differences in meaning in a conversation	Unit 9 p96
☐ talk about my experiences in an interview	Unit 9 p98
☐ identify words which need spelling changes and predict answers before attempting an activity	Unit 9 p99
☐ use descriptive language to improve a story	Unit 9 p100
☐ understand the writer's purpose in an online article	Unit 10 p102
☐ understand responses to questions in conversations	Unit 10 p106
☐ reach a decision in a discussion	Unit 10 p108
☐ create verb forms and collocations accurately	Unit 10 p109
☐ introduce and conclude an essay appropriately	Unit 10 p110

READING | Gapped text | A travel article

1 **In pairs or as a group, answer the questions.**

1 Which is more important when creating a good film/series: the plot, the set and location or the actors?

2 Why do you think people might like to travel to locations where a film or series has been made?

2 **Read the article and find the following information.**

1 The price of a tour to visit a favourite series location. _____

2 How much tourism revenue might increase over a period of time. _____

3 The approximate percentage of people whose travel plans are influenced by what they see on TV series and films. _____

4 The number of jobs created in one area affected by film/series tourism. _____

5 Some European cities and other countries that have benefited from film/series tourism. _____

6 The type of jobs people can get because of film/series tourism. _____

3 **Look at the words and phrases in bold in the text. Match each one with a description in 1–5.**

This is used to …

1 introduce a reason or result: _____ , _____ , _____ , _____

2 add information: _____ , _____

3 contrast information: _____ , _____

4 show someone thinks they're stating something obvious: _____

5 show someone is happy about something: _____

OPTIMISE YOUR EXAM

Gapped text

- Linking words and phrases make a text logical and coherent, and make it easier for the reader to understand the writer's main points.
- They also indicate if the writer wants to explain, give reasons why, add information, contrast ideas, etc.
- Pay careful attention to linking words that come just before or after a gapped sentence.

AN *Alternative* HOLIDAY

Are you a *Game of Thrones* or *Star Wars* fan and looking for the holiday of your dreams? It might seem incredible but nowadays, around 80% of tourists are motivated to visit places after seeing the top locations in their favourite TV programmes and films.

Although it all started with New Zealand and *The Lord of the Rings* trilogy, *Game of Thrones* and *Star Wars* have really become the big draws in more recent years. Tourism in Spain is booming with organised tours to visit real-life locations in Seville, Girona and Peñiscola. **1 ____** In Croatia, fans of the series can go on a themed tour of Dubrovnik and a hike up to Mount Srd for amazing views over the 'kingdom'. **What's more**, as casting dates for extras are regularly posted on Twitter, many fans are keen to try their luck by getting a place on set and visiting the locations at the same time.

We met Jon, a tall, blond-haired Swede in the main street in Dubrovnik who told us he'd arrived a few years ago hoping to be an extra in the next series. **2 ____** But he was still living there **due to** the many opportunities for working for film and series tour companies. Two friends from Madrid, Juan and Lucia,

had just finished a $75 walking tour of Dubrovnik and a trip to the Fortress of Klis. Lucia told us, 'I'm not really a Thrones fan at all, but **thankfully** I love looking at old cities so I don't really mind going with Juan to see King's Landing and The Pile Gate where King Joffrey was faced with a riot. Juan is trying to persuade me to go to Belfast next to see The Iron Throne.'

3 ____ Fans who previously never thought of travelling to windswept sites such as the Giant's Causeway are now coming in their hoards to see where all the big *Game of Thrones* scenes took place. **Consequently**, nearly a thousand full-time jobs and many part-time jobs have been created in a region with a population of only two million.

4 ____ **However**, he said that the opportunity to work as a carpenter building film sets had changed his life. He added that now more series, including *Line of Duty*, were moving to locations in the area. 'The work's interesting and I hope it goes on for at least a few more years. **Besides**, it's great for young people to have jobs in hotels and the possibility to show people around. **5 ____** **So**, it may mean we have a lot more filming in the future over here.'

Fans who saw the *Harry Potter* films will have been surprised to recognise some of the same scenery in the 2015 *Star Wars: The Force*

Awakens. The Wye Valley and Forest of Dean have created a trail for viewers who want to follow in the footsteps of their screen heroes through the main areas used in the film. **As a result**, tourism revenue was predicted to rise by at least £50 million over a period of five years. 'We loved it', said Petra. She told us that she'd done the *Game of Thrones* tours in her native Croatia but seeing where *Star Wars* was filmed was even better. 'I saw the first film with my dad years ago when I was seven and have seen them all. I really want to visit Skellig Michael Island now to see where part of *Star Wars VII* was shot.'

6 ____ Experts believed that this was certain to increase in the future. We asked the Director of Tourism in Northern Ireland if he thought it would continue to be a growing industry. 'Young people are fed up with package tours to beach resorts and **of course** they want to see the real places where their favourite series and films are made', he told us.

So, it would seem that long format television series and the search for beautiful areas to film in will certainly benefit economies worldwide for many years to come.

4 🔊 3.06 **Read the text again. Choose which sentence A–G fits each gap 1–6. There is one extra sentence you do not need.**

A Brendan had been unemployed for more than three years.

B Initially, he'd been disappointed as the producers didn't take him on for a part.

C In 2015, the UK alone was making as much as £140 million from screen tourism, according to film consultancy services.

D Finally, the cost of filming here compared to the United States is lower.

E All of these places were used for sets in *Game of Thrones*.

F Unfortunately, he didn't get a part and decided to move on to another filming location.

G Northern Ireland has also benefited from the same series and with an increase in tourism, the economy is sure to start growing.

5 **Find these words and phrases in the article. Work out what they mean from the context.**

a trail (n)	booming (v)
big draws (noun ph)	fed up with (phr v)
hoards (n)	windswept (adj)

▶ **Workbook Unit 11:** Reading, pages 84–85, exercises 1, 2, 3, 4

Grammar in context

Choose the correct word or phrase to complete these sentences from the article on page 115.

1 *He **said** / told that the opportunity to work as a carpenter had changed his life.*

2 *We asked if he thought **it would continue** / would it continue to be a growing industry.*

✓ REMEMBER

- We use reported speech when we are reporting or summarising what someone else said without giving their exact words.

- Reported speech usually uses different tenses, modals and pronouns compared to direct speech, and other time words. For example: *'**We're** going to visit an amazing castle **tomorrow**', said Ben.* → *Ben said (that) **they were** going to visit an amazing castle **the next day**.*

- When we use reported speech for *yes/no* questions, we use *if/whether*: *'Do you want to borrow my tent?'* → *I asked Anna **if** she wanted to borrow my tent.*

- When we use reported speech for *wh-* questions, we don't use the question form of the verb: *'Where are you going on holiday?'* → *I asked Lia **where they were** going on holiday.*

- As well as *say*, there are many other verbs we can use to report what someone else said, including *agree, apologise, ask, beg, claim, command, deny, order, refuse, state, suggest, tell.* Many of these are followed by different grammatical patterns to *say*, e.g. *Matt **suggested** meeting up at the weekend.*

▶ **See Grammar reference, Unit 11,** page 159

1 Read the sentences and correct the mistakes.

1 The tour guide said that we are the first tourists to visit the forest for many years. _____

2 The hotel owner told us that the shops were closed today because there was a festival. _____

3 The captain said that the plane is flying at over 800 kilometres per hour. _____

4 Sally asked the waiter was the fish fresh. _____

5 The security guard at the airport asked us if we packed our bags ourselves. _____

6 Mum wanted to know where had we been the previous evening. _____

7 The taxi driver refused take us to our hotel. _____

8 Marcus denied to taking us in the wrong direction. _____

2 Look at the messages and complete the reported speech sentences 1–10.

> **Hey Jamie! How are you? How was your holiday?** 12:16
>
> **Hi Lisa! I'm OK but I had a really bad holiday. My sister had an accident in the mountains. She's still in hospital.** 12:17
>
> **Oh no! What happened?** 12:17
>
> **We were skiing and someone crashed into her. She fell over and broke her ankle.** 12:18
>
> **Is she OK?** 12:18
>
> **She can't fly home until next week, but she'll be OK. Thanks.** 12:18
>
> **Good. I'm happy to hear that. So, do you fancy going to the cinema on Saturday?** 12:20
>
> **Sure! That sounds great. What do you want to see?** 12:20
>
> **How about the new Pirates of the Caribbean film?** 12:20
>
> **Maybe we can see something else? I saw it last week!** 😊 12:21

SEND

1 Lisa asked Jamie _____

2 Jamie replied that he _____

3 He explained that his sister _____

4 Lisa asked what _____

5 Jamie said that they _____

6 Lisa asked if _____

7 Jamie explained that she _____

8 Lisa invited Jamie _____

9 She suggested _____

10 Jamie explained that _____

THINK | RESEARCH | CULTURE | LEARN | ME

Have you or has someone you know ever had an accident on holiday? What happened?

Words connected with *travelling*

1 🔊 3.07 **Write a word from the box in each gap. Don't use all the words. Listen and check.**

> arrive | get | reach

1 Do you know what time we'll _____ to New York?
2 I'll call you when we _____ at the port.

> excursion | flight | journey | ride
> route | travel | trip | voyage

3 My dad's going on a business _____ to China next week.
4 A GPS, or satnav, is handy for working out the best _____ to take.
5 All the _____ arrangements have been made, so I've just got to pack now and I'll be ready to go!

> fare | fee | ticket

6 How much is the entry _____ into the music festival?
7 How much will the taxi _____ to the airport be, do you think?

> entrance | gate | platform | reception

8 Make sure you're at the departure _____ at least 30 minutes before your flight.
9 The train won't be here for another 20 minutes – do you want to stand on the _____ or wait in the waiting room?
10 Remember to ask if the room has Wi-Fi when you check in at the hotel _____ .

> commuters | passengers

11 Everyone has to wear a seatbelt, even _____ in the back of the car.
12 Roadworks in both directions are making life a misery for _____ .

2 **Write a sentence for each of the eight words you didn't use in Exercise 1, showing you know what they mean and how they are used.**

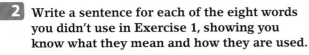

Phrasal verbs

3 🔊 3.08 **Write a word from the box in each gap. Listen and check.**

> check | drop | get | head
> pick | see | set | turn

1 We've definitely gone the wrong way. Do you think we should _____ *round*?
2 Thanks for the lift. If you could just _____ me *off* by the library, that'd be great.
3 There's a café at the other end of the beach. Let's _____ *for* that, shall we?
4 The taxi is going to _____ us *up* at 7 o'clock in the morning.
5 We all went to the station to _____ Ed *off*. It was really exciting!
6 We're hoping to _____ *away* for a couple of days next weekend if Angie's free.
7 Please _____ *out* of the hotel by 11 am on the morning of your departure.
8 To be at the port by nine, we'll have to _____ *out* from here at half past six.

Words + prepositions

4 🔊 3.09 **Write one preposition in each gap to complete the sentences. Use the words in italics to help you. Listen and check.**

1 I'm *looking forward* _____ going on the adventure holiday because I'm really *keen* _____ experiencing new things.
2 This travel visa's *valid* _____ the next three months.
3 The beach was so *crowded* _____ sunbathers that we decided to leave.
4 On holiday, it's important that nobody has the chance to *interfere* _____ your luggage.
5 If we get *separated* _____ each other, let's meet back at the hotel in an hour.
6 There was a sign in the bathroom *warning* us _____ drinking the tap water.
7 This app is *useful* _____ translating different words and phrases into the local language.
8 There's no *point* _____ getting *upset* _____ the delay – there's nothing we can *do* _____ it.

● SAY IT **RIGHT**

> **Resource centre: Unit 11**
> Stress in phrasal verbs (4)

> THINK | RESEARCH | CULTURE | LEARN | ME
>
> What's the furthest you've ever been from home? Who did you go with? What did you do there?

1 In pairs or as a group, ask and answer the questions.

1 Look at the photo. What is the man doing? How has he prepared for his trip?

2 Why do you think people choose to do this?

2 Look at the beginnings and endings of the sentences in Exercise 4. Write a word or phrase that has a similar meaning to each of these words and phrases.

1 issues _____

2 incident _____

3 had a mechanical problem _____

4 pursued _____

5 positively affected _____

6 be aware of _____

7 communicated _____

8 get lost _____

9 cope with _____

10 journey _____

3 Look at Exercise 2 again. Can you think of any other ways of saying the same things?

OPTIMISE YOUR EXAM

Sentence completion

- This type of task has distractors – extra options which are partly related to something you hear but which don't match exactly.

- For example, an option may mention being jealous of a work colleague and one of the speakers mentions being jealous, but not about a colleague.

- Remember that the whole option must match what you hear.

4 🔊 3.10 Listen to an interview about a young man who cycled around the world. Match sentence beginnings 1–8 with sentence endings A–J. There are two extra sentence endings you do not need.

1 In 2015, Tom Davies set out on a trip to ____

2 Because of political and visa problems, he ____

3 He was impressed by the people who offered to ____

4 In Australia, he had to ____

5 Cycling for hours a day, Tom needed to ____

6 Justin thought it was easy to ____

7 Tom thinks drivers in India need to ____

8 It was a common occurrence for Tom to ____

A help him when his bike broke down.

B tell how Tom was feeling from the way he expressed himself.

C cycle around the world.

D pay more attention to cyclists.

E meet his family in Australia.

F deal with strong desert winds.

G be chased by dogs.

H had to avoid conflictive situations.

I become disorientated in the middle of the desert.

J eat a lot of food every day.

5 🔊 3.10 Listen again and check your answers.

THINK | **RESEARCH** | CULTURE | LEARN | ME

Research and plan a round-the-world trip that you would like to take. Think about where you'd like to go, what the weather will be like, where you will stay and what dangers you might encounter.

Grammar in context

Look at these sentences from the audio in the listening lesson and answer the questions.

a) *I wonder if you could <u>tell us what you look for</u> in a blog.*

b) *And do you know <u>how far he cycled</u>?*

1 The first sentence starts with *I wonder if*. Does that mean the speaker is uncertain and speculating?

2 Do both sentences end with a question mark?

3 Are the underlined sections in the question form?

☑ REMEMBER

● In a direct question, we start with the question word (*What time does the train leave?*) or an auxiliary verb (*Does the train leave from platform 6?*).

● With indirect questions, we use an introductory phrase to make the question more polite. Because of this phrase, we don't use question word order: *Can you tell me what time **the train leaves**?* NOT *Can you tell me what time ~~does the train leave~~?*

● Some of the introductory phrases we can use are like questions, and end with a question mark: ***Do you know if/whether** the train leaves from platform 6?*

● Some of the introductory phrases aren't like questions, and don't end with a question mark: ***I'd be grateful if** you could tell me what time the train leaves. / **I wonder if/whether** you know if it leaves from platform 6.*

▶ **See Grammar reference, Unit 11,** page 160

---

1 **Complete the dialogue with indirect questions.**

A: Excuse me, (**1**) _____ you tell me why the 19:30 train to Manchester was cancelled?

B: I'm afraid there was a signalling problem outside London.

A: OK, thanks. I (**2**) _____ if you could tell me what time the next train to Manchester leaves.

B: The next one leaves in 15 minutes.

A: Thanks! And (**3**) _____ you let me know if I can take a bike on board?

B: Yes, you can. There's a special carriage at the front.

A: That's fantastic. In that case, I'd like to know (**4**) _____ there is an extra charge to pay.

B: No, travelling with your bike is free.

A: That's great!

B: Let me know if I can help with anything else.

A: Oh, yes! I'd be (**5**) _____ if you could help me carry my bike on to the train.

B: Of course – it looks very heavy!

A: It is! Oh, I forgot to ask, do you know (**6**) _____ there is Wi-Fi on the train?

B: Yes, there is. It's really easy to connect with the network and it's free!

2 **Write indirect questions using the prompts.**

1 I / grateful / tell me / any places left on the studio tour

_____

2 I wonder / you know / why the trip was cancelled

_____

3 Could / tell me / what time / we land in Moscow

_____

4 You know / I can change my hotel reservation

_____

3 **Rewrite the direct questions as indirect questions using the words given.**

1 Where did they film the new *Star Wars* film?

COULD

_____

2 Are we going to arrive on time?

KNOW

_____

3 Why did you decide to travel around the world by bike?

CAN

_____

4 How do I get to the station?

TELL

_____

THINK | RESEARCH | CULTURE | LEARN | ME

Do you have ways of making questions more polite in your first language? How do you make questions more polite?

▶ **Workbook Unit 11:** Grammar 2, page 87, exercises 1, 2

Talk2Me

It's hard to say, but ...

Flipped classroom

1 ▷ Watch the *Talk2Me* video and make notes about the types of holiday the people go on and what kinds of things they like doing when they are on holiday.

_____

_____

_____

_____

_____

_____

_____

2 ▷ Watch the video again. Write the name of the person who says the expressions in the *Phrase expert* box.

PHRASE EXPERT

I'd be tempted to say … | I haven't really thought about it, but … | I'm not sure about that … | I'm the kind of person who … | It's hard to say, but … | Let's see … | That's an interesting / a difficult question … | To be honest …

3 Look at photographs A and B. In pairs, discuss some of the advantages and disadvantages of each type of holiday. Say which holiday you would prefer to go on and why.

A

B

4 Complete the dialogue with the words and phrases in the box.

difficult question | honest | kind of person
see | tempted | thought about

Would you prefer to go sightseeing in a city or spend the day by the beach?

That's a (**1**) _____ ! I love going anywhere on holiday. Let's
(**2**) _____ … I haven't really
(**3**) _____ it, but I'm the
(**4**) _____ who is very active.
So I'd be (**5**) _____ to say that I'd prefer to go sightseeing. However, to be
(**6**) _____ , I'd be happy with any type of holiday right now!

▼

OPTIMISE YOUR EXAM

Interview

● Remember to try and answer the questions promptly and say more than one sentence. If you aren't sure what to say immediately, try to use a phrase to give yourself some time to think quickly.

● It's not a good idea to learn a speech before the exam on specific topics. Try to be natural and say what you can in three or four sentences.

▼

5 Take turns to be the examiner and candidate to ask and answer the questions. Use expressions from the *Phrase expert* box.

● Would you prefer to go camping in the mountains or stay in a hotel?

● Where's the most interesting place you've visited?

● What are the good and bad points for going on holiday with family or friends?

● Have you ever been abroad? If so, where did you go? If not, would you like to go abroad? Where would you like to go?

● Would you like to travel or live abroad when you're older?

● What are the good or bad points about travelling by plane?

● Do you think it's better to go on holiday in a different country or in your own country? Why?

1 **Look at the text and the words in capitals in Exercise 2 and answer the questions.**

1 Which of the gaps will be filled by an adjective? _____

2 Which of the gaps will be filled by a noun? _____

3 Which nouns will be plural? _____

▼

OPTIMISE YOUR **EXAM**

Word formation

● Answer every question. If you aren't sure, make a sensible guess.

● English spelling is sometimes difficult. Always check carefully when you think you might have to change a vowel or part of a word to form the new word in the gap.

● Read the whole text again when you have completed the task.

2 **Write a form of the word in capitals in each gap to complete the text.**

A holiday with a difference

Are you interested in doing something **(1)** _____ when you next go abroad? Would you like to spend a couple of weeks living with like-minded young people from all over the world while **(2)** _____ local communities? Then why not consider registering for a volunteering project with the SCI (Service Civil International) network? You can choose from hundreds of different projects all around the world, from helping to build footpaths in the mountains of Slovenia to organising **(3)** _____ at a summer camp for children in Russia. **(4)** _____ get free food and accommodation in exchange for five or six hours work a day. But best of all, they also get a **(5)** _____ opportunity to experience another culture, its people and traditions.

The projects are organised by local groups in the host countries, but you can find out about all of them on the SCI website. **(6)** _____ are then made through a partner organisation in your own country. After that, you just have to make **(7)** _____ to get there. SCI has been bringing people from different countries together for nearly a hundred years, so why not join them for a unique and **(8)** _____ worthwhile experience?

MEANING

HELP

ACTIVE
PARTICIPATE
VALUE

APPLY
ARRANGE

HUGE

3 **Look at the sentences in Exercise 4 and answer the questions.**

Which of them test your knowledge of …

1 phrasal verbs? _____

2 word patterns? _____

3 reported speech? _____

4 direct speech? _____

▼

OPTIMISE YOUR **EXAM**

Sentence transformation

● Make sure you give yourself some time to go over your final answers. Always check you haven't written more than five words. If you have written more than five words in any of the sentences, the answer isn't correct.

4 **Complete the second sentence so it has a similar meaning to the first. Do not change the word given. Use two to five words, including the word given.**

1 Will was met at the airport by Lea. **PICKED**

It was Lea who _____ the airport.

2 'Remember to call Fiona when you get there, Jake.' **TOLD**

Jake _____ forget to call Fiona when he got there.

3 'Are you flying to Australia via Singapore, Dionne?' asked Megan. **SHE**

Megan _____ flying to Australia via Singapore.

4 Steve's dad said he'd warned him to keep his passport safe. **LOSING**

'I _____ passport, Steve,' said his dad.

5 'Sorry I didn't meet you at the station, Greg,' said Guy. **APOLOGISED**

Guy _____ at the station.

6 Don't get a ticket in advance – it's a waste of time. **POINT**

There _____ a ticket in advance.

1 In pairs or as a group, answer the questions.

1 What was the best/worst school trip you went on? Why was it good/bad?

2 What things do you like seeing on school trips?

2 Read this email and answer the questions.

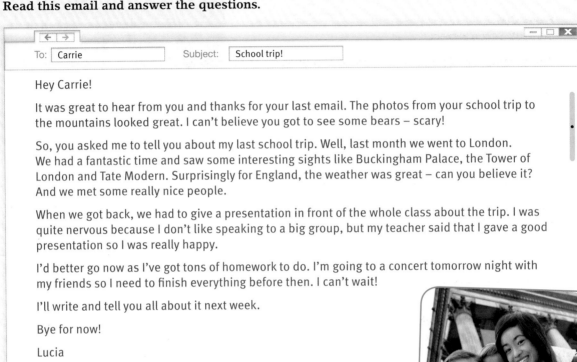

To: Carrie   Subject: School trip!

Hey Carrie!

It was great to hear from you and thanks for your last email. The photos from your school trip to the mountains looked great. I can't believe you got to see some bears – scary!

So, you asked me to tell you about my last school trip. Well, last month we went to London. We had a fantastic time and saw some interesting sights like Buckingham Palace, the Tower of London and Tate Modern. Surprisingly for England, the weather was great – can you believe it? And we met some really nice people.

When we got back, we had to give a presentation in front of the whole class about the trip. I was quite nervous because I don't like speaking to a big group, but my teacher said that I gave a good presentation so I was really happy.

I'd better go now as I've got tons of homework to do. I'm going to a concert tomorrow night with my friends so I need to finish everything before then. I can't wait!

I'll write and tell you all about it next week.

Bye for now!

Lucia

1 Find at least three examples of informal words or phrases.

_____

2 Find at least three examples of informal grammar and punctuation.

_____

3 Write a more formal equivalent for each word or phrase in bold. There may be more than one correct answer.

Example: I**'ve got** some geography homework to do.   *have*

1 My brother **got** stung by a bee on holiday.   _____
2 I **got** the train tickets yesterday.   _____
3 I **got** a model plane for my birthday.   _____
4 We **got** separated at the airport.   _____
5 We finally **got** a taxi home.   _____
6 Susie **got** me to promise I'd go shopping with her.   _____
7 You need to **get** a visa before you can enter the country.   _____
8 What time do you have to **get to** the station tomorrow?   _____
9 Why don't you **get** a job to pay for the trip?   _____
10 I don't know how they **got on** the train without a ticket.   _____

OPTIMISE YOUR EXAM

A letter / An email

- Before you start writing, read the task carefully and underline the key points to help you organise your ideas.
- If the task includes questions, make sure you answer them all and include relevant information.

4 **Look at this writing task and make notes to answer the questions. Use your imagination if necessary.**

You've received this email from your friend, Carl.

> **From:** Carl
> **Subject:** School project
>
> We're doing a project at school on what makes a holiday special. What was the best holiday you've ever been on? What made it so special? Tell me all about it!

Write your **email**.

• What was the best holiday you've ever been on?

_____

• Where did you go?

_____

• Who did you go with?

_____

• What did you do there? What made it so special?

_____

• What other information do you want to tell Carl about it?

_____

5 **Plan**   Make a paragraph plan.

Part	Purpose	Useful phrases	My notes
Paragraph 1	greeting – ask Carl how he is, tell him what you have been doing recently	_It was great to hear from you!_	
Paragraph 2	answer his question – what was the best holiday you've been on? where did you go? what made it so special?	_So, you asked me to tell you about …_	
Paragraph 3	other information you want to tell Carl about	_I'll write and tell you about it next week._	
Paragraph 4	say goodbye to Carl	_Bye for now!_	

6 **Write**   Write your email in an appropriate style. Write 140–190 words.

7 **Check**   Before you hand in your email, complete this checklist.

Checklist

○ I've thanked Carl for his email and referred to something in it other than the project.

○ I've written an informal email in a chatty, conversational style.

○ I've started and ended my email in an appropriate way.

○ I've followed my paragraph plan.

○ I've described my holiday in detail.

○ I've checked my spelling and grammar.

12 Achieve the impossible

READING | Multiple matching | A magazine article

1 **In pairs or as a group, answer the questions.**

1 What do you think it takes to be successful in life?

2 How do you feel when you are in a difficult situation?

2 **Read the article quickly and match each person to a statement. There is one extra statement you do not need.**

1 Guled Adan Abdi ____

2 Mursal ____

3 Olivia Hallisey ____

4 Xiuhtezcatl Roske-Martinez ____

This young person …

a) works with others to try and improve the natural conditions on our planet.

b) won an important prize after giving a speech at the United Nations.

c) creates things from materials that other people dispose of.

d) discovered a way to monitor the symptoms of a life-threatening illness.

e) teaches other young people and helps them realise their potential.

3 **Look at extracts 1–4 from the questions in Exercise 4. Match them to similar phrases in a)–f). There are two extra items in a)–f) you do not need.**

1 didn't receive any official schooling ____

2 was educated to appreciate the natural world ____

3 was able to keep on investigating ____

4 was taught to deal with everyday situations ____

a) was allowed to continue her research

b) was taught in a rural environment

c) missed out on any formal education

d) wasn't able to get to classes every day

e) learnt valuable life skills

f) was brought up to respect the land

OPTIMISE YOUR **EXAM**

Multiple matching

● Read the texts quickly first for general understanding.

● Remember to read the lead-in line to the questions carefully. Then read the questions and underline any key words.

● Look for words and expressions which are similar in the questions and the relevant part of the text.

● If you can't find the answer, leave it and move on to the next question. Check your answers once you have finished.

Get inspired!

Read about four young people from around the world who have achieved great things.

A **Guled Adan Abdi** from Somalia was only 13 when he became famous for his electronic toys. From an early age he had a passion for making toys from unwanted objects that other people were throwing away. He started observing cars in his local town and by using his natural mechanical skills he worked out how to motorise his toys. Without any formal training he came up with a way to construct items from plastic containers used for cooking and powered them with batteries costing only $0.25. Although he missed out on any formal education for several years, he finally returned to school and was encouraged by his teacher, who bought him batteries to power his creations and pushed him to continue with his experiments. His education was eventually fully funded by the local government. They were so impressed by his skills that not only did the government pay for his education but they also invited him to meet the President. Of course Guled's ambition is to learn how to build real cars in the future.

B **Mursal**, a young Afghani girl, has represented Afghanistan's non-profit organisation Skateistan at a global conference in Doha, Qatar. She is one of the many girls who have benefited from the organisation's aim to empower young people.

She reported on the Skateistan blog how she had begun skateboarding several years before through Skateistan, an organisation started by avid skateboarder Oliver Percovich. As a result, she has learnt valuable life skills and she is now teaching other young people about one of these skills: leadership. Mursal has learnt to make choices for herself through multimedia educational programmes offered by the organisation, including environmental studies and world cultures. What started with three skateboards and a few keen Afghani skaters is now an organisation that combines skateboarding with education for young people in three different countries. Mursal's message in her classes is particularly aimed at young women and their empowerment in the local and global community. Rarely do a few skateboards lead to such an inspirational outcome!

C **Olivia Hallisey** from Connecticut was still a teenager when she made a great start in her ambition to become a doctor and to work for a global health organisation. She was the grand prize winner of the 2015 Google Science fair with her invention of a test for Ebola, the disease which caused a devastating loss of life in West Africa in 2014. Olivia designed an economical test which not only offered results in 30 minutes but also used a card which can store antibodies for up to a week without refrigeration. This was a considerable improvement on current tests, which involve the use of chemicals and need storage at very low temperatures.

Not only will the prize money allow her to continue her research into the use of her test for other fatal diseases but it will have an impact on the consequences of these diseases, which leave many children orphaned and lacking basic human needs.

D Little did people in the United Nations conference hall in New York know what was going to happen when a young boy called Xiuhtezcatl stood up. 15-year-old **Xiuhtezcatl Roske-Martinez**'s cool and confident composure must have amazed them all when he became one of the youngest speakers ever to campaign about climate change at a UN summit. Xiuhtezcatl had been a climate change activist since he was six years old. In his home state of Colorado, he was brought up to respect the land and has worked with environmental organisations on many projects, including introducing a fee for plastic bags and stopping fracking in Boulder, an idyllic mountain city. He works mainly with his group, Earth Guardians, which has more than 400 groups worldwide, to spread awareness of environmental issues. Despite his fame, Xiuhtezcatl likes to do the same things that most young people do and he believes that it is for world leaders to be at the forefront of environmental change.

---

4 ◁))) 3.11 **For each question, choose from the people A–D. The people may be chosen more than once.**

Which person

educates and inspires other young people to take action about vital issues which affect their future? `1`

didn't receive any official schooling for a period of time? `2`

was able to keep on investigating due to a financial reward? `3`

was taught important ways to deal with everyday situations? `4`

behaves in a similar way to their age group, even though they are well known? `5`

had their education completely paid for by regional authorities? `6`

was educated to appreciate the natural world from an early age? `7`

went to an international forum in a different part of the world? `8`

invented something that was cost effective and a great advance on existing products? `9`

used a mixture of instinct and specific abilities to devise a way to make their invention function? `10`

5 **Find these words and phrases in the text. Work out what they mean from the context.**

at the forefront (adj phr)	came up with (phr v)
composure (n)	empower (v)
encouraged by (v + prep)	orphaned (adj)
outcome (n)	spread awareness (v phr)

Grammar in context

Look at these sentences from the extract on page 125 and answer the questions.

a) *Not only will the prize money allow her to continue her research … but it will have an impact …*

b) *Rarely do a few skateboards lead to such an inspirational outcome!*

c) *Little did people … know what was going to happen when a young boy called Xiuhtezcatl stood up.*

1 What do you notice about the underlined words?

  a) They have positive meanings.

  b) They have negative meanings.

2 What do you notice about the word order in the clause after the underlined words?

  a) It is like a question.

  b) It is like a statement.

✓ REMEMBER

● When some negative adverbial words and phrases are used at the beginning of a sentence, the subject and the verb 'invert'. We use the question form of the verb, even though the sentence is not a question. For example:

○ **Never** *had I tried so hard in all my life.*

○ **Hardly** *had he got on the plane when the problems began.*

○ **No sooner** *had they started their journey than the GPS failed.*

○ **Not only** *was she thirsty, but she was hungry too.*

○ **Rarely/Seldom** *have I heard such an empowering story.*

○ **Little did** *the passengers know what was about to happen.*

○ **Only** *when they saw the news did they realise the seriousness of the situation.* (Note that with *only*, the verb in the second clause is inverted.)

▶ **See Grammar reference, Unit 12,** page 160

---

1 **Complete the second sentence so it has a similar meaning to the first. Do not change the word given. Use two to five words, including the word given.**

1 I reached the top of the mountain when it began to snow.

          HARDLY

  _____ the top of the mountain when it began to snow.

2 We took off and our plane ran into difficulties.

          SOONER

  _____ off than our plane ran into difficulties.

3 We didn't realise she was at the forefront of the exciting discoveries.

          LITTLE

  _____ that she was at the forefront of the exciting discoveries.

4 We found our way through the jungle and discovered a small village.

          WHEN

  _____ our way through the jungle did we discover a small village.

5 We lost our way and night began to fall.

          NOT ONLY

  _____ our way but night began to fall.

6 Young people don't often speak at international conferences.

          SELDOM

  _____ young people speak at international conferences.

---

2 **Underline six phrases in the text which could be rewritten using inversion. Rewrite those phrases.**

Lucky to be alive!

Sixteen-year-olds rarely sail around the world and those who do it alone are even rarer. But that's exactly what Californian teenager Abby Sunderland tried to do a few years ago.

An experienced sailor, it had been Abby's dream to sail around the world for some time, but she didn't know how it would end up. Things had been going well and she was over half way round when she found herself in a terrible storm in the Indian Ocean. There were both very strong winds and also 15-metre-high waves. She had never had to face such difficult conditions so far from land.

The winds damaged her sail, which she had to take down and repair while the ship was navigating the huge waves. Immediately after she had done this, the winds became stronger again and caused more damage.

When her satellite phone failed, and her sail broke and ended up in the sea, Abby knew that she would have to set off her emergency satellite beacons, which would tell everyone she needed rescuing.

For nearly 24 hours, everyone was very worried about Abby, but eventually aeroplane pilots were able to make contact with her and report back to her parents that she was fine, before a French fishing boat in the area was sent to rescue her.

A 16-year-old has seldom had such a brave story to tell.

1 _____

2 _____

3 _____

4 _____

5 _____

6 _____

Easily-confused words

1 🔊 3.12 **Write a word from the box in each gap. Don't use all the words. Listen and check.**

| infamous | famed | unknown |

1 Despite his talent, Van Gogh was relatively _____ during his lifetime.

2 Jesse James was a(n) _____ outlaw in the Wild West.

| effort | job | work |

3 It took a huge _____ to get to the top of the mountain.

4 You'll be rewarded for all the hard _____ you've put in this term.

| achieve | earn | succeed |

5 Don't give up. I'm sure you'll _____ your goal one day.

6 To _____ in passing the exam, you need to focus on what's important.

| fail | lose | miss |

7 If you _____ the exam, don't let it stop you from following your dreams.

8 Some people become more determined when they _____ a contest.

2 **Write sentences with the unused words from Exercise 1.**

_____

_____

_____

_____

3 **Write the correct form of one word from Exercise 1 in each gap to complete the sentences.**

1 With all the _____ you've made recently, you're bound to pass the exam.

2 My grandma _____ many things in her life and I like listening to her stories.

3 Some singers go from being _____ to being household names in a very short time.

4 Every time I _____ at something, I quickly pick myself up and try again.

5 To _____ in surviving in the wild, you need to know where to find water.

6 Unfortunately, Sadie _____ her flight to Barcelona so she couldn't go on the school trip.

7 After university, I want to go travelling before I get a full-time _____ .

8 I left my coat on the train. I'm going to call the station's _____ property office!

Phrasal verbs

4 🔊 3.13 **Put each of the phrasal verbs into the correct column. Listen and check.**

1 The heavy snowfall meant the village was *cut off* for days.

2 Jackie's stupid joke *sparked off* a huge argument.

3 Did you *finish off* the curry that was in the fridge?

4 I almost didn't recognise my dad when he *shaved off* his beard!

5 Police *roped* the area *off* so that no-one could get in the area.

6 I finally managed to *wipe* the dirty mark *off* the window.

7 Wait until everyone moves back before you *set off* the fireworks.

8 When you've finished, make sure you *log off* from the computer system.

start / make sth start	prevent, keep away	finish, complete	remove

Idioms with *keep* and *lose*

5 🔊 3.14 **Choose the correct word to complete each sentence. Listen and check.**

1 If you don't *lose your **brain** / **nerve** / **vein***, you'll reach your goal!

2 Try to *keep **look** / **sight** / **vision** of* what you want to achieve at all times.

3 Make sure you *keep your **face** / **head** / **hair*** during all the excitement and you'll have a good chance of winning.

4 Try to focus your energy and not *lose your **anger** / **emotion** / **temper*** during the game.

5 I was determined to *keep my **letter** / **word** / **sentence*** and do what I had promised to do.

6 When you really concentrate on a task, it's easy to *lose **sight** / **track** / **way** of* time.

1 **In pairs or as a group, ask and answer the questions.**

1 How do you think success should be measured? In financial terms or in some other way?

2 What do you think is your greatest achievement so far in your life?

2 **Look at the questions in Exercise 4 and underline all the adverbs in the questions and answer options.**

3 **Complete each statement with an adverb you underlined in Exercise 2. There may be more than one correct answer for some gaps.**

1 'The music was great, but it was the dancing that I enjoyed _____ .'

2 'The building was _____ destroyed by fire.'

3 'It's _____ important that you read the next chapter.'

4 'They _____ visited Madrid when they lived in Spain.'

5 'She _____ wears red but today she is wearing black.'

OPTIMISE YOUR EXAM

Multiple choice (extracts)

● Remember you may hear the speakers talk about all three points in the options.

● Read the questions carefully and look for specific words like *most*, *particularly*, *mainly*. These may help you identify the correct answer if more than one option is mentioned.

---

4 🔊 3.15 **You will hear people talking in eight different situations. For questions 1–8, choose the best answer (A, B or C).**

1 You hear two friends talking about an important day.
How does the woman feel?
A disappointed about what happened
B proud of someone close to her
C afraid of something

2 You hear a news report about a woman.
What is special about the woman's achievement?
A It happened on a particular day.
B It had never been done before.
C It was totally unexpected.

3 You hear a boy telling a friend about rescuing someone.
What did he enjoy most about it?
A The attention he received.
B The reward he was given.
C The sense of achievement he got.

4 You overhear a girl talking about a book she has read.
How did she feel when she finished the book?
A sad there wasn't more of it
B relieved to get to the end of it
C confused by the ending

5 You hear part of a programme on an extraordinary place.
What is the presenter mainly doing?
A recommending a visit to the place
B explaining something about the place
C complaining about something

6 You hear a teacher talking about someone he admires.
What does he particularly admire about the man?
A his talent
B his determination
C his kindness

7 You hear a girl talking about something she did for charity.
What is she most proud of?
A being a good example to others
B helping someone else to keep going
C refusing to give up

8 You hear part of an interview with a musician.
What does he find most surprising about Beethoven's ninth symphony?
A people's reaction to the work
B his use of voices in the work
C his hearing when he wrote it

5 🔊 3.15 **Listen again and check your answers.**

THINK | RESEARCH | CULTURE | **LEARN** | ME

Talk together about what you have learnt about doing multiple-choice tasks. What should you do first? What should you do next?

Grammar in context

Look at these extracts from the audio in the listening lesson and match them to make sentences.

1 *What is really remarkable* ____

2 *It was the way everyone else reacted* ____

a) *that felt really good.*

b) *is the fact that he was deaf when he wrote it.*

 REMEMBER

- In cleft sentences, we put what we want to emphasise first and then everything else in the sentence goes into a relative clause beginning with *that*.

- Cleft sentences can begin with:
  - ○ **What** *I like is that the skyscraper is so tall.*
  - ○ **The reason why** *I like it is that the bridge is so long.*
  - ○ **It** *was the diverse culture that I found amazing.*
  - ○ **It was not until** *I saw it from a distance that I realised how big it was.*

▶ **See Grammar reference, Unit 12,** page 160

1 **Choose the correct word or phrase to complete each sentence.**

1 What many people don't realise **that / is that** the Romans achieved remarkable feats of engineering.

2 **What / It** is the tunnel under the English Channel that really impresses me.

3 The reason why so many people visit the Great Wall **that / is that** it's a breathtaking sight.

4 It was not until we visited the Pyramids **that / is that** we saw what all the fuss was about.

5 What you notice about the building **that / is that** it is so tall you can't see the top clearly.

6 It was **only / not** when I learnt how old Stonehenge is that I realised how amazing it was.

2 **Underline the mistake in each sentence and rewrite it correctly.**

1 That amazes me is that the bridge is over six miles long. _____

2 It is the length of the railway tunnel what I find so great. _____

3 The reason which it is so special is that it's the tallest in the world. _____

4 It impresses people about Dubai's Palm Island is that it's completely artificial. _____

5 It was not when I saw the Golden Gate Bridge that I realised how long it was. _____

6 What do I love about the Taj Mahal is that it looks pink in the morning. _____

3 **Read the text. Rewrite each numbered sentence as a cleft sentence, starting with the word or phrase given.**

A feat of engineering

[1]When you see the Burj Khalifa, you are impressed that it is so tall. It is 828 metres high and has 162 floors. [2]The engineering process involved is really incredible. For example, the builders had to build over 40 wind tunnels just to test how various parts of the building coped in high winds. [3]You only realise what a feat it is when you visit the observation deck on the 124th floor. Looking at the view over Dubai is like looking out of the window of a plane. The building contains over 28,000 hand-cut glass panels and is topped by a spire that is more than 200 metres long. [4]The spire was built inside the tower and then lifted into position, which is incredible. If you cut across the building, you would see that it is shaped like the letter Y. [5]Most people don't know it is based on the shape of a flower. While it was being built, it was known as Burj Dubai. [6]The building was named Burj Khalifa when it was finished.

1 What _____

2 It _____

3 It is not _____

4 What _____

5 What _____

6 It was not _____

● **SAY IT RIGHT**

Resource centre: Unit 12
Intonation in cleft sentences

☆

| THINK | RESEARCH | **CULTURE** | LEARN | ME |

What feats of amazing engineering are there in your own country? What do you think of them?

Talk 2 Me

Sorry, do you mean ...?

1 ▷ Watch the *Talk2Me* video and answer the questions.

1 What advantages and disadvantages of being famous do people discuss in the video?

2 How many of the people would like to be famous?

2 ▷ Read the sentences. The underlined words are incorrect. Rewrite the sentences with the correct words. Watch the video again and check your answers.

1 So, what you're <u>mean</u> is …

_____

2 Sorry to <u>say</u>, but…

_____

3 Sorry, but I don't <u>interrupt</u> your point.

_____

4 I think you <u>get</u> …, don't you?

_____

5 Can I just <u>sorry</u> …?

_____

6 <u>Saying</u>, do you mean…?

_____

3 In pairs, discuss the following statements. Try to explain your reasons.

> 'Nowadays, it's easy to become a celebrity. Anybody can become a celebrity.'

PHRASE EXPERT

Can I just say …? | I think you mean …, don't you? | Sorry, but I don't get your point. | Sorry, do you mean …? | Sorry to interrupt, but … | So, what you're saying is …

4 Look at the questions in Exercise 5. For each one, make notes for your main ideas and one or two reasons or an example to justify your points.

OPTIMISE YOUR EXAM

Discussion

- Listen carefully to what your partner says. If you aren't sure what they mean or what point they are trying to make, ask them to explain or check you understand.

- You may need to interrupt your partner sometimes because you want them to explain something or if you disagree with them. Try to be polite!

5 In groups of three, discuss the questions. Take turns to be the examiner and candidates. Try to interrupt your partner politely if you disagree, ask for clarification or want to add a point.

- How important is it to be successful at work?
- Is it good to be ambitious?
- Is it important not to give up when you find something difficult to do?
- If you could be famous for something, what would it be and why?
- What responsibilities do famous people have as role models for young people?

1 Look at the words in capitals in Exercise 2 and answer the questions.

1 Which of them are adjectives? What nouns can you form from them? ____
2 Which of them are verbs? What nouns can you form from them? ____
3 Which of them are nouns? What adjectives can you form from them? ____

OPTIMISE YOUR EXAM

Word formation

● Check that your answers are the correct part of speech, have the correct prefix or suffix, and that you've used a negative form where necessary.

2 Write a form of the word in capitals in each gap to complete the text.

Ada Lovelace: A true pioneer

In 2015, **(1)** _____ were held across the world to mark the 200th anniversary of Ada Lovelace's birth. But who was this extraordinary woman and what did she discover that was so significant? Ada Lovelace is **(2)** _____ thought to be the world's first computer **(3)** _____ . She was the daughter of the famed Romantic poet Lord Byron, but had a difficult **(4)** _____ separated from her father. She was often ill, which eventually lead to a **(5)** _____ . But with the support of her mother, she developed her interest in mathematics. As a teenager, she became friends with the **(6)** _____ Charles Babbage, and began working with him on his Analytical Engine, a machine often regarded as one of the earliest computers. While studying the machine, she wrote a computing code known as an algorithm. The code could potentially be used by the machine to 'read' data – an **(7)** _____ which had never been done before. Unlike Babbage, who was more interested in numbers and building a calculator, Ada had the vision to see the future **(8)** _____ of a computer. And it was this vision that has earned her the highest respect from experts around the world.

CELEBRATE

WIDE
PROGRAM

CHILD
ABLE

MATHEMATICS

ACCOMPLISH

CAPABLE

3 Read the text in Exercise 4 quickly. Answer the questions.

1 Which gaps test vocabulary from this unit and which gaps test grammar? ____
2 What is gap 1 testing: a phrasal verb or an idiom? ____
3 Gap 8 is testing an idiom with *keep*. What idioms with *keep* have you learnt in this unit? ____

OPTIMISE YOUR EXAM

Multiple-choice cloze

● Before you decide on your answer, read the complete sentence carefully.
● Cross out any options that are definitely wrong.

4 Choose the correct word to fill each gap.

Achievements in space

Which is the bigger human feat, landing on the moon or building the International Space Station (ISS)? The moon landings may have **(1)** ____ off an interest in space exploration, but nothing useful came out of them. **(2)** ____ makes the ISS special is that it is a floating laboratory. If we ever **(3)** ____ the goal of sending people to Mars, it will be because of what we learn from the experiments on board the ISS.

The ISS started life in the 80s as an American project named Freedom. Only when it became an international project in the 90s **(4)** ____ it start to take shape. Over the years, many missions have added various sections to the ISS. **(5)** ____ has a project brought so many people together. This massive **(6)** ____ , made in a spirit of peaceful cooperation, contrasts with the dangerous rivalry that prompted the moon landings. It's possible to argue that the moon landings **(7)** ____ in their aim of starting the space age. The ISS, however, allows us to keep **(8)** ____ of what is important: exploring space peacefully together.

1	**A** come	**B** made	**C** brought	**D** sparked
2	**A** What	**B** Which	**C** It	**D** This
3	**A** get	**B** achieve	**C** succeed	**D** make
4	**A** was	**B** has	**C** did	**D** that
5	**A** Hardly	**B** Barely	**C** Rarely	**D** Only
6	**A** work	**B** feat	**C** effort	**D** success
7	**A** failed	**B** stopped	**C** quit	**D** lost
8	**A** vision	**B** look	**C** sight	**D** view

1 **In pairs or as a group, answer the questions.**

1 What do you imagine it would be like to visit the place in the photo?

2 What impressive landmarks are there in your country?

2 **Read this review and choose which structure from a)–c) the writer has used.**

a) • introduction, say what, where and when
  • give detailed information about the place
  • say what else you did when you were in the area
  • say how much you are looking forward to going back

b) • introduction, say what, where and when
  • describe the main plus points of the place
  • give one or two positive details and your reaction to them
  • mention any negative points and make a recommendation

c) • introduction, say what, where and when
  • explain one main thing you didn't like and say why
  • explain another thing you didn't like and say why
  • mention any positive points and make a recommendation

3 **Which other structure in Exercise 2 could you use to write a review?**

4 **Read the review again and underline any facts about the skywalk that the writer mentions.**

The Grand Canyon Skywalk

One of the most amazing feats of engineering in the world is the Grand Canyon Skywalk. The skywalk is a kind of bridge made out of steel and glass and it sticks out over the Grand Canyon in the USA. My family and I visited it last summer.

What is most impressive about the skywalk is that you can step out over the canyon with a drop of 1,200 metres! If you can keep your head while looking through the glass, it certainly is an incredible feeling.

Access to the skywalk may seem expensive. However, not only does the ticket include transport and a meal, but you also get a certificate to show you visited. My family and I thought it was actually quite a reasonable price.

My only criticism of this fantastic site is that you are not allowed to take your own camera onto the skywalk. This is to prevent items being dropped into the canyon, but it means you have to buy a professional photo of yourself on the skywalk. Overall, though, I highly recommend the Grand Canyon Skywalk.

OPTIMISE YOUR EXAM

A review

● When you are reviewing a place, describe the key positive and negative features and include your opinion or a personal reaction.

● Describe any important facts, such as size, price of admission, what exactly you can see or do there.

● Try to balance the good and bad points about the place and make a recommendation in the final paragraph.

5 Look at this writing task and make notes to answer the questions. Use your imagination if necessary.

You see this advert on an English-language website for teenagers.

> ## Reviews wanted!
> Have you visited a place that you think could be described as a wonder of the world or an amazing piece of engineering? We want your reviews. Tell us what you liked about the place, anything you didn't like, and your view of what the place has to offer other young people. Would you recommend it? Tell us and you could appear on the website!

Write your **review**.

- What place are you going to write about?

  _____

- What is the best thing about this place?

  _____

- How did you feel when you visited it?

  _____

- Write one or two details about the place. It could be the size, the number of visitors, the price of admission, the facilities.

  _____

- What was your reaction when you visited the place? Were you impressed/disappointed/annoyed?

  _____

- Are you going to make any negative points? About what?

  _____

- What recommendation are you going to make to other young people?

  _____

6 **Plan**   Make a paragraph plan.

Part	Purpose	Useful phrases	My notes
Title	introduction and a short phrase to summarise your opinion		
Paragraph 1	a positive aspect of the place – what's the best thing about it? how did you feel?	*What is most impressive about ...* *The best thing about ...*	
Paragraph 2	a few details about the place and some interesting facts – what can you do there? what is interesting to see?	*Some interesting things to do are ...* *There are lots of attractions in ...*	
Paragraph 3	mention any negative points	*My only criticism is ...* *On the downside ...*	
Paragraph 4	your final recommendation	*Overall, I highly recommend visiting ...* *It's ideal for ...* *I wouldn't recommend it for people who ...*	

7 **Write**   Write your review in an appropriate style. Write 140–190 words.

8 **Check**   Before you hand in your review, complete this checklist.

Checklist

- ◯ I have briefly said what, where and when.
- ◯ I've written at least four paragraphs.
- ◯ I've described the main positive/negative points of the place.
- ◯ I've given my personal reaction to the place.
- ◯ I've said what it has to offer other young people.
- ◯ I've made a recommendation.
- ◯ I've checked my spelling and grammar.

GRAMMAR AND VOCABULARY

1 Write a form of the word in capitals in each gap.

198 COUNTRIES BEFORE TURNING 40!

Gunnar Garfors from Norway is the youngest person to have visited all 198 countries in the world. Along the way, he has taken a huge number of (1) _____ , driven thousands of kilometres and made friends all over the world. Everywhere he went, he learnt to rely on the people he met, who were nearly always (2) _____ and kind. In many countries, he was invited to (3) _____ and festivals and in a few places became quite friendly with the local people. He has also become an expert in making the necessary (4) _____ to visit so many places in such a short time.

The (5) _____ to plan, while at the same time being flexible when plans change at the last minute are both (6) _____ skills to have if you want to follow Gunnar's example. It helps to speak a few widely-spoken languages so you can communicate (7) _____ with the people you meet, but even a few expressions in the local tongue can go a long way. Finally, don't forget to take photos to show the world you really have achieved this remarkable (8) _____ !

FLY

HELP
CELEBRATE

ARRANGE

ABLE
VALUE

MEANING

ACCOMPLISH

___/8

2 If a sentence is correct, tick it. If a sentence is incorrect, underline the mistake and correct it.

1 What do I like about Archie is that he's got a great sense of humour. _____

2 I wonder whether you know where is the entrance to the Underground. _____

3 Had I known then what I know now, I would have acted differently. _____

4 It was the size of the country what really impressed me. _____

5 Ella claimed that she had seen Oliver two days ago, but I didn't believe her. _____

6 Little I knew that my life was about to change for ever. _____

7 Damien actually denied to tell Ash my secret when I know it was him. _____

8 It was until I met Honey that I realised what a lovely person she is. _____

9 No sooner had we set off when it started to rain heavily. _____

10 It only was when Mum got home that she realised she'd left her bag at work. _____

___/10

3 Choose the correct word.

1 How was your school skiing **excursion** / **trip** to the Alps?

2 I put all my **effort** / **work** into one last push and finally the door opened.

3 How much is the entrance **fare** / **fee** at the new skating rink?

4 Ned got out the map and showed me the **journey** / **route** he was planning to take.

5 I'll be so relieved when we finally **get** / **reach** our destination.

6 My parents have warned me not to **fail** / **lose** another test this term.

7 There's no **point** / **reason** in telling Molly you're upset because she never listens.

8 I believe an honest person always keeps their **saying** / **word**.

9 Some singers can be **infamous** / **unknown** for years before they become popular.

10 It's easy to lose **sight** / **track** of time when you're having fun.

___/10

4 Complete each gap with the correct form of a phrasal verb from the box.

| check out | cut off | drop off | get away | log off |
| make for | pick up | rope off | set off | turn around |

1 Alex yawned, _____ the university computer and left the library.
2 If this snow continues, we could be _____ for days.
3 I've forgotten the passports! We'll have to _____ and go back to get them!
4 Our car broke down on the country road so we _____ the only light we could see.
5 Could you call reception and find out what time we need to _____ in the morning?
6 The gardener _____ a section of the park where he was planning to plant some trees.
7 We'd better _____ early if we want to avoid the rush hour traffic.
8 Running a restaurant is very demanding and we don't often _____ on holiday.
9 When he goes out, I'll ask my dad to _____ the book you wanted me to lend you.
10 A driver was waiting to _____ us _____ at the airport when we arrived.

___/10

5 Complete the second sentence so it has a similar meaning to the first. Do not change the word given. Use two to five words, including the word given.

1 The phone began to ring and immediately went silent again.   **BEGUN**
  Hardly _____ to ring when it went silent again.
2 Why don't you do your homework before you go out with your friends?   **OFF**
  I suggest _____ before you go out with your friends.
3 I only realised how much I was going to miss her when she left.   **UNTIL**
  It _____ that I realised how much I was going to miss her.
4 I was both soaking wet from the rain and exhausted.   **BUT**
  Not _____ I was also soaking wet from the rain.
5 Try not to get angry when you speak to Isobel.   **LOSE**
  Try _____ , when you speak to Isobel.
6 People only saw how difficult Danny's life had been when they read his book.   **SEE**
  Only when they read his book _____ a difficult life Danny had had.

___/12

Total score ___/50

▼
EXAM SKILLS

Tick the statements that are true for you. Review the skills in the unit if you need more help.

I can ...	Unit/page
☐ understand linking words and phrases in a travel article	Unit 11 p114
☐ identify synonyms in s short talk	Unit 11 p118
☐ answer questions promptly in an interview	Unit 11 p120
☐ identify where spelling changes are needed in word formation tasks and remember to double-check answers for accuracy	Unit 11 p121
☐ use informal language in a letter / an email	Unit 11 p122
☐ identify synonyms in a magazine extract	Unit 12 p124
☐ identify speakers' opinion and attitude in conversations	Unit 12 p128
☐ ask for clarification in a discussion	Unit 12 p130
☐ use parts of speech and negative forms accurately and identify incorrect options when completing activities	Unit 12 p131
☐ usc my imagination in a review	Unit 12 p132

OPTIMISE

- Remember to check what type of texts you will read and what type of exam questions you will have to answer.
- Managing your time in the exam is important. Divide your time equally between all the exam questions.
- If you aren't sure about the answer to one question, move on to the next one and go back and try again before you write your final answers.

1 Look at some text types you might read in an exam. Can you add any more?

newspaper articles, reports _____

2 Look at three different types of exam questions and some ideas to help you manage your time for each question on the exam day. Put the ideas in a logical order as quickly as you can.

1 Multiple-choice questions

A Look at the multiple-choice options. Check them all before you make your choice. ____

B Write your answers on the mark sheet. ____

C Read the text quickly first for a general idea. _1_

D Scan the paragraph to find information which relates to the main question. Make any short notes now. ____

E Look at the main question, underline key words and then find the relevant paragraph for the question. ____

2 Gapped text

A Look at what comes before and after the gap in each sentence. ____

B Make your choice and read the text one more time to make sure it is coherent. ____

C Write your answers on the mark sheet. ____

D Read the whole text to get an idea of its structure and development. ____

E Read the gapped sentences and try to put them in the gaps. Check they fit logically. ____

3 Multiple matching (questions)

A Read the questions and underline key words. ____

B Find any specific information which relates to each question. Check it against words you underlined in the question. ____

C Read the texts to get a general idea. Pay attention to people's thoughts and ideas. ____

D Write your answers on the mark sheet. ____

E Scan each text in more detail. ____

3 Read the instructions to a multiple-choice exam question and the first part of the text. Time yourself for a maximum of two minutes.

You are going to read an article about Shakespeare's 400th anniversary celebrations. For questions 1–6 choose the answer (A, B, C or D) which you think fits best according to the text.

2016 was the 400th anniversary of Shakespeare's death, so I was truly excited when I was invited to write about the celebrations for an international arts magazine. Having been a Shakespeare fan since studying his plays at school, I was keen to discover whether the events would increase public interest in the great writer. Would other areas of the arts, such as film or poetry be included in the celebrations as well as the plays on stage? Luckily, the magazine editors were happy for me to go out in search of both performances and audiences which is exactly what I did.

Initially, while looking for information online I was pleased to see that it was not only in England that the anniversary was being celebrated but also all over the world. Sometimes there were unusual celebrations such as jazz concerts and rap music in the United States and an English language production of _The Tempest_ in the mountains outside Granada, in southern Spain. Additionally, an international programme of events took place where 18 Shakespeare films were screened in 110 countries around the world. To my mind, the playwright's influence on the arts, and most of all on cinema can't be underestimated. The festival of Shakespeare films organised in the UK highlighted how filmmakers have been inspired by his plays over the years.

On my travels, I discovered that one of the films that proved most popular with younger audiences was Baz Luhrmann's 1996 version of _Romeo and Juliet_. The setting was changed from Verona in Italy to the fictional Verona Beach and the rival families from the play became street gangs. The big pull for the new audience was the actor who played Romeo, Leonardo DiCaprio. As fresh and modern as when it was filmed 20 years ago and introduced a whole youthful generation to the joys of Shakespeare on the big screen, the re-screening of the film had a similar effect on a completely new, young audience. Leaving the cinema, Ryan chatted to us about the film. 'We've been studying Shakespeare at school, and I could never really get what he was on about. The language just didn't make any sense but when it's set in California and it's about gangs then the language doesn't bother you so much and you can understand it. And Leo's great as Romeo. I can't believe how young he looked!'.

OPTIMISE

- Remember, with multiple-choice questions only **one** option can be right.
- Sometimes one word in the question/sentence or options can be key to get the right answer.
- Be careful when you read the exact same words or phrases in a question and then find them in the text. They may not always help you with the correct answer.

4 A student has <u>underlined</u> some key points for three questions and made some notes before answering them. Decide if you agree with their ideas.

---

1 In <u>paragraph two</u> the <u>writer</u> tells us that the Shakespeare <u>anniversary celebrations</u> …

A were most <u>popular</u> in <u>English-speaking countries.</u>
Not just the English speaking world

B were <u>original in content</u> and <u>successful globally.</u>
Content?
global = international

C <u>underestimated the influence</u> of <u>Shakespeare</u> in <u>films.</u>
Yes: influence, underestimated cinema

D hoped to <u>influence people</u> by <u>showing Shakespeare</u> plays <u>via film.</u>
No: influence on the arts not people

2 <u>According to the writer</u>, what is the main <u>reason</u> for <u>the popularity</u> of the <u>film</u>, *Romeo and Juliet*?

A The set was <u>changed</u> to make it more <u>contemporary.</u>
Yes: setting was changed

B It <u>introduced</u> a <u>new generation</u> to <u>Shakespeare</u> via the <u>screen.</u>
That was the first time it was screened

C It had a <u>star actor</u> in the <u>leading role.</u>
Yes: Leo de Caprio

D It was a <u>fresh, modern play</u> that <u>appeals</u> to <u>young people.</u>
Fresh modern film?

3 What does <u>Ryan</u> say about <u>seeing</u> the film, *Romeo and Juliet*?

A The <u>main actor</u> was <u>good</u> but <u>too young.</u>
Can't believe how young he was?

B <u>Shakespearian language</u> was <u>impossible to understand.</u>
Never really get it = can't understand, R also says didn't make any sense

C <u>Not understanding</u> the <u>language bothered</u> him.
Not bothered ... didn't bother ... can understand: no

D <u>Shakespearian language</u> was <u>less challenging</u> in a <u>modern context</u> and <u>setting.</u>
Set in California, gangs?? So, quite modern

---

5 Discuss what type of mistakes the student made. Use the Optimise box on page 136 to help you. Which question has one word which is key to get the correct answer?

---

6 Now read the second part of the text and answer questions 4–6. Try to read and complete the questions in five to six minutes.

But in addition to promoting Shakespeare through film it was the big screen film stars of the moment who also played their part, literally, by going on stage and taking on some of the most respected roles in theatre. Eager crowds of all ages queued up to see Benedict Cumberbatch of *Sherlock* and *The Imitation Game* fame starring as Hamlet at the Barbican theatre. His performance was highly praised, although not everyone was convinced that having a film star in the role was the best way to encourage more theatre-goers. When I spoke to 16-year-old Serena, who saw the performance to complement her school studies of the play, she disagreed 'I thought it was amazing and Benedict was fantastic in the role. Of course it helps if you've got a top actor playing the part, it's true. But, in the end, I don't think it matters what your motivation for going to the theatre is, as long as you enjoy yourself'.

Other actors from both the stage and the big screen such as Sir Kenneth Branagh, whose films and performances have popularised Shakespeare for many years, contributed to the anniversary's success. Branagh's theatre company presented their own version of *Romeo and Juliet* on stage, with a star-studded cast and set in the 1950s. Who could resist seeing Richard Madden (Robb Stark in the series *Game of Thrones*) and Lily James (Cinderella in Disney's 2015 film) in the leading roles? Audiences enjoyed a wonderful soundtrack and stunning costumes.

So, it would seem that Shakespeare lives on for everyone through both film and on the stage. I'm sure Ryan and Serena would agree.

4 What does *eager* mean in paragraph 4?
 A large **B** nervous **C** enthusiastic **D** popular

5 What main point does Serena make about going to the theatre?
 A A top actor in a leading role attracts more people.
 B People's motivation for going to the theatre varies a lot.
 C Going to the theatre complements school studies.
 D It's not important why people go if they are well entertained.

6 What does the writer imply in the last part of the text?
 A An original set and popular actors help draw people to the theatre.
 B The theatre attracts an older generation more than a younger one.
 C The anniversary was mainly successful due to Sir Kenneth Branagh.
 D Soundtracks and costumes are key to a good theatre performance.

▼

OPTIMISE YOUR READING EXAM

Remember to …

- [ ] read any titles or subtitles in texts if they are there.
- [ ] read all possibilities or options carefully before you decide on your answer.
- [ ] move on to the next question if you aren't sure of an answer and go back after.
- [ ] be aware of distractors in answer options.
- [ ] use skimming and scanning techniques in reading texts.

- Remember to think about who is speaking and what they are talking about the first time you listen.
- It's a good idea to make some notes next to the options while you listen.
- Be careful if you hear the exact same words as in the options. These may not always help you choose the correct answer!

1 ◁))) 3.16 **Listen to three short parts from extracts of people talking in different situations. Who is talking and what are they talking about? Choose from the list.**

1 _____

2 _____

3 _____

people	topic
a parent	dangerous sports
a sports instructor	how to be a good actor
a teacher	a difficult situation in the mountains
two actors	a film and the actors' performance
two friends	a class presentation
different family members	the plot of a book
a teenager	how reading can help students with homework

OPTIMISE

- Remember to listen to the whole extract before you decide on your answer.
- Sometimes the correct information comes at the end of the conversation.
- Try to think about what the question is asking you to listen out for. Underline key words to help you focus.
- Focusing on key words in the question will help you to avoid distractors!

2 ◁))) 3.17 **Read the main questions for the first three multiple-choice questions and underline any key words. Then listen to the extracts and make some notes to answer the questions. Compare your answers in pairs.**

1 What do the two friends agree about?

_____

2 Why is the teacher talking to the class?

_____

3 How does the teenager feel about the experience?

_____

3 **Now read the multiple-choice options in Exercise 4 for each question. Are the notes you made in Exercise 2 similar to any of the answer options?**

4 3.17 **Listen and choose the correct option.**

1 What do the two friends agree about?

  A The plot of the film was disappointing.

  B The actors could have been given more sensitive roles.

  C The survival scenes weren't tough enough.

2 Why is the teacher talking to the class?

  A To remind them they should do a lot of homework for a presentation.

  B To insist they use the internet to help them develop ideas for a presentation.

  C To encourage them to use their own ideas and plan well for a presentation.

3 How does the teenager feel about the experience?

  A Secretly pleased that they had stopped the dangerous climb.

  B Terrified that they might fall and have an accident.

  C Surprised and happy that they had had the experience.

- Before you listen, use the time you **OPTIMISE** have to read through the sentences carefully and think of any ideas to fill the gaps.
- Remember to fill in the exact words you hear and don't write extra words.
- Don't forget to read what comes before and after the gap. This may help you decide how many words you need or what part of speech is missing.
- Check your spelling.

5 Read the instructions for a listening task. Underline any words or phrases you think are important.

> You'll hear a student called Suzanne Wilson talking about a volunteer project in the Canary Islands in Spain. For questions 1–10 complete the sentences with a word or short phrase.

6 Before you listen, look at the possible answers a student has predicted for the first six sentences. Can you think of any more words or ideas?

Suzanne's school organised a volunteer working trip with a (**1**) _____ organisation.

what type of organisation: nature? local?

She explains that bottlenose dolphins can form (**2**) _____ with different species and human beings.

a noun? Form + ? form a friendship? families?

Suzanne uses the word (**3**) _____ to describe how the colour of bottlenose dolphins helps them hide themselves.

similar word to hide ... disguise? cover?

Suzanne insists that the protection of the bottlenose dolphin is crucial as once they are captured about half of them may die in approximately (**4**) _____ .

a number/years, days, months?

Suzanne was amazed by the Atlantic green turtle which is the largest of its species with a (**5**) _____ .

noun: part of the turtle? long neck, big head?

Suzanne warns us that the turtles are under threat for a number of reasons and may lose their (**6**) _____ .

homes, habitat? place where they lay eggs: nests?

7 🔊 3.18 **Listen and check the answers another student wrote for questions 1–6. Correct any mistakes.**

Suzanne's school organised a volunteer working trip with a (**1**) *conservationist* organisation.

She explains that bottlenose dolphins can form (**2**) *strong relationships with species* with different species and human beings.

Suzanne uses the word (**3**) *camaflage* to describe how the colour of bottlenose dolphins helps them hide themselves.

Suzanne insists that the protection of the bottlenose dolphin is crucial as once they are captured about half of them may die in approximately (**4**) *19 days* .

Suzanne was amazed by the Atlantic green turtle which is the largest of its species with a (**5**) *hard shell* .

Suzanne warns us that the turtles are under threat for a number of reasons and may lose their (**6**) *nesting sights* .

8 Look at the Optimise box again. What type of mistakes did the student make in Exercise 7?

9 🔊 3.19 **Now listen to part 2 of the recording and complete sentences 7–10.**

Suzanne liked the volunteer accommodation and says that that volunteers are responsible for the (**7**) _____ of the place.

Suzanne preferred volunteering at the research centre because it offered her an (**8**) _____ into research project management.

There are other activities that volunteers can do in their free time, such as diving, canyoning, (**9**) _____ or

_____ .

Suzanne suggests that to volunteer you need to be positive, hardworking, cooperative and able to (**10**) _____ .

▼

OPTIMISE | **YOUR LISTENING EXAM**

Remember to ...

☐ listen to each task twice before you decide on your answers.

☐ make any notes on the exam paper the first time you listen.

☐ take time to write your answers on to the final answer sheet at the end of the complete listening test.

☐ check that spelling is correct.

☐ be clear what the question is asking.

1 Match the topic area (A–C) with the questions (1–7). Then think of two more possible questions for each section.

A Free-time activities and going out

B Family, friends and home

C Experiences and plans

1 What are your plans for this weekend? ____

2 Tell us about someone interesting in your family. ____

3 Who do you usually spend your free time with? ____

4 If you could choose to do something new, what would it be? ____

5 What are you most looking forward to in the next few months? ____

6 Tell us something about the area where you live. ____

7 How often do you go to the cinema? ____

> **OPTIMISE**
> - In the first part of a speaking exam you usually answer some questions about yourself, your interests, experiences, etc.
> - Don't prepare or learn a speech for this part of the exam. Try to speak naturally.
> - Try to extend your answers with a short explanation or give an example.

2 ▷ Watch two students answering questions about themselves. Complete the information about each student. Make some notes.

	Which questions from Exercise 1 do they answer? (Note down any different questions)	Do they extend their answers? (Note down any examples, reasons, explanations)	What language do they use? (Note down any structures and tenses, words or expressions and linking words)
Student A			
Student B			

> **OPTIMISE**
> - In a speaking exam you usually get a mark for pronunciation. This means the examiners will listen to how you stress words and whole sentences, if your intonation is generally correct and how well you pronounce different sounds.
> - Try to speak clearly so the examiners and your partner can hear you. You don't have to have a perfect accent!

3 ▷ Watch the video again and complete the table.

	Do they speak clearly?	Do they stress the right words and parts of sentences?	Do they use the correct intonation?	Do they pronounce most sounds well?
Student A	Yes, all of the time. ☐ Yes, most of the time. ☐ No, not very often. ☐ No, not at all. ☐	Yes, all of the time. ☐ Yes, most of the time. ☐ No, not very often. ☐ No, not at all. ☐	Yes, all of the time. ☐ Yes, most of the time. ☐ No, not very often. ☐ No, not at all. ☐	Yes, all of the time. ☐ Yes, most of the time. ☐ No, not very often. ☐ No, not at all. ☐
Student B	Yes, all of the time. ☐ Yes, most of the time. ☐ No, not very often. ☐ No, not at all. ☐	Yes, all of the time. ☐ Yes, most of the time. ☐ No, not very often. ☐ No, not at all. ☐	Yes, all of the time. ☐ Yes, most of the time. ☐ No, not very often. ☐ No, not at all. ☐	Yes, all of the time. ☐ Yes, most of the time. ☐ No, not very often. ☐ No, not at all. ☐

4 ▷ **Watch two students each talking about a different set of photographs. Answer the questions while you watch.**

1 How many photographs are there in each set of exam questions? _____

2 How long does each student have to talk about the photographs and answer the question about them? _____

3 Can both students see their partner's set of photographs? Why / Why not? _____

4 How long does the other student have to answer an additional question about their partner's photos? _____

5 Can the students talk together about the photographs or questions? _____

OPTIMISE

- Timing is important in a speaking exam. The examiner will guide you but make sure you know exactly how much time you have to answer each part of a question, usually around one minute.
- You often talk about photos in a speaking exam. Remember to listen carefully. In this task, it's important to **compare** the photos, not describe them in detail.
- Try to find two or three similarities or differences between the photos. This will help you extend the first part of your answer.
- Then answer the question about the photographs. Give your opinion or a reason for your answer: *I think / don't think … because …* Use any examples in the photographs to help you focus.

5 **Work in pairs. Student A look at set 1 photographs. Student B look at set 2 photographs. Make a note of any words or expressions related to your set. Then find some similarities or differences between them. You have three minutes to write down your ideas. Compare your lists and add any more ideas together.**

| What are the advantages of studying in these different ways? | 1 |

| How might the people be feeling? | 2 |

Example: classroom

Set 1

formal style class room, inside, informal/relaxed way to study, outside, students collaborating, sharing, project work

In the first photo we can see a more formal style classroom with a teacher talking and the students are inside whereas/ but/while in the second photo the students are outside, talking together, and sharing ideas, it might be a project …

6 **Work in pairs. Take turns to talk about the set of photographs you made notes about and answer the question. Time your partner for one minute. How well do they manage the time? How could they improve?**

OPTIMISE

- In a speaking exam you usually get a mark for grammar and vocabulary.
- Try to use a variety of different structures, words and expressions. Try not to repeat yourself too much.
- Use a variety of linking words or phrases to help you structure what you say.

7 Work in pairs. Look at the two questions the examiner asks each student after they have talked about the photographs and some example answers. How can you improve them? Add your own ideas.

1 Which of these situations would you prefer to be in?

I like studying outside. It's more fun than studying in the classroom. It's good to work in teams and you learn from different people.

2 What's the best way to travel around where you live?

The best way to travel is by train. It's cheap. It's quite fast. It's also clean. It's better than the bus because the bus is always crowded.

8 Work in pairs. Take turns to answer each question in Exercise 7. Time your partner. How well do they manage the time? How could they improve?

9 ▷ Watch the video again. Complete the table for each student. Is there anything they could improve? Give examples for each question in the table.

	Does the student compare the photographs and find similarities and differences?	Does the student use a variety of grammar structures, vocabulary and linking words and phrases?	Does the student answer the question and give reasons, explain their ideas?
Student A			
Student B			

10 ▷ Watch two students talking about a discussion topic. Choose the correct option in the sentences while you watch.

1 First, the students have to talk together for about *two / three* minutes.

2 The discussion topic is about important things for *families / young people* today.

3 The students talk about the *positive / negative / future* effects.

4 The students have *one / two* minutes to make a decision.

5 The students talk about *some / all* of the different points.

6 The students finally make a decision and *agree / disagree*.

11 ▷ In pairs, watch the video again. Choose one student each. Make some notes using the questions below. Is there anything the students could improve?

Do the students ...

1 organise the discussion in a logical way? How?

2 listen to each other and develop new ideas to discuss? How?

3 talk about all the options? If not, which ones?

4 ask for and give opinions? How?

5 agree or disagree? How?

6 interrupt each other? How?

7 check they understand or ask for clarification? How?

8 agree or disagree at the end?

> **OPTIMISE**
> - Remember, you have approximately 30 seconds to answer a question about your partner's photographs.
> - Try to give reasons and examples when you answer. You need to say more than one or two sentences to speak for 30 seconds.
> - Connect your ideas with linking words and expressions (*because, this is why, but, so, for example …*).

> **OPTIMISE**
> - In a speaking exam you usually get a mark for how you interact with your partner (and also the examiner).
> - Remember to listen carefully to what your partner says. This will help you focus and develop your own arguments.
> - It's a good idea to organise a discussion. Remember to use words and phrases to help you start off, move on, keep talking and come to a final conclusion.
> - If you want to interrupt your partner, be polite! Try not to dominate the discussion!

12 Look at the exam question again on page 142. Tick the questions below you think the examiner might ask the students after they have finished the discussion.

1 What new developments have there been in technology? ____

2 Do you think young people have enough free time these days? ____

3 How important is it to find time to relax or do sport and exercise? ____

4 What food do you like or dislike? ____

5 Who influences young people more, their family or their friends? ____

6 Is it a good idea for young people to work and study at the same time? ____

13 ▷ Now watch the students answering some questions after a discussion. Which questions did they answer from Exercise 12? Write down any other questions they answered.

14 ▷ Watch the video again. In pairs, choose one student. Complete the table. Is there anything they could improve? Give examples in the table.

▼

OPTIMISE

- In a speaking exam you usually have to develop ideas after a discussion. The examiner will ask you questions about the topic.
- You may answer a question individually or together.
- Try to develop your ideas when you answer. Explain what you mean and why, give examples, from **your experience** if you can, and give your opinion.
- It's a good idea to ask your partner what they think about your comments.

▼

OPTIMISE

- In a speaking exam, express your ideas clearly and give a logical, relevant answer.
- Try not to hesitate too much. Speak as fluently as you can.
- Connect your ideas with relevant linking words and expressions.
- Try not to repeat your ideas or the same ideas as your partner. Develop new ideas and arguments about the topic.

	Does the student give clear, logical answers?	Does the student speak fluently?	Does the student use linking words and expressions to connect their ideas?	Does the student develop ideas and arguments? (Are there any from their own experience?)
Student A				
Student B				

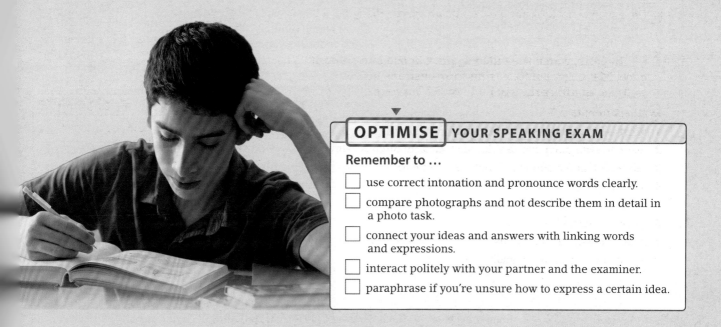

▼

OPTIMISE YOUR SPEAKING EXAM

Remember to …

☐ use correct intonation and pronounce words clearly.

☐ compare photographs and not describe them in detail in a photo task.

☐ connect your ideas and answers with linking words and expressions.

☐ interact politely with your partner and the examiner.

☐ paraphrase if you're unsure how to express a certain idea.

OPTIMISE

- Always read the instructions carefully and look at any examples in each part of the test.
- Remember, it's important to know what you have to do in each part of the test and what you may be tested on.

1 Look at four different exam instructions. Match a question type (A–D) to the instructions (1–4). What language might you be tested on?

A Key sentence transformation ____

B Word formation ____

C Multiple-choice cloze ____

D Open cloze ____

1 For questions 1–8, read the text below and decide which answer (A, B, C or D) best fits each gap.

2 For questions 1–8, read the text below and think of the word which best fits each gap. Use only one word in each gap.

3 For questions 1–8 read the text. Use the word given in capital letters at the end of some sentences to form a word that fits in the gap in the same line.

   Write your answers in CAPITAL LETTERS on the separate answer sheet.

4 For questions 1–6 complete the second sentence so that it has a similar meaning to the first sentence, using the word given. Do not change the word given. You must use between two and five words, including the word given.

2 Look at exam tips 1–8. Match them to exam questions in Exercise 1 (A–D). There may be more than one possible answer.

1 Read the words before and after the gap. ____

2 Read the title and whole text first to give you a general idea. ____

3 Decide if a missing word is positive or negative. ____

4 Check your spelling carefully. ____

5 Use the key word and don't change its form. ____

6 Write only between two and five words. ____

7 Try all the options in the gap first to see if they make sense in the sentence. ____

8 Don't leave anything blank. You may get the answer right! ____

3 Read the exam instructions, the title and the text to get a general idea of the topic. Then answer the questions below.

   Which gap(s) needs ...

1 a noun? _____

2 an adjective? _____

3 an adverb? _____

4 a verb? _____

For questions 1–8 read the text. Use the word given in capital letters at the end of some sentences to form a word that fits in the gap in the same line. There is an example at the beginning. Write your answers in CAPITAL LETTERS.

Becoming a successful crime writer

Some of us are gifted with the extraordinary (0) _CAPABILITY_ to write or tell a good story but not many have the patience or (1) _____ to write professionally. Nor will the majority of enthusiastic authors experience that (2) _____ feeling of seeing their novel reach number one as a best seller. Crime fiction is generally still high on people's reading list and, as a result, many crime authors have become (3) _____ successful. It is (4) _____ that famous detectives, such as Sherlock Holmes, Hercule Poirot and Miss Marple are still very appealing to many readers. In addition, films and more recent TV series such as the modern day Sherlock Holmes, (5) _____ Benedict Cumberbatch, have increased the interest in crime novels.

CAPABLE
DETERMINE
SATISFY
EXTREME
DENY
STAR

So, if you want to follow in the footsteps of Dame Agatha Christie or Sir Arthur Conan Doyle, here are some tips: it's (6) _____ to read as many good crime writers as possible and don't forget to keep a note of anything you find curious or (7) _____ .

ADVISE
SURPRISE

At the same time, try observing everyday life around you as this might also stimulate your (8) _____ and help inspire you to write the next great crime story.

CREATE

OPTIMISE

- For word formation questions, read the text and title to get a general idea of the topic.
- Look at the words in capitals and think about what part of speech the new word should be.
- If you aren't sure of the new word, try different forms in the gap before you decide on your answer.
- Remember to write your answers in CAPITAL LETTERS and check your spelling carefully when you finish.

4 Look at a student's answers to the first four questions in the text in Exercise 3. Decide if you agree with the answers. If not, correct them and write why they are incorrect.

1 *DETERMINED*

_____

2 *SATISFYING*

_____

3 *EXTREMLY*

_____

4 *DENYING*

_____

5 Now complete the answers for 5–8 in Exercise 3. Time yourself doing the task – try not to go over five minutes.

6 Read the exam instructions and three questions for a sentence transformation task. Then look at a student's answers for 1–3. What mistakes have they made?

For questions 1–6 complete the second sentence so that it has a similar meaning to the first sentence, using the word given. Do not change the word given. You must use between two and five words, including the word given. 0 is an example.

0 The holiday break we had was so relaxing.

SUCH

It *WAS SUCH A* relaxing holiday break.

1 'Let's buy Dave a new sweater.' Gill said to us.

SUGGESTED

Gill *SUGGESTED THAT ALL OF US BUYING* Dave a new sweater.

2 They can't wait to take part in the competition.

LOOKING

They're *LOOKING FORWARD TO TAKE* part in the competition

3 I don't know how to solve this maths problem.

FIGURE

I *DON'T FIGURE UP* a way to solve this maths problem.

7 Now complete the answers to questions 4–6. Time yourself doing the task – try not to go over five minutes.

4 We only went to the concert because Steve recommended it.

HAVE

We _____ to the concert if Steve hadn't recommended it.

5 I regret not having studied harder for the exam.

WISH

I _____ harder for the exam.

6 Everyone thinks that Linda is the best candidate for the job.

THOUGHT

Linda _____ the best candidate for the job.

1 **Write true (T) or false (F) for each sentence. Compare answers with a partner.**

1 There are usually two pieces of writing in an exam. ____

2 You can choose what you want to write in both parts of the exam. ____

3 You need to include all the information from any instructions to get a good mark. ____

4 You shouldn't waste time making a plan. It's best to start writing quickly. ____

5 You should write between 140–190 words. ____

6 If you write too much or too little you can lose marks. ____

7 You normally have about 40 minutes to write an essay. ____

2 **Read the exam questions. Write a plan for each question. Spend about five minutes on each one. Compare your notes in pairs.**

> **1** You have received an email from your English-speaking penfriend, Simon.
>
> ---
>
> **From:** Simon   **Subject:** I need your help!
>
> I've been playing chess with a group of people after school for fun. Now, they want to get more professional and go in for competitions with other clubs but I don't think I'm good enough! What do you think I should do? I don't want to upset the group.
>
> Help, please!
> Simon

> **2** You have seen this announcement in a new English-language magazine for young people.
>
> ---
>
> **Stories wanted!**
>
> We are looking for stories for our new English-language magazine for young people. Your story must **begin** with this sentence:
>
> *When Claire heard the doorbell ring she had never felt so nervous in her life.*
>
> Your story must include:
>
> • an invitation   • a location

> **3** You see this announcement in your school English-language magazine.
>
> ---
>
> ## Film reviews wanted
>
> Have you ever seen a film where the main character(s) did something inspiring?
>
> Write a review of a film, explaining what the main character(s) did and why it was inspiring. Tell us if you would recommend the film to others or not and why.
>
> The best reviews will be published in our next edition!

 OPTIMISE

- Remember to check exactly what you have to do in a writing exam and how much time you have to be able to organise yourself effectively.
- Spend about five minutes writing a plan before you start writing.
- Remember to include all the information asked for in a question.

OPTIMISE

- It's important to think about the style and language you will need for each different type of exam question.
- Register is important in **a letter or email**, e.g. is it formal or informal? Think about who you are writing to. Open and close the letter/email in the appropriate way.
- **A story** needs to be well organised, have a clear storyline and include a good use of narrative tenses and adjectives/adverbs to make it interesting for the reader. Try to surprise the reader and keep their attention.
- Describing and explaining clearly are important in **a review.** Give your opinion, reasons why and examples. Remember to make a recommendation.

3 **Look at extracts from a student's essays for the exam questions in Exercise 2. How could you improve them? Compare your answers in pairs.**

> *1 Firstly, in my opinion, it does not seem advisable to commit to something which you think will be quite a challenge. Personally, I don't believe you must always be concerned about other people will react.*
>
> *2 Claire wasn't believing that the room had been chose for a special party. It wasn't nice ... it was small, cold and dark. What was she going to do? She had wanted the event to be special and already was invited over fifty people but there wasn't room to fit all. It was very small.*
>
> *3 Although many difficulties the main actor can overcome all difficulties in the end of the film. Because she has a personality strong. She is also very, very honest. So, the other characters forgive her. I like this film very much.*

OPTIMISE

It's a good idea to read all the instructions carefully and <u>underline</u> important points.

4 Look at the exam question for an essay. A student has <u>underlined</u> key points in the instructions. Would you underline any more?

In your English class you have been talking about young <u>people</u> and <u>health</u>. Now your English teacher has asked you to <u>write an essay</u> for homework.

Write the essay using **all** the notes and giving <u>reasons</u> for your point of view.

Some <u>people think</u> that nowadays <u>young people</u> are not as <u>fit and healthy</u> as they were in the past. What's your opinion?

Notes

Write about:

1 <u>exercise and diet</u>
2 <u>medicine and illness</u>
3 ………….. (your own ideas)

---

5 Look at some notes the student made to plan their ideas before they wrote the essay. Can you add any more ideas to their notes?

Introduction: explain main idea and main reasons, e.g. we have a busy life, young people study a lot, no time to exercise.

young people in the past: different way of life to now. Less medicine and illness?

young people today: sport, food and diet, other things: e.g. no time for sport, exercise?

Conclusion: give general opinion: I agree: exercise more, learn about diet and health at school, but say why it's difficult to change?

---

6 There are four main areas an examiner will use to mark your writing in an exam. Match the areas (1–4) to the questions (A–D).

1 Content ____   3 Organisation ____
2 Communication ____   4 Language ____

A Are the ideas clear? Is it interesting for the reader, e.g. does it keep your attention? Is the style correct, e.g. formal, informal, semi-formal?

B Is the correct language and vocabulary used? Is it accurate? Is there a variety of structures and vocabulary? Is there punctuation? Is the spelling correct?

C Are all parts of the question included? Does the person (e.g. a friend, a teacher, a magazine editor) reading it get all the information they need?

D Is the writing logical and coherent? Are there linking words or phrases to connect ideas?

---

7 Read the student's answer to the essay. Look at the questions in Exercise 6 (A–D) and put a tick (✔) or cross (✗) next to each question. Compare your answers in pairs or groups. Find any examples to justify your answers.

8 Look at the underlined words or sections in the essay. Can you correct any mistakes? Where would you divide the essay into logical paragraphs?

Today young people lead very busy lives and, as a result, they are less <u>healthier</u> than in the past. They <u>frequently can</u> suffer from <u>ilness</u> or stress. This is mainly due <u>for</u> the fact that teenagers spend a lot of time studying, sitting down or using technology. <u>In past time</u>, I believe young people didn't take care of <u>themselve</u> in any special way, but they may had a better diet and eaten less <u>food fast</u>. in addition, they probably spent more time in a natural environment and would have done more <u>pysical</u>, outdoor activities so they were less sick and didn't need much medical treatment.<u>Despite</u> a lot of young people nowadays do sport and are conscious of their appearance, they don't always pay attention to what they eat. Fast food is cheap but this doesn't give you a <u>balance</u> diet. Some teenagers lead a <u>sitting down</u> life and <u>prefer stay</u> at home with the latest technology. To sum up, young people could be fit and healthy because there are a lot of medical advances to cure illness. What's more, schools teach us about health. However, stress and lack <u>in</u> time make us forget about our health.

▼

OPTIMISE YOUR WRITING EXAM

Remember to …

☐ copy the exact words from the exam question if appropriate.

☐ make a plan before starting the task.

☐ organise your task answer into paragraphs.

☐ if there is a choice of questions, select one which requires a style of writing you are confident in.

☐ use a variety of adjectives and tenses.

GRAMMAR REFERENCE

Countable and uncountable nouns

Countable nouns can be counted and have a singular and plural form.

Uncountable nouns are often abstract ideas (*truth, information*, etc.), materials (*iron, glass, water, wood*, etc.) and collections (*furniture, luggage, baggage, money*, etc.).

Nouns like these are followed by a verb in the singular, even if they're describing more than one object:

*All the food **was** delicious.*

*Wood **isn't** as strong as metal.*

! To talk about one object in a collection, we can use *piece of, sheet of, item of*, etc. and we can use plural verbs where appropriate:

*Can you buy me a **packet of** tissues?*

*One piece of luggage **is** enough for the two of us.*

! Some nouns are both countable and uncountable. Often, this is because the word refers to a substance/material or a thing that's made of that substance:

• <u>material/substance – uncountable</u>: *glass, chocolate, coffee, paper*, etc.

• <u>a thing containing that material/substance – countable</u>: *a glass* (to drink from), *a chocolate* (one from a box), *a coffee* (a drink), *a paper* (a newspaper), etc.

! There are a few nouns which only have a plural form. These include: *clothes, scissors, trousers, jeans, groceries*. They cannot be counted, i.e. we can't say ~~a trouser~~ or ~~three clothes~~, but we use *many* rather than *much*:

✔ *How **many** clothes did you buy today?*

✘ *How **much** clothes did you buy today?*

Articles

• **indefinite article (*a(n)*)**

USE: with singular countable nouns (when we are not being specific or when we mention something for the first time):

*We saw **a** family friend last weekend.*

! Whether we use *a* or *an* depends on the sound, not the spelling:

*I lent him **a** euro.*

*We'll arrive in **an** hour, more or less.*

• **definite article (*the*)**

USE: with singular countable nouns (specific or general):

***The** internet has changed the way we communicate.*

*That's **the** book I was telling you about.*

plural countable nouns (when we are being specific):

*Here are **the** pens I borrowed from you yesterday.*

uncountable nouns (when we are being specific):

***The** truth isn't always very nice to hear.*

! We usually use *the* when there is only one of something: *the sun, the sky, the internet*, etc.

• **no article**

USE: with plural countable nouns (when we are talking generally):

People use smartphones more than computers these days.

uncountable nouns (when we are talking generally):

Would you like some help with your project?

! Notice how we use articles in these phrases:

time: *in **the** 2000s, in **the** morning, in June, on Friday, at night*

people and work: *work as **a** …, have **a** job, go to work, **the** Queen, **the** Chinese*

places: ***the** Alps, **the** USA, **the** UK, Madrid, Russia*

entertainment: ***the** media, on **the** radio, on TV, go to **the** cinema*

organisations: ***the** army, **the** police, **the** fire brigade*

travel: *on **the** bus, catch **a/the** bus, take **a** taxi*

Quantifiers show the number or amount of something

USE: with countable and uncountable nouns (*a lot of, lots of, some, the*).

with countable nouns (*a, an, one/two/*etc.*, a number of, a few, few, many, how many*).

with singular uncountable nouns (*a piece of, an amount of, a little, little, much, how much*).

• *many* and *much* are usually only used in questions and negative statements (unless you want to sound very formal). In positive sentences where you don't want to sound very formal, use *a lot of / lots of*. (It's also common to use *a lot of / lots of* in questions and negative statements.)

• *few = only a few = not many*:

***Few** people have climbed that mountain. = **Only a few** people*

have climbed that mountain.

• *a few = some but not many*:

*Yes, **a few** people have managed to climb to the top.*

• *little = only a little = not much*:

*They gave us **little** information. = They **only** gave us **a little** information.*

• *a little = some but not much*:

*Yes, I have got **a little** money left.* (Note: don't confuse this with *a little* which we can use with countable nouns to mean *small*, e.g. *I was only a little boy then*.)

• *a number of = some*:

*There were a small/large **number of** people in the park.*

• *an amount of = some*:

*There was a small/large **amount of** snow on the mountain.*

! We can also use *too many* and *too much*:

Too many people were queuing for the museum, so we went somewhere else. (= such a lot of … that)

and *much/far too*:

The tickets were **much too** expensive.

! Some quantifiers (*all, both, each, either, every, many, much, neither, some*) can come immediately before a noun (e.g. *all people*). When we want to use these quantifiers before

an article, a possessive or a pronoun, we use *of* – *all of my friends, both of the people, neither of us*. With *all* and *both*, we can leave out *of* before an article or a possessive, but not before a pronoun.

! When we want to use *every* before an article, a possessive or a pronoun, we use *one of* (e.g. *every one of my friends*).

! With *no* and *none*, we use *no* when we are talking generally (e.g. *No dogs are allowed.*) and *none* before an article, a possessive or a pronoun (e.g. *None of the cats was black.*)

GRAMMAR REFERENCE | Unit 2 | Tenses (1): present/past simple, *used to*, *would*, *be/get used to*

Present simple

FORM: *I/You/We/They* **live** / **don't live** …
He/She/It **lives** / **doesn't live** …
Do *I/you/we/they* **live** …? **Does** *he/she/it* **live** …?

! We form the emphatic present simple with *do/does*:
Yes, you're right. He **does live** *around the corner from me!*

USE: to talk about: **1** general truths and facts, **2** current habits, **3** how often things happen, **4** permanent situations, **5** states, and **6** the future in schedules:

1	Water **boils** at 100 °C.
2	I **walk** to school.
3	We **have** exams three times a year.
4	He **lives** in the city centre.
5	I **love** your shoes!
6	My plane **departs** at 6 o'clock tomorrow morning.

Past simple

FORM: Regular verbs in the past simple end in *-ed* (*explained, tried, wanted*, etc.); irregular verbs don't follow a pattern (*get, have, said, taught, went*, etc.). You need to learn the past simple of irregular verbs.

USE: to talk about: **1** single completed actions in the past, **2** main events in a story, **3** habits and repeated actions in the past, **4** permanent situations in the past, and **5** general truths and facts about the past.

1	I **walked** over 20 kilometres on Sunday.
2	He **opened** the door, **went** outside and **looked** up at the stars.
3	We always **went** to dance class on Friday evenings.
4	I **was** always the worst at playing football.
5	The Mesopotamians **invented** the wheel over 5,000 years ago.

! We form the emphatic past simple with *did*:
We **did** *understand the instructions!*

! When we repeat a verb in the past simple, we usually just use the auxiliary verb. We don't repeat the main verb:
✔ *I didn't like the food but Joe* **did**.
✘ *I didn't like the food but Joe* **liked**.

Stative verbs

USE: to refer to states rather than actions. Stative verbs include verbs about thinking (*believe, know, think*, etc.), existence (*be, exist*, etc.), emotions (*love, like, hate*, etc.), human senses (*hear, see, smell*, etc.), appearance (*appear, look, seem*, etc.) and possession or relationships between things (*belong to, have, include*, etc.).

! Some verbs can refer to either states or actions (e.g. *feel, have, imagine, look, see, smell, think* and *taste*).
Does *your big brother* **have** *a car?* (state)
Did *you* **have** *a party for your last birthday?* (action)

would / used to

FORM: *would / used to* + bare infinitive

As a child, I **would** *always* **do** *my homework in the evenings. / As a child, I always* **used to do** *my homework in the evenings.*

USE: we use *would* to talk about past habits and *used to* to talk about past habits or states. Both forms are commonly used to talk about the distant past.

! We can't use *would* to talk about past states.
✔ *My dad* **used to** *have a beard when he was younger.*
✘ *My dad* **would** *have a beard when he was younger.*

be/get used to

FORM: *be/get used to* + *-ing* form / noun
She's **used to getting up** *early so she isn't tired.*
Eventually, we **got used to life** *in New York.*

USE: to talk about something that is familiar or no longer strange. *Get used to* refers to the process of adapting to a new situation and means *become familiar with*. *Be used to* refers to the end result and means *be familiar with*.

! We can use this form to talk about the past and the future:
I **was used to getting** *up early when I was a baker.*
Don't worry – you'll soon **get used to having** *short hair.*

used to / be/get used to – negative

FORM: *never used to / didn't use to / wasn't/weren't used to / never got used to / couldn't/can't get used to*

They **never used to** */ **didn't use to** *like parties but these days they never miss one!*

We **weren't used to swimming** *in the sea and got very cold!*

I've lived in Spain for twenty years but I **can't get used to having** *dinner at 10 o'clock at night!*

USE: to talk about negative situations.

used to / be/get used to – questions

FORM: **Did** *you/he/etc.* **use to** …? / **Are** *you* **used to** …? / **Is** *he/she/etc.* **used to** …? / **Have** *you* **got used to** …?

Did *they* **use to** *live next door to you?*
Are *you* **used to** *singing in front of people?*
Have *you* **got used to** *the cold winters in Moscow?*

USE: to ask questions.

Present perfect simple

FORM: *I/You/We/They***'ve lived** / *haven't lived* …

*He/She/It***'s lived** / *hasn't lived* …

Have *I/you/we/they* **lived** …? **Has** *he/she/it* **lived** …?

USE: to talk about: **1** situations that started in the past and are still true, **2** completed actions at a time in the past which is not mentioned, **3** completed actions where the important thing is the present result, and **4** a series of actions continuing up to now:

1	*I***'ve lived** *here for many years.*
2	*We***'ve watched** *this film at least once before!*
3	*He***'s** *just* **arrived** *so we can start the class now.*
4	*So far this year, I***'ve passed** *all my exams.*

We can also use the present perfect simple: **5** to refer to the future, in time clauses (*when, as soon as, once,* etc.), **6** with words/phrases like *already, ever, for, just, never, since, so far, up to now, yet,* **7** with superlatives, and **8** with ordinal numbers**.**

5	*He'll phone you* **as soon as** *he***'s arrived** *– don't worry.*
6	*We***'ve** *already* **bought** *a new tent for our camping holiday.*
7	*That was the* **best** *film I***'ve** *ever* **seen***!*
8	*This is the* **first** *time we***'ve** *ever* **been** *to the theatre.*

! We use *for* + a period of time, and *since* + the moment when it started:

We've had this flat **for three months** / **since July.**

Past perfect simple

FORM: regular verbs

had + past participle

I/You/He/She/It/We/They **had ('d) walked** *far.*

I/You/He/She/It/We/They **had not (hadn't) walked** *far.*

Had *I/you/he/she/it/we/they* **walked** *far?*

Yes, I/you/he/she/etc. **had.** *No, I/you/he/she/etc.* **hadn't.**

irregular verbs

You need to learn the past participle of irregular verbs.

See the Irregular verbs reference, page 175.

USE: to talk about: **1** completed actions before a moment in the past, **2** situations and states before the past, and **3** completed actions where the important thing is the result at a moment in the past:

1	*He* **had finished** *cooking dinner by the time we got home.*
2	*They* **had lived** *in France for several years before they started learning French.*
3	*We didn't tell him the truth because he***'d** *just* **had** *another piece of bad news.*

! Phrases such as *It was the first/second/etc. time* … are followed by the past perfect simple.

It was the third time he **had seen** *the man in the grey hat outside his house.*

FORM: *be* + *-ing*

USE: to talk about: **1** actions or situations in progress at a particular moment, **2** temporary actions or situations, and **3** unfinished actions or situations:

1	*What* **were** *you* **doing** *when I called?*
2	*I'm* **living** *here for a few months.*
3	*I***'ve been working** *on a new invention recently.*

More specifically:

Present continuous

events happening at a particular moment now	*It***'s pouring** *with rain.*
temporary situations or events now	*I'm* **reading** *an interesting book at the moment.*
changing or developing situations now	*It***'s getting** *colder each day.*
annoying habits (usually with *always*)	*You***'re always taking** *my clothes without asking! It really annoys me!*
future arrangements	*I'm* **taking** *the exam next week.*

Past continuous

events happening at a particular moment in the past	*It* **was pouring** *with rain when I woke up.*
temporary situations or events in the past	*I* **was sleeping** *in my brother's bedroom while mine was being repainted.*
changing or developing situations in the past	*It* **was getting** *colder each day.*
future arrangements in the past	*I* **was taking** *the exam the following week.*
two actions in the past in progress at the same time	*While I* **was doing** *my homework, my sisters* **were playing** *music very loudly*

Present perfect continuous

events and actions continuing up to the present moment	*I***'ve been writing** *this essay for the past hour and still haven't finished.*
events and actions that finished just before the present moment	*I***'ve been dealing** *with emails all morning and only finished about ten minutes ago.*

Past perfect continuous

events and actions continuing up to a particular moment in the past	*I***'d been writing** *my essay for over an hour and still hadn't finished when the lesson started.*
events and actions that finished just before a particular moment in the past	*I***'d been dealing** *with emails all morning and only finished about ten minutes before Sean arrived.*

See Grammar reference, Unit 4 for information about the future continuous and the future perfect simple/continuous.

FORM:

Type of adjective	Normal	Comparative	Superlative
Regular adjective (one syllable)	*old*	*+ -er older*	*+ -est oldest*
Regular adjective (one/two syllables) ending in *-e*	*wide*	*+ -r wider*	*+ -st widest*
Regular adjective (one syllable) ending in a vowel + consonant	*big*	double the final letter + *-er bigger*	double the final letter + *-est biggest*
Regular adjective (two syllables) ending in *-y*	*silly*	replace *-y* with *-ier sillier*	replace *-y* with *-iest silliest*
Other regular adjective (two or more syllables)	*difficult*	*more* + adjective *more difficult*	*most* + adjective *most difficult*
Irregular adjective	*good* *bad* *far* *little* *many/much*	*better* *worse* *farther/further* *less* *more*	*best* *worst* *farthest/furthest* *least* *most*

Regular adverb	Comparative	Superlative
quickly	*more/less quickly*	*most/least quickly*

Irregular adverb	Comparative	Superlative
hard	*harder*	*hardest*
early	*earlier*	*earliest*
well	*better*	*best*
badly	*worse*	*worst*
far	*farther/further*	*farthest/furthest*
fast (run fast)	*faster*	*fastest*
late	*later*	*latest*
often	*more/less often*	*most/least often*

USE: We use **comparative** adjectives and adverbs to show that things or people are different or separate from each other:

*John is a **better swimmer than** me.*

*John swims **better than** everyone else at his school.*

We use **superlative** adjectives and adverbs to show that one member of a group is at the top or bottom of the group:

*John is **the best swimmer** at his school.*

*John swam **the best** in the swimming competition.*

! We don't always use *than* with comparatives:

*That is my **younger** sister.* (the comparative describes the noun)

*In Mediterranean countries, the weather is usually **hotter**.* (= hotter than it is in other places)

! We don't always use *the* with superlatives:

*This portrait is **his best painting** by far.*

! We can use *even* and *much* with comparatives:

*Jenny's story is good, but Mike's story is **even/much** better!*

! To talk about the result of something increasing, we can use *the* + comparative, *the* + comparative:

*The **harder** you study, the **better** exams results you get.*

Other ways of comparing

as + adjective + *as*	To describe how things are the same in some way	*He is **as tall as** Josh (is).*
not as/so + adjective + *as*	To describe how things are different	*She didn't practise **as hard as** David (did).*

Predictions

For a prediction saying what we think or guess will happen, we often use *will*.

*Do you think they **will** find our house without a GPS? Yes. I'm sure they **will**.*

For a prediction based on evidence seen at the time of speaking, we often use *be going to*.

*Look at those clouds! I think it's **going to** rain!*

! Sometimes *will* and *be going to* are both correct. In general, *be going to* is more informal and is common in speech.

*Jo **will** be at the meal. / Jo's **going to** be at the meal.*

For a prediction when we are not certain what will happen, we can also use *may/might* (possibility) *or should* (probability).

Do you think Ellie will win the race tomorrow?

*I'm not sure. She **might** do. / She **should** do.*

Intentions and arrangements

To talk about intentions (something planned but not yet arranged), we often use *be going to*.

*My parents said we can have a party! We're **going to** invite about twenty people!*

To talk about arrangements (something agreed and arranged), we often use the present continuous.

*I'm **making** some sandwiches and my friends are bringing the games!*

! Sometimes the present continuous and *be going to* are both correct.

*We're **getting** / **going to get** a new car! Tomorrow we're **going to visit** / **visiting** the garage to help Mum and Dad choose it!*

Instant decisions

For decisions made at the moment of speaking, we often use *will*.

Don't worry! I'm free all day tomorrow. I'll help you with your project!

Timetabled future events

To talk about things that happen according to a schedule, we often use the present simple.

*His train **leaves** at 7 o'clock.*

! Words/phrases used with the present simple include: *as soon as, before, once, the moment that, unless, until, when.*

Offers, requests, promises, suggestions, refusals

To make offers or requests, we use *will or shall. Shall* is quite rare except in questions.

I'll collect you from the party if you like.

***Will** you collect me from the party, please?*

***Shall** I collect you from the party?*

! We don't use *will* in questions to make offers.

✗ ***Will** I collect you from the party?*

! To make or ask about promises, we use *will.*

*I **will** keep that information secret.*

*Do you promise you'**ll** remember to bring my dictionary?*

! To make suggestions and offers (for *I* and *we* only), we use *shall.*

***Shall** I ask the teacher to give us some help?*

*Let's stay at home and watch TV, **shall** we?*

Future continuous

FORM: *will/won't + be + -ing (will be working, won't be travelling,* etc.)

USE: to talk about actions happening (in progress) at a point in the future. This use is similar to how we use the present continuous to talk about actions happening now and how we use the past continuous to talk about actions happening at a point in the past. (See Grammar reference, Unit 3.)

*This time tomorrow, I'**ll be sitting** on the beach in the sunshine.*

(Compare: *Now, I'm sitting on the beach in the sunshine. / This time yesterday, I was sitting on the beach in the sunshine.*)

We can also use the future continuous to refer to future events that are expected to happen, in a similar way to how we use the present continuous for the future.

*Next week, we'**ll be learning** more vocabulary to talk about technology.*

Future perfect simple

FORM: *will/won't + have + past participle (will have finished, won't have started,* etc.)

USE: to talk about actions completed at a time between now and a point in the future. This use is similar to how we use the present perfect simple to talk about actions completed between some point in the past and now and how we use the past perfect simple to talk about actions completed before a point in the past. (See Grammar reference, Unit 2.)

*Francis **will have finished** his homework by 6 o'clock.*

! We can also use other modals with these tenses, including *may* and *might* for possible actions, and *should* for probable actions.

*This time on Friday, I **might be meeting** Jane and Tony at the shopping centre. I'll let you know.*

*My dad **should have finished** work by six thirty this evening. He isn't usually late home.*

Future perfect continuous

FORM: *will/won't + have been + -ing (will have been living, won't have been working,* etc.)

USE: to talk about actions happening up to a point in the future. This use is similar to how we use the present perfect continuous to talk about actions happening up to now and how we use the past perfect continuous to talk about actions happening up to a point in the past. (See Grammar reference, Unit 3.)

*Next month, we **will have been studying** English for exactly four years.*

GRAMMAR REFERENCE | Unit 4 | Conditionals (1): zero and first conditionals

Zero conditional

FORM: *If* + present simple, present simple

USE: general truths, scientific facts:

*If you **exercise** regularly, your body **gets** stronger.*

*Your body **gets** stronger if you **exercise** regularly.*

! All conditional sentences have two parts: the *if* clause and the result clause. We separate the clauses with a comma when the *if* clause comes first.

! We can also use other present tenses in the *if* clause, depending on the meaning:

*If you'**re walking** to their house, walk along the roads, not across the park.*

First conditional

FORM: *If* + present simple, *will/won't* + bare infinitive

USE: possible or likely situations now, generally, or in the future:

*If you **revise** tonight, it **will help** you in your test tomorrow!*

*It **will help** you in your test tomorrow if you **revise** tonight.*

unless, as/so long as, provided (that), in case

unless (= 'except if', and replaces *if not*)

*If you don't / **Unless you** work harder, you won't get a good mark in the final exam.*

as/so long as / provided (that) (= 'if the following situation is true or happens' or 'on condition that', and replaces *if*)

*If / **As/So long as / Provided (that)** you arrive on time, you'll be free at 4 o'clock.*

in case (= 'because the following might happen')

*Don't forget your umbrella **in case** it rains.*

FORM: Modals have only one form and are followed by the bare infinitive:

I/He/They **can** *come to our party.*

You **must** *try and relax more!*

We can also use the continuous infinitive (*You should* **be wearing** *your sports kit.*), the perfect infinitive (*I could* **have swum** *all afternoon.*) and the perfect continuous infinitive (*She shouldn't* **have been playing** *with that injury.*)

USE: some modals (*can, could, may, might, must, should*), semi-modals (*have to, ought to, need to*) and other phrases (*be able to*) can express the following:

ability, possibility, probability, advice or criticism, obligation and permission

We can use the modals *shall, will* and *would* to talk about the future, to make offers and to talk about hypothetical situations.

Ability – *can / could / be able to*

To talk about ability now or generally. *I* **can** *play the violin.*

To make a decision now about future ability. *I* **can** *meet you this evening.*

To talk about ability in the past. *I* **could** *speak English quite well when I was younger.*

To talk about hypothetical situations. *If only I* **could** *be a pop star.*

! To talk about ability in the future, use *will be able to*.
I **will be able to** *finish the project over the weekend.*

! We don't use *can* as an infinitive. We use *be able to*.
✔ *I'd love* **to be able to** *speak Italian.*
✘ *I'd love* **to can** *speak Italian.*

Permission – *can / could / may / be allowed to*

To talk about permission now, in the future, or generally:
Can/Could/May *I use your phone for a moment?*

! *Can* and *may* are both more polite than *could*.

! To talk about permission in the past, we don't usually use a modal.
✔ *I* **was allowed to** *go to the party.*
✘ *I* **could** *go to the party.*

! *Could* might refer to permission in the past, in reported speech.
Dad said I **could** *go to the cinema.*

Advice or criticism – *should / ought to*

To ask for / give advice, or to criticise someone, now, in the future/past, or generally:

You **ought to** *tell Jason the truth.*

You **shouldn't** *believe everything Neil tells you.*

You **should have told** *me about your new job!*

She **ought to have handed** *in her report yesterday.*

! *Should* is much more common in spoken and written English than *ought to*.

Obligation – *must / have/has to / have/has got to / need to*

To talk about personal obligation now, in the future, or generally:

I **must** *remember to get my mum a birthday present before the weekend.*

To talk about external obligation now, in the future, generally or in the past:

I **have to** *see the doctor tomorrow afternoon.*

Susie **had to** *study until midnight on Sunday.*

! In official contexts, such as notices and rules, *must* is sometimes used for external obligation.
Everyone **must** *scan their ticket before boarding the train.*

! *Must* cannot be used as an infinitive. Use *have to*.
✔ *I'd hate* **to have to** *study in August.*
✘ *I'd hate* **to must** *study in August.*

! *Mustn't* and *don't have to* mean different things.
You **mustn't** *do that!* = Don't do that!
You **don't have to** *do that.* = You can do that if you want to but it's not necessary.

! We can also use *didn't need to* to describe a lack of obligation:
I **didn't need to** *take the test again because I passed.*

We can use *needn't* + *have* + past participle to describe a past action which turned out to be unnecessary:
I **needn't have worried** – *they offered me the work experience placement!* = I did worry but it wasn't necessary.
You **needn't have asked** *for an extension for your project. I'd already decided to give you one.* = You asked for an extension but it wasn't necessary.

Possibility – *can/could*

To talk about possibility now or generally.
It **can** *be hard making new friends.*

To talk about general possibility in the past.
When my parents were younger, teachers **could** *be very strict.*

Possibility – *may/might/could*

To talk about possibilities in the present, the future and generally.
They **may/might/could** *win the match.*

Probability – *should / ought to*

To talk about what is probably true.

His new novel **should** / **ought to** *be available online today.*

He **should** / **ought to have left** *work by now.*

! Be careful with *should* + *have* + past participle because it can be used both for situations which happened and for situations which didn't happen:

He should have finished his homework by now. = He's probably finished it. (probability)

He should have finished his homework by now. = He hasn't finished it. (criticism)

Certainty – *must / can't / could/may/might*

When we make deductions, we use different modals to show how sure we are about something.

must

If we are certain that something is true or is the case, we use *must*.

*John **must** be happy. He just got top marks in all his exams.*
*He **must have left** work by now.*

can't/couldn't

If we are certain that something is not true or is not the case, we use *can't* or *couldn't*.

*It **can't/couldn't** be our neighbours at the door, they're on holiday.*
*Harry **can't/couldn't have been** in PE. He's off sick today.*

could/may/might

If we think something is possibly true or may be the case, we use *could*, *may* or *might*.

*Max **could/may/might** be home sick. I'm not sure but I haven't seen him today.*
*The film **could/may/might have ended** by now.*

GRAMMAR REFERENCE | Unit 6 | Verb patterns (1): verb + infinitive/-*ing*

Verbs/phrases usually followed by the full infinitive (+ *to*)

aim, be able, afford, agree, appear, arrange, ask, attempt, choose, decide, hope, manage, offer, plan, prepare, pretend, promise, refuse, seem, tend, want, would like, would prefer

! Some of these verbs/phrases can be followed by an object before the full infinitive.

*His mum and dad want **him** to go to university.*

Verbs/phrases usually followed by the -*ing* form

admit, appreciate, avoid, can't, consider, deny, discuss, dislike, enjoy, fancy, feel like, imagine, involve, mention, mind, miss, practise, put off, risk, succeed, suggest, understand

! Some of these verbs and phrases can be followed by a possessive form (more formal) or an object (more informal) before the -*ing* form.

*Do you mind **me/my** borrowing your dictionary?*

! Verbs and phrases with prepositions can often be followed by the -*ing* form.

*She's **interested in talking** to you about your experience.*
*Stephen didn't **succeed in convincing** his parents to let him go away for the weekend.*
*Thanks **for showing** me how to solve that maths problem.*

Verbs/phrases usually followed by an object + bare infinitive

feel, hear, let, make, notice, see, watch

Verbs/phrases followed by the full infinitive or -*ing* form with little or no change in meaning

begin, continue, hate, intend, love, prefer, start

Verbs/phrases followed by the full infinitive or -*ing* form with a change in meaning

forget, go on, like, mean, regret, remember, stop, try

*He **forgot to tell** his parents he would be late home from school. / I'll never **forget seeing** the sea for the first time.*
*I **regret to inform** you that I cannot help you on this occasion. / Does he **regret making** that decision?*

GRAMMAR REFERENCE | Unit 6 | Verb patterns (2): infinitives of purpose

FORM: *to / in order to / so as to* + bare infinitive

USE: to show the reason why we do something:

*I went to the shopping centre **to** get a present for my brother.*
*The Minister resigned **in order to** spend more time with her family.*
*The company lowered prices **so as to** attract new customers.*

! When the reason is negative and includes *not*, we don't usually use an infinitive on its own. We use *in order not to* or *so as not to*.

*I sent her a text message **so as not to** interrupt her with a phone call.*

prefer, would prefer, would rather, had better

FORM:

prefer (+ object) + -*ing*	*I prefer swimming to I rather than playing football.*
prefer (+ object) + full infinitive	*I prefer to swim rather than to play football.*
prefer + noun	*I prefer the sea to I rather than the pool.*

would prefer (+ object) + full infinitive	*I would prefer (us) to go to the cinema on Saturday evening.*
would prefer + noun	*I would prefer the cinema on Saturday evening.*
would rather (+ object) + bare infinitive	*I would rather not go to his party tomorrow night.*
subject + *would rather* + different subject + past tense	*I would rather you didn't touch my things without asking.*
had better + bare infinitive	*We had better arrive on time tomorrow morning.*

! We use *prefer* to talk about general preferences. We use *would prefer* to talk about specific preferences.

*I **prefer** tennis to rugby. / I'**d prefer** to meet up for a coffee rather than go to the shops.*

! The negative form of *I prefer to* is *I prefer not to*.

✔ *I **prefer not to** study at weekends.*

✘ *I **don't prefer to** study at weekends.*

! The phrase *had better* can be confused with *would rather*, but is not used to talk about preferences. It means *should* and is followed by the bare infinitive.

*I'**d better** not tell him or he'll get really angry.*

USE: There are various different types of pronoun, including relative pronouns (*who, which, that,* etc.), personal pronouns (*I, you, her, him, us,* etc.) and reflexive pronouns (*myself, yourself,* etc.). They are usually used in place of nouns and noun phrases.

Reflexive pronouns

myself, yourself, himself, herself, oneself, itself, ourselves, yourselves, themselves

These are used when the subject and object are the same (e.g. *I had to make **myself** lunch today as my parents were out*.) and for emphasis (e.g. *Did you make that pizza **yourself**?*).

Other

We use *there + to be* to talk about something that exists: ***There's** a film about his life that I think you would enjoy.*

We use *it + to be* to refer to the weather and temperature (***it's** snowing, **it was** really hot*), distances (***it's** not very far*), situations (***it was** a fantastic concert*) and phrases such as *It is believed/thought/said that …, It has been found that …,* etc.

! We use *one* when we're not being specific (*Those T-shirts are great! I might buy **one**.*), and *it* when we're being specific (*That T-shirt is great! I might buy **it**.*).

! We usually use *something, someone/body* and *somewhere* in positive statements and *anything, anyone/body* and *anywhere* in negative statements and questions. However, we can sometimes use *something, someone/body* and *somewhere* in questions to sound more positive and encouraging. For example, *Did you do **anything** interesting in art today?* is asking a straight question, while *Did you do **something** interesting in art today?* expects a positive answer.

so and *such*

USE: to talk about amounts, and their results and effects:

so + adjective/adverb + (*that*) clause	*It's **so difficult** (that) not many people pass.* *They worked **so slowly** (that) they didn't finish.*
so + *many/much* + noun + (*that*) clause	*There are **so many** films I want to see (that) I can't choose.* *I had **so much** homework (that) it took me all day to do it.*
such + *a(n)* + adjective + singular noun + (*that*) clause	*It was **such a long novel** (that) I didn't get to the end!*
such + adjective + plural noun + (*that*) clause	*They're both **such brilliant books** (that) I don't know which one to recommend.*
such + *a lot of* + noun + (*that*) clause (= *so many/much*)	*We had **such a lot of time** (that) we started to get a bit bored.*

! We can also use *so* and *such* without a *that* clause. This has a similar meaning to *really* or *very*, but it's more emphatic.

*He's **so tall**! = He's **very/really** tall!*

*It was **such** a difficult test! = It was **very/really** difficult!*

too

USE: to criticise, to say that something is negative or bad, or to show that something prevents us from doing something:

too + adjective/adverb (**+ for** someone/something) (+ full infinitive)	*It's **too hot** (for me) (to sunbathe). She runs **too fast** (for me) (to keep up with her).*
too many + plural countable noun	*There were **too many** people at the concert. I couldn't see the band.*
too much + uncountable noun	*Can you really have **too much** money?*

! *too* is not followed by a *that* clause.

! When the meaning is positive, we don't use *too*. We use other words and phrases, such as *really* or *extremely* (with adjectives or adverbs) or *lots of* (with nouns).

enough

USE: *enough*: the right amount/number of;

not enough: less than the right amount/number of:

(*not*) *enough* + noun (+ full infinitive)	*I've / I haven't got **enough time** (to finish everything).* *Because **enough people** came, the school show was a success.* *Because **not enough people** came, the charity concert didn't make much money.*
(*not*) *enough* + noun/ adjective/adverb (+ *for* someone/something)	*There were **enough exhibits** in the exhibition to keep everyone interested.* *There's / There isn't **enough time** (**for** us to rehearse.)*
(*not*) + adjective/adverb + *enough* (+ *for* someone/ something) (+ full infinitive)	*I'm (not) **good enough for** the school orchestra.* *You're (not) **talented enough to be** an artist.* *It was (not) **difficult enough for me to feel** challenged.*
(*not*) + *a(n)* + adjective + *enough* + singular noun	*I'm (not) **a good enough actor** to be in the school play.*
(*not*) + adjective + *enough* + uncountable noun or plural countable noun	*We're (not) **good enough musicians** to be in the band.* *They're (not) **good enough students** to be able to take that exam.*

USE: The word *enough* is not followed by a *that* clause.

Connectors of contrast

USE: *although, even though, though, in spite of, despite* and *however* are used to contrast one idea with another:

although **/** *even though* **/** *though* + clause, clause	**Although / Even though / Though** his house is in the city centre, it's very quiet at night.
in spite of **/** *despite* + *-ing*, clause	**In spite of / Despite** his house being in the city centre, it's very quiet at night.
in spite of **/** *despite* + *the fact (that)* + clause, clause	**In spite of / Despite** the fact (that) his house is in the city centre, it's very quiet at night.
in spite of **/** *despite* + noun, clause	**In spite of / Despite** the location of his house, it's very quiet at night.
However, clause	His house is in the city centre. **However**, it's very quiet at night.

! With *although, even though, though, in spite of* and *despite*, the clauses can come in a different order:

*His house is very quiet at night **although / even though / though** it's in the city centre.*

*His house is very quiet at night **in spite of / despite** being in the city centre.*

! *However* can also come at the end or in the middle of a sentence.

*His house is in the city centre. It's very quiet at night, **however**.*

*His house is in the city centre. It's, **however**, very quiet at night.*

Second conditional

FORM: *If* + past simple, *would/wouldn't* + bare infinitive

USE: impossible, unlikely or hypothetical situations now, generally, or in the future:

*If you **lived** in Italy, you **would** probably **have** a very different diet.*

*You would probably **have** a very different diet if you **lived** in Italy.*

! Remember that all conditional sentences have two parts: the *if* clause and the result clause. We separate the clauses with a comma when the *if* clause comes first.

! We can also use past continuous in the *if* clause, depending on the meaning:

*If you **were living** in Italy, you **would** probably **have** a very different diet.*

! We can also use other modals in the result clause, depending on the meaning:

*If you **lived** in Italy, you **could** practise speaking Italian every day. (= would be able to)*

! With the verb *to be*, there are two forms with the second conditional:

*If I **were** a teacher, I'd ... more formal and often used in writing.*

*If I **was** a teacher, I'd ... more informal and often used in speech.*

Third conditional

FORM: *If* + past perfect, *would have* + bare infinitive

USE: to talk about the hypothetical past (i.e. to imagine a past that didn't happen):

*If we'd **known** about the problem, we'd **have done** something about it. = We didn't know about the problem. We didn't do anything about it.*

! Both clauses in the third conditional are hypothetical (i.e. they didn't really happen).

! Instead of *would*, we can also use *might* and *could*:

*If we'd known about the problem, we **might/could** have done something about it.*

! Be careful with verbs in the negative in third conditional sentences.

*He would have come with us if he **hadn't** been so busy. = He didn't come with us. He was very busy.*

Mixed conditionals

FORM: 1 *If* + past perfect, *would* + bare infinitive; **2** *If* + past simple, *would have* + bare infinitive

USE: 1 to talk about the hypothetical present result of a past condition:

If I hadn't already seen that film, I would go with you to the cinema.

2 to talk about the hypothetical past result of a present condition:

If you had a better sense of humour, you would have found Harriet's joke funny.

! Instead of *if*, we can use an inversion in conditionals. This is more formal.

***Had** we **known** what was going to happen, we would have been more careful. (= If we had known what)*

USE: We sometimes use the past simple and past continuous to describe the present, the future or general situations. Often, these are hypothetical situations.

If clause in second conditionals

*If I **had** more free time, I wouldn't be so stressed all the time.* = I don't have much free time at the moment.

*My parents couldn't afford to give up work unless they **won** the lottery.* = except if they won the lottery in the future

Unlikely hypothetical situations using *suppose, supposing, what if, imagine (if)*

*Suppose / Supposing you **wanted** a new pet. What animal would you choose?*

*What if you **wanted** a new pet? What animal would you choose?*

*Imagine (if) you **wanted** a new pet. What animal would you choose?*

Expressing preference with *would rather*

*I'd rather you **turned** the TV off and read a book.*

! We can't follow this structure with *I*:

✗ *I'd **rather** I helped your father in the garden.*

✔ *I'd **rather** you/we/she/he helped your father in the garden.*

Expressing preference or making suggestions with *It's (high/about) time*

*It's time we **went** home.* = We should go home now.

*It's high time you **went** home.* = You should go home now.

*It's about time they **went** home.* = They should go home now.

To be very polite in questions, requests, hopes, etc.

***Did** you ask to see me Mrs Wilson?*

*I **was wondering** if you could explain that to me again, please.*

*I **thought** you could use some help with your project.*

Wishes and regrets about hypothetical situations with *wish, if only*

• wishes about the present:

*I wish I **didn't have** to do so much homework. / If only I **didn't have** to do so much homework.*

• wishes about the past (regrets):

*Don't you wish you **had started** learning the piano sooner?*

! We can use *would* with *wish* to express criticism.

*I wish people **wouldn't** drop litter in the streets!*

! We can use *could* with *wish* to express hypothetical ability.

*I wish I **could** sing as well as you can.*

FORM: *be* + past participle (+ *by/with/of/from/as/to*)

We don't use the passive in the present perfect continuous or past perfect continuous.

We can use it in all other tenses, plus with modals, *-ing* forms and infinitives:

*You **should be given** a prize for being the fastest runner in the school.*

*He loved **being asked** to play the main role in the school play.*

*It was nice **to be told** that my story was the most original.*

! Some verbs are not usually used in the passive. These include intransitive verbs (verbs which don't take objects), such as *appear* and *seem*, and some transitive verbs, such as *have* and *let*.

USE: We often use the passive: **1** when we don't know who 'does' the action, **2** when it's not important who 'does' the action, **3** when it's obvious who 'does' the action, and **4** for emphasis, or to sound more formal:

1	His school bag **has been stolen** from under his desk.
2	The classroom **is tidied** every afternoon.
3	I**'ve been given** extra homework for talking in class.
4	The football tournament this weekend **has been cancelled**.

We use *by* to show who or what does the action:

*She was taught to play the clarinet **by** her big sister.*

We often don't use *by* if we don't know who does the action, if it's not important or if it's obvious:

Josh's skateboard has been taken by someone.

The books are put away every evening by people working in the library.

They were arrested and taken to the police station by police officers driving a police car.

We can use *with* for tools and equipment:

*The cats were rescued from the tree **with** a long ladder.*

We can use *of* for materials:

*This jacket is made **of** wool.*

Sometimes we use other prepositions, such as *to, as*, etc. depending on the meaning.

*A free dictionary was given **to** every student.*

*It's been described **as** the easiest language to learn.*

! Instead of saying *People say (that) …*, or *Scientists have estimated (that) …*, etc., we can use the passive with *It* as the subject: *It is said (that) …, It has been estimated (by scientists) (that) …*

The causative

FORM: *have* (in the right form) + object + past participle

I'm having my hair cut tomorrow afternoon.

We can also use *get* instead of *have*. *Get* is a little less formal.

Where did you get your hair cut? I love it!

USE: to talk about asking or paying someone else to do something for us. We can use it when the person who does the action is unimportant or obvious, in the same way as we can with the passive. We can also use the causative to put the topic (the thing we are talking about) first in a sentence and the new information later.

! The causative can also be used to talk about (usually bad) things that happen to us, such as things being stolen, broken, etc. We don't usually use *get* with this meaning.

Jade had her phone stolen last week.

The causative and the passive

The causative has a number of things in common with the passive.

• We use *by* to show who or what 'does' the action:

We had our house painted by a local company.

• We can use *with* to describe tools and equipment:

I've had my coat cleaned with a special chemical.

• We often don't use *by* if we don't know who 'does' it:

Rob had his gym bag stolen by someone.

• We often don't use *by* if it's obvious who 'does' it:

She's having her 'autobiography' written for her by someone else.

• We often don't use *by* if it's not important who 'does' it:

The producers of the film had a new language invented by language experts.

Direct and indirect objects

Some verbs can be followed by two objects:

The writer (subject) read (verb) us (object 1) a short story (object 2).

We can also say this with the objects in the opposite order, but we need to use a preposition (usually *to* or *for*):

The writer read a short story to us.

In the passive, there are often two ways of expressing this:

We were read a short story by the writer. / A short story was read to us by the writer.

Verbs which take two objects include: *bring, buy, call, cook, cost, get, give, leave, lend, make, offer, owe, pass, pay, play, promise, read, refuse, send, show, sing, take, teach, tell, wish, write.*

USE: to tell us exactly who or what we are talking about (defining relative clause) or give us extra information about who or what we are talking about (non-defining relative clause). Relative clauses are often introduced by relative pronouns.

Relative pronouns

who – for people (and sometimes animals):

The man who teaches us French is from Paris.

which – for things (and sometimes animals):

Playing football, which is my favourite sport, doesn't cost anything.

that – for people and things, in defining relative clauses only:

Is this the book that you were talking about the other day?

where – for places:

That is the hotel where we stayed last time we were here.

when – for time:

The day when I met my girlfriend was the best day of my life.

why – used after *reason*:

Does he know the reason why you don't want to talk to him?

whose – possessive:

Will the students whose bags are over there please move them?

whom – people as the object of the relative clause and after prepositions (very formal):

The students with whom you will be competing are all highly intelligent.

Defining relative clauses

FORM: In defining relative clauses we:

• don't use a comma.

The woman who I met was called Sarah.

• can use *that* instead of *who* or *which*.

The woman that I met was called Sarah.

• often leave out the relative pronoun when it is the object of the clause.

The woman I met was called Sarah.

Non-defining relative clauses

FORM: In non-defining relative clauses we:

• separate the relative clause with commas.

My sister, who lives with me, is a vet.

• can't use *that* as a relative pronoun.

✗ *My sister, that lives with me, is a vet.*

• can't leave out the relative pronoun.

✗ *My sister, lives with me, is a vet.*

Relative pronouns and prepositions

We can use a preposition + *which* instead of *where*.

The hotel where / in which we stayed last summer was beautiful.

We can also put the preposition at the end of the clause. This is less formal and we can replace *which* with *that*.

The hotel which/that we stayed in last summer was beautiful.

FORM: Participle clauses can be formed using present participles (ending in *-ing*), past participles (usually ending in *-ed,* although there are many irregular forms) and perfect participles (*having* + past participle).

USE: 1 to define in a similar way to defining relative clauses (present and past participle clauses):

*Anyone **working in this company** can make a lot of money.* (= *Anyone who is working* …)

*The first novel **written by Charles Dickens** was* The Pickwick Papers. (= *… which was written by* …)

2 to express conditions (*if*) (past participle clauses):

***Given the chance**, I would love to visit the USA.* (= *If I was given the chance,* …)

3 to describe reasons and results (present participle, past participle and perfect participle clauses):

***Needing a break**, I stood up from the desk and went into the garden.* (= *Because I needed a break,* …)

***Left on its own**, the neighbour's dog barked all day.* (=

Because it was left on its own …)

***Having played golf before**, I knew that it was a difficult game.* (= *Because I had played golf before* …)

4 to describe time relations (present participle and perfect participle clauses):

***Opening the door**, I spotted the man running down the road.* (= *As/When I opened the door,* …)

***Running along the path** by the sea, I had some wonderful views of the coast.* (= *While running* …)

***Having reached our hotel room**, we started to unpack.* (= *After we had reached* …)

! The subject of the participle clause and the subject of the main clause have to be the same.

✔ *Leaning out of the window, I could see a hot-air balloon passing overhead.*

✘ *Leaning out of the window, a hot-air balloon passed overhead.*

FORM: In reported speech, we don't use all the words and tenses of direct speech.

Be careful with tenses and time/place words.

Direct speech	Reported speech
present simple *'I play tennis.'*	past simple *Dan said (that) he **played** tennis.*
present continuous *'I'm playing tennis.'*	past continuous *Dan said (that) he **was playing** tennis.*
past simple / present perfect simple / past perfect simple *'I played / have played / had played tennis.'*	past perfect simple *Dan said (that) he **had played** tennis.*
past continuous / present perfect continuous / past perfect continuous *'I was / have been / had been playing tennis.'*	past perfect continuous *Dan said (that) he **had been playing** tennis.*
will/can *'I will/can play tennis.'*	would/could *Dan said (that) he **would/could play** tennis.*
must *'I must play tennis.'*	had to *Dan said (that) he **had to play** tennis.*

! We sometimes **don't** need to change the verb tense:

	Direct speech	Reported speech
scientific facts / situations that are still true	*'The tennis court is near my house.'*	*Dan said (that) the tennis court **is** near his house.*
somebody just said something, so it's still true	*'I'll see you there at 5 o'clock.'*	*Dan's just called and said (that) he **will** see us there at 5 o'clock.*
the reporting verb (e.g. *say*) is in a present tense	*'I love all sports.'*	*Dan **says** (that) he **loves** all sports.*

! With reported *yes/no* questions, we use *if* or *whether* and change the tense and word order:

Direct speech	Reported speech
'Do you play tennis?'	*Dan asked me **if/whether** I **played** tennis.*

! With questions with *who, why, how,* etc., we repeat the question word and change the tense and the word order:

Direct speech	Reported speech
'When did you start playing tennis?'	*Dan asked me **when** I **had started** playing tennis.*

! Time and place words are often different, because of the different perspective:

Direct speech	Reported speech
here	*there*
today	*that day*
now	*then / at that moment*
tomorrow	*the following/next day*
next week/month/year	*the following week/month/year*
yesterday	*the day before / the previous day*
last week/month/year	*the previous week/month/year*
ago	*before*
this/that + noun	*the/that*
this/that (subject/object)	*it*
these/those + noun	*the/those*
these/those (as a subject)	*they*
these/those (as an object)	*them*

Reporting verbs

Apart from *say*, there are lots of other verbs we can use to report what someone said. They each have their own grammar, so be careful when using them. They include: *claim, command, deny, order, promise, refuse, state, suggest, tell, warn* and many others.

FORM: Although all indirect questions are questions, some have a question mark at the end, and some don't. It depends on the introductory phrase that you use.

USE: Indirect questions are a way of being more polite when asking a question. We can use indirect questions in spoken and written English.

Introductory phrases which need a question mark at the end

Can/Could you tell me/us/etc. / let me know …?

Do you know / think you could tell me …?

Would/Will you tell us …?

! The basic rule is that if it starts like a question, it ends in a question mark.

Introductory phrases which don't need a question mark at the end

I'd be grateful if you could tell me/us/etc. …

I wonder if you could tell us / let us know …

I wonder if you know …

I'd be interested in hearing if you …

I'd like to know …

! The basic rule is that if it doesn't start like a question, it doesn't end in a question mark.

Word order

We don't use question word order in the main question.

Short, direct questions (less formal)	Longer, indirect questions (more polite)
Why did you choose that trip?	*I'd be grateful if you could tell us **why you chose** that trip.*
What is that machine for?	*Do you know **what that machine** is for?*
When is your next excursion to Peñiscola?	*I'd like to know **when your next excursion to Peñiscola is**.*
Where can I find a travel agent?	*I wonder if you know **where I can find** a travel agent.*
Are you an adventurous person?	*Could you tell me **if/whether you're** an adventurous person?*

FORM: negative adverbial word/phrase + question word order

USE: to express a negative meaning in a formal style:

never, e.g. ***Never** have I heard such nonsense!*

hardly, e.g. ***Hardly** had the project begun when the problems started.*

no sooner, e.g. ***No sooner** had we got to the beach than it started to rain.*

not only, e.g. ***Not only** was the train late, but it was full too!*

rarely/seldom, e.g. ***Rarely/Seldom** does anyone visit this remote island.*

little, e.g. ***Little** did I expect to see such a fantastic show.*

only + clause, e.g. ***Only** after the guests left did the manager notice that they had forgotten a suitcase. (Note that with only, the verb in the second clause is inverted.)*

! Remember that we use *when* after *hardly* and *than* after *no sooner.*

***Hardly** had we set off on our journey **when** the coach broke down.*

***No sooner** had we set off on our journey **than** the coach broke down.*

FORM: 1 introductory clause beginning with *What* or *The reason (why)* clause + *be* + *that* clause

***What** I love about Gabriel is **that** he's always smiling.*

***The reason (why)** I went home early was **that** I was feeling a little unwell.*

2 introductory clause beginning *It* + *be* clause + *that* clause

***It's** the terrible traffic and pollution **that** I don't like about that city.*

***It** was **not until / only when** we got to the beach **that** we realised that the sea was dirty and cold.*

USE: to put what we want to emphasise at the beginning of the sentence.

! In cleft sentences starting with *What* and *The reason (why),* we can also use a noun instead of the *that* clause.

*What I don't like about Thomas is **his bad temper**.*

*The reason (why) the holiday was a disaster was **the weather**.*

! In cleft sentences starting with *It is, It was,* etc. we can also use relative pronouns in place of *that.*

*It was my best friend **who**/**that** organised my surprise birthday party.*

*It was a moment **which**/**that** I will never ever forget.*

VOCABULARY REFERENCE

Introduction

This *Vocabulary reference* contains all the target vocabulary from *Optimise B2* Student's Book. The words and phrases are arranged unit by unit, so you can refer to them as you work on vocabulary lessons throughout the book. You can also use the pages as a revision tool when you're preparing for a test or an exam.

The target vocabulary has been subdivided into six groups:

Topic vocabulary

The **Topic vocabulary** sections focus on language connected to the unit topic. Learning these words and being able to use them correctly will help you in your exams. Having a wide vocabulary is particularly relevant for Use of English, Speaking and Writing exams.

Word formation

The **Word formation** sections present you with all the different parts of speech – verbs, adjectives, nouns and adverbs – that come from root words that appear in *Optimise B2* Student's Book. Most exams will test your knowledge of word formation, so learning all the forms of a word is a good way to make sure you are well prepared for your exam.

Collocations

Collocations are phrases with combinations of words which naturally go together in English. Learning collocations will help you in exam tasks, such as open cloze, multiple-choice cloze and sentence transformations. It will also improve your productive English and therefore help you with speaking and writing.

Idioms

Idioms are common phrases in a language, whose meaning is often not literal, so can be difficult or impossible to guess. You will find a good knowledge of idioms is particularly helpful in sentence transformation tasks.

Word patterns

Word patterns are phrases which use specific grammatical structures. For example, phrases with dependent prepositions (*regardless of*), or phrases that require a certain verb form or sentence structure (*find* (sth) *strange* (+ *that*)).

Phrasal verbs

Phrasal verbs consist of a verb (*take, come, look,* etc.) plus a particle. The particle can be an adverb (*away, down,* etc.) or a preposition (*in, on,* etc.). Remember that some phrasal verbs have more than one meaning; in the tables, the meaning given for the phrasal verb always matches the one used in the unit.

These are the main types of phrasal verbs:

Type 1: the verb is transitive (has an object). When the object is a noun, we can put the particle before or after the noun:

*Let's **act** the story **out** instead of reading it! / Let's **act out** the story instead of reading it!*

And when the object is a pronoun, the pronoun **must** separate the two parts of the phrasal verb:

✔ *Let's **act** it **out**.* ✗ *Let's **act out** it.*

Type 2: the verb is intransitive (does not have an object) and you cannot separate the two parts of the verb:

✔ *At weekends we just **hang out** in the park.*
✗ *At weekends we just **hang** in the park **out**.*

❗ Some phrasal verbs may have different meanings when they are used transitively or intransitively:

*Do you mind if I **turn over** and watch MTV instead of these cartoons? (= change TV channel)*

*You may now **turn** your exam paper **over** and begin. (= turn a piece of paper towards you)*

Type 3: the verb is transitive (has an object) but you cannot separate the two parts of the verb:

✔ *I can never **sit through** the news – it's so boring.*
✗ *I can never **sit** the news **through** – it's so boring.*

✔ *The police **looked into** the robbery but never arrested anyone.* ✗ *The police **looked** the robbery **into** but never arrested anyone.*

Type 4: the phrasal verb is three words – verb + adverb particle + preposition:

*You scared me – don't **creep up behind** me like that ever again!*

❗ These phrasal verbs are always transitive and you can never separate the words with an object or pronoun:

✔ *I'll have to study a lot to **catch up with** my classmates.*
✗ *I'll have to study a lot to **catch up** my classmates **with**.*

Throughout the *Vocabulary reference*, you will see various abbreviations. This key explains what they all mean.

> **KEY:** adj = adjective; adv = adverb; n = noun; ex = exclamation; p = preposition; phr = phrase; pl = plural; sb = somebody; sth = something; swh = somewhere; US = American English; v = verb

UNIT 1

TOPIC VOCABULARY | Words connected with *TV* and *cinema*

Word	Example sentence
audience (n)	The audience was a mix of adults and children. They all loved the theatre performance.
box office (n)	There were no tickets at the box office for the new *Star Wars* film.
broadcast (v)	Every day, lots of new programmes are broadcast on television.
cast (n)	Jen was excited to be part of the cast for the new movie.
channel (n)	The BBC broadcasts over different channels in the UK.
credits (n)	Credits usually feature at the end of a film or TV show.
director (n)	Steven Spielberg is one of the most successful cinema directors.
flop (n)	Everyone hated the last dinosaur movie – it was a complete flop!
on demand (adj)	Remember, if you miss the TV show tonight on Channel 3, you can record it and watch it on demand afterwards.
producer (n)	J.K. Rowling wrote the *Harry Potter* books and was also the producer of the last two films.
programme (n)	*Dragon's Den* is my favourite TV programme.
reality show (n)	*MasterChef* is a popular reality show.
release (v)	When is the new film by Peter Jackson released?
satellite (n)	There are more TV channels on satellite.
screenplay (n)	The movie's screenplay was difficult to learn for the actors.
series (n)	*Game of Thrones* is a series adapted from novels.
sitcom (n)	My favourite sitcom is *The Big Bang Theory* – it makes me laugh so much.
viewer (n)	Viewers usually watch TV shows from their homes.

PHRASAL VERBS

Phrasal verb	Meaning	Example sentence
act out (Type 1)	perform (often sth, e.g. a story, that already exists)	In the game *charades*, you have to act out the title of a book, film, or song.
chill out (Type 2)	relax	Let's just chill out at home tonight.
come on (Type 2)	start to be broadcast	Oli's favourite programme comes on TV in a few minutes.
hang out (Type 2)	spend time doing nothing in particular	On Saturdays, my friends and I often just hang out in the park.
sit through (Type 3)	stay until the end of sth, particularly if you're not enjoying it	I couldn't sit through the film till the end – it was too long!
take up (Type 1)	use space or time	I've got exams soon, so revising takes up most of my evenings.
turn over (Type 2)	change channel	This programme's boring. Let's turn over and watch something else.

COLLOCATIONS | Collocations with *do, have, make* and *take*

Collocation	Example sentence
do nothing	I love doing nothing on Sundays!
do sb a favour	Could you do me a favour and lend me a dictionary?
do your best	As long as you do your best, it doesn't matter if you win or lose.
have a good time	Did you have a good time at the party last night?
have a holiday	Are you having a holiday abroad this year?
have sth to do	I can't come out today as I have lots of things to do at home.
make a difference	Being able to speak English really makes a difference when you go abroad.
make an effort	You really need to make more of an effort to pass the exam.
take a break	Let's take a break for five minutes and then play again.
take part in	Let me know if you want to take part in the art competition.
take time off work	Dad had to take two weeks off work when he broke his leg.
take your time	Take your time – we're not in any hurry.

WORD FORMATION

Core word	Derivatives
appear (v)	disappear (v), (dis)appearance (n), apparent (adj), apparently (adv)
decide (v)	(in)decision (n), deciding (adj), (in)decisive (adj), (in)decisively (adv)
end (v/n)	ending (n), unending (adj), unendingly (adv), endless (adj), endlessly (adv)
exist (v)	existence (n), existing (adj)
impress (v)	impression (n), impressionist (n), impressionism (n), (un)impressive (adj), (un)impressively (adj)
late (adj)	latest (adj), lateness (n), lately (adv), later (adj/adv)
please (v)	(dis)pleasure (n), (un)pleasurable (adj), (dis)pleased (adj), (un)pleasant (adj), (un)pleasantly (adv)
popular (adj)	popularise (v), (un)popularity (n), unpopular (adj), (un)popularly (adv)

UNIT 2

TOPIC VOCABULARY | Words connected with *studying* and *learning*

Word	Example sentence
certificate (n)	I got a certificate when I finished the summer course.
coach (n)	To be a successful football team, you need a great coach.
degree (n)	You usually have to study for three or four years to get a degree.
graduate (n)	That company only hires graduates, so you need to have completed your university studies.
instructor (n)	When I'm old enough to learn to drive, I'm going to have lessons with my mum – she's an instructor!
lecturer (n)	My aunt is a lecturer at university. She teaches economics.
licence (n)	Did you know that in the UK you need a licence if you have a TV?
pass (an exam / a test) (v)	He passed the test easily because he had studied very hard.
pupil (n)	My dad's a primary school teacher with 32 four-year-old pupils in his class.
qualification (n)	He left school without a single qualification, so I'm not surprised he can't find a job.
revise (for an exam / a test) (v)	I need to revise all weekend because I have four big exams next week.
take (an exam / a test) (v)	The best thing about being an adult? Maybe that I haven't had to take an exam for 15 years!
undergraduate (n)	She's still an undergraduate but she'll finish her final year at university next summer.

PHRASAL VERBS

Phrasal verb	Meaning	Example sentence
catch up with (Type 4)	get to the same level as	If you work hard, you'll soon catch up with the rest of the class.
creep up behind (Type 4)	slowly and quietly get closer to sb	Oh! You frightened me! Don't creep up behind me like that!
dig up (Type 1)	find/discover information about sth by investigating it	Where did you dig that article up from? It's perfect!
end up (Type 2)	be in a particular place or state after doing sth	We took a wrong turn and ended up in completely the wrong place.
hurry up (Type 2)	do sth more quickly	If we don't hurry up, we'll be late.
look up (Type 1)	try to find a particular piece of information	Look the word up online.
set up (Type 1)	start a business, club, etc.	I've set up a group on WhatsApp so we can organise the party.
speak up (Type 2)	talk louder	The phone line is terrible so you'll have to speak up.
think up (Type 1)	create/invent an excuse for sth	I need to think up a good reason for being late.
use up (Type 1)	use all of sth	Have you used all the paper we had in the printer?

WORD PATTERNS | Words + prepositions

Core words	Example sentence
bored of/with (-ing)	I'm so bored of/with practising the piano!
concentrate on (-ing)	I couldn't concentrate on doing my homework because of the noise outside.
criticise (sb) for (-ing)	People criticised the government for increasing taxes.
decide against (-ing)	We've decided against going abroad on holiday.
experienced in (-ing)	They need a coach experienced in working with players of all different levels.
interested in (-ing)	I'm not really very interested in watching TV.
pay attention to	Make sure you pay attention to any announcements.
qualify as	After seven years, I finally qualified as a doctor.
succeed in (-ing)	The burglar succeeded in opening the door and got in.
wrong with (-ing)	What's wrong with telling someone you find them annoying?

WORD FORMATION

Core word	Derivatives
believe (v)	(un)believable (adj), (dis)belief (n), believer (n), unbelievably (adv)
champion (n)	championship (n)
compete (v)	competition (n), competitor (n), competing (n), (un)competitive (adj), (un)competitively (adv)
difficult (adj)	difficulty (n)
inform (v)	informative (adj), information (n), informer (n), informant (n)
maths (n)	mathematics (n), mathematical (adj), mathematician (n), mathematically (adv)
relate (v)	relative (adj/n), (un)related (adj), relatively (adv), relation (n), relationship (n)
success (n)	succeed (v), (un)successful (adj), unsuccessfully (adv)

UNIT 3

TOPIC VOCABULARY | Words connected with *manufacturing* and *tools*

Word	Example sentence
appliance (n)	The most useful appliance in our house is the washing machine.
create (v)	When inventors create things that make a difference to people's lives, I'm sure it's an amazing feeling.
develop (v)	My sister is only 19 but she has a great job developing IT systems.
discover (v)	Alexander Fleming discovered penicillin in 1928, nearly 100 years ago.
engine (n)	The steam engine was invented by James Watt in the 18th century and was very important in the industrial revolution.
generate (v)	This radio doesn't use batteries, you generate electricity by moving this handle in a circle.
invent (v)	Tim Berners-Lee invented the World Wide Web in 1989.
machine (n)	There are machines at the bus stops where you can buy tickets.
manufacture (v)	Germany manufactures over 5 million cars every year.
motor (n)	Some cars now have motors which use petrol and electricity.
remote control (n)	This programme is boring … You've got the remote control, can you change channel?
tool (n)	You need a special tool to open the smartphone.

PHRASAL VERBS

Phrasal verb	Meaning	Example sentence
carry out (Type 1)	do work, research, experiments, etc.	They're carrying out a survey about recycling.
come on (Type 2)	develop, make progress	The building work on our new house is coming on nicely.
come up with (Type 4)	think of an idea or a plan	We need to come up with some good ideas for raising money.
figure out (Type 1)	calculate, solve a problem, understand a situation	I'm trying to figure out the answer to this crossword clue.
look into (Type 3)	investigate	Police are looking into a series of burglaries in the local area.
plug in (Type 1)	connect to a machine, the electricity supply, etc.	Plug the printer in, then turn it on. It's that simple.

COLLOCATIONS | Collocations with *top* and *high*

Collocation	Example sentence
high priority	Getting a part-time job isn't a high priority for me, but it would be nice.
high speed	Be very careful crossing that road – cars often drive down it at very high speed.
high time	It's high time the council did something about this problem.
high-definition	The latest high-definition TVs have amazing picture quality.
high-performance	Ferrari make high-performance cars.
high-powered	A high-powered telescope allows you to see stars really clearly.
high-tech	Tim always has the latest high-tech equipment and gadgets.
top award	Winning an Academy Award is considered the top award for a film actor.
top priority	Getting a part-time job is my top priority right now. I'm desperate to earn some extra money!
top secret	This information is top secret, so don't tell anyone!
top speed	My mum's car has a top speed of 120 km/h, but she never drives that fast.

WORD FORMATION

Core word	Derivatives
achieve (v)	achievement (n), achiever (n)
create (v)	creation (n), creator (n), creativity (n), (un)creative (adj), (un)creatively (adv)
discover (v)	discovery (n), discoverer (n)
explore (v)	explorer (n), exploration (n), exploratory (adj)
fortunate (adj)	unfortunate (adj), (un)fortunately (adv), fortune (n)
science (n)	scientist (n), (un)scientific (adj), (un)scientifically (adv)
simple (adj)	simply (adv), simplicity (n), simplify (v)
solve (v)	solution (n), solver (n), solving (n)

UNIT 4

TOPIC VOCABULARY | Words connected with *law* and *order*

Word	Example sentence
accused (n)	The accused said she was home alone all evening, but of course it was impossible to be sure.
evidence (n)	There was very little evidence against him, so the police released him.
fine (n)	You'll get a fine if they catch you on the train without a ticket.
guilty (adj)	The thief was guilty because his fingerprints matched the ones found at the crime scene.
imprisonment (n)	He got life imprisonment for the robbery and his wife got two years for not telling the police what she knew.
judge (n)	The judge delivered the final sentence after the accused was found guilty by the jury.
jury (n)	I'd love to be on a jury – I think it would be really interesting to be in a court and see how it works.
justice (n)	In some parts of the world it's very hard to get justice, particularly if you are in a minority group.
trial (n)	The trial lasted for four months and then, because of a problem, they had to stop and start again.
verdict (n)	We have no idea what the verdict will be – it's impossible to predict what might happen.
victim (n)	We could hardly understand the victim in court because he was crying and in such distress.

PHRASAL VERBS

Phrasal verb	Meaning	Example sentence
beat up (Type 1)	hit or kick sb many times to hurt them	They beat him up and stole his phone, but he'll be all right.
break in (Type 2)	enter a building in order to steal sth	The thieves broke in by smashing a window.
come forward (Type 2)	offer help or information	A young man came forward to help the police with their investigation.
get away with (Type 4)	manage to do sth bad without being punished	How did they get away with robbing the bank?
hold up (Type 1)	steal from sb by threatening with violence, usually with a weapon	The robbers held up a bank in the city centre yesterday.
let off (Type 1)	give sb little or no punishment	I can't believe you let Ed off with just a warning!
make for (Type 3)	move towards a place	When the fire alarm went off, everyone made for the car park.
turn in (Type 1)	tell the police about sb	His mother found stolen goods in his car so she turned him in.

COLLOCATIONS | Collocations with *crime*

Collocation	Example sentence
crime lab	The fingerprint results should be back from the crime lab soon.
crime prevention	We had a chat at school about crime prevention.
crime rate	The crime rate around here has fallen dramatically.
crime scene	Members of the public were kept away from the crime scene.
crime wave	The police have promised to tackle the recent crime wave.
hate crime	They said that the attack on the disabled man was a hate crime.
organised crime	Large gangs are responsible for a lot of organised crime.
petty crime	After a life of petty crime, Ethan found himself in jail.
youth crime	Do you think boredom is the cause of a lot of youth crime?

WORD FORMATION

Core word	Derivatives
burgle (v)	burglary (n), burglar (n)
grow (v)	growing (adj), grown (adj), growth (n)
prevent (v)	preventable (adj), preventive (adj), prevention (n)
satisfy (v)	dissatisfy (v), (un)satisfying (adj), (un)satisfactory (adj), (dis)satisfaction (n)
shock (v/n)	shocking (adj), shockingly (adv)
understand (v)	misunderstand (v), understandable (adj), (mis)understanding (n)
vandal (n)	vandalise (v), vandalism (n)
young (adj)	youngster (n), youth (n), youthfulness (n)

UNIT 5

TOPIC VOCABULARY | Words connected with *sports*

Word	Example sentence
ball (n)	Hockey balls are harder than tennis balls.
bat (n)	Cricket bats are usually made from wood.
beat (v)	The other team played very badly so we beat them easily.
competitor (n)	Are the competitors ready for the race? Get set, GO!
course (n)	There's a golf course near my house but I've never played.
court (n)	Shall we hire a tennis court on Saturday morning?
cue (n)	Sam forgot his cue for the snooker game and had to go home!
draw (v)	They are drawing at the moment and it isn't long until the final whistle. They'll have to play extra time.
field (n)	Our local sports centre has a football field which it shares with the school.

Word	Example sentence
opponent (n)	It's a good idea to find out information about an opponent before an important match.
pitch (n)	It's an artificial football pitch but I really like playing on it.
racket (n)	After a period of time, rackets need to be restrung.
referee (n)	Do you think the referee was fair in the game yesterday?
ring (n)	The two boxers are in the ring now and the fight is about to start.
rink (n)	In the winter, they build an ice skating rink in the square in town.
rod (n)	I never travel to the sea without a fishing rod!
score (v)	They scored two goals in the first five minutes. It was amazing!
spectator (n)	There was a great atmosphere in the stadium thanks to the spectators.
stick (n)	The two players' sticks smashed against each other and broke!
track (n)	If you want to watch the motor racing, you'll find you get a much better view of the track on television.
umpire (n)	The umpire awarded the final point to Joe's opponent.
viewer (n)	Millions of viewers watched the opening ceremony on TV.
win (v)	He's won gold three times at the championships, he's so fast!

PHRASAL VERBS

Phrasal verb	Meaning	Example sentence
check out (Type 1)	look at sth in order to evaluate it	Check out this website – it might help us with our project.
knock out (Type 1)	make sb leave a competition after losing	She was knocked out of the singing competition in the fourth round.
listen out for (Type 4)	listen carefully to try to hear sth	Let's listen out for any announcements about trains being delayed.
make out (Type 3)	see, hear, understand, distinguish	Can you make out what that sign over there says?
mind out (Type 2)	be careful	Mind out! That car's reversing.
pull out (Type 2)	stop being involved in an activity, event, situation, etc.	Tina was going to be in the team but had to pull out because of an injury.
stand out (Type 2)	be more visible, better, etc. than others	One camera stood out from all the others in terms of design.
stick out (Type 2)	be more visible, etc. than others	She wasn't a great player so she really stuck out in the basketball team.

WORD PATTERNS | Words + prepositions

Core words	Example sentence
adjust to (-ing)	It took me a few months to adjust to my new school.
anxious about (-ing)	Are you anxious about tomorrow's exam?
ban (sb) from (-ing)	The player was banned from participating in the match after cheating.
benefit from (-ing)	I really benefited from doing more exercise.
cheat at	Athletes who cheat at their sport by using banned substances should be banned.
consist of	The Reading paper consists of five tasks.
difference between (-ing)	What's the difference between tennis and badminton?
insist on (-ing)	She insisted on including pictures in her project.
participate in (-ing)	More than 100 people participated in the fun run.
prevent (sb) from (-ing)	We were prevented from going on the trip because of bad weather.

WORD FORMATION

Core word	Derivatives
anxious (adj)	anxiety (n), anxiousness (n), anxiously (adv)
argue (v)	argument (n), argumentative (adj), arguable (adj), arguably (adv)
compete (v)	competitive (adj), competition (n), competitor (n), competitively (adv)
develop (v)	development (n), developer (n), developing (adj), (un)developed (adj)
fail (v)	failure (n)
long (adj)	length (n), lengthen (v), elongate (v)
swim (v/n)	swimming (n), swimmer (n), swimmingly (adj)
win (v/n)	winner (n), winnings (n), winning (adj)

UNIT 6

TOPIC VOCABULARY | Words connected with *the world of work*

Word	Example sentence
bonus (n)	They get a bonus in December if the company has had a good year.
off sick (phr)	Ms Weber isn't in the office today, she's off sick.
on maternity/ paternity leave (phr)	My teacher is on paternity leave at the moment, he'll be back in a couple of weeks.
on strike (phr)	They went on strike because of unfair pay.
resign (v)	He resigned from his job last month as it was too stressful.
retire (v)	My grandparents retired last year.
salary (n)	My salary isn't very good, but thankfully my rent is cheap.
tip (n)	Do you always leave a tip in restaurants after a meal?
unemployed (adj)	He's been unemployed for months and can't find another job.
wage (n)	My wages aren't very high as I only work part time.

PHRASAL VERBS

Phrasal verb	Meaning	Example sentence
burn out (Type 2)	become unable to work through working too hard	Jake burnt out after a few years in show business.
copy in (Type 1)	send a copy of an email to sb	When you reply to Amy's email could you copy me in?
fill in for (Type 4)	do sb's job while they are away	Noah's off sick, so could you please fill in for him?
get ahead (Type 2)	be more successful than other people	If you want to get ahead, you need to work hard.
key in (Type 1)	put information into a computer using a keyboard	I keyed in my security number and the door opened.
lay off (Type 1)	end sb's employment because there isn't enough work for them to do	The company laid off over 1,200 people when it got into difficulties.
take on (Type 1)	start to employ sb	We'll take you on for a month and see how things go.
work (your way) up (Idiomatic)	gradually get to a higher position in an organisation	Martine worked her way up from shop assistant to director of the whole company.

COLLOCATIONS | Collocations with *go* and *get*

Collocation	Example sentence
get a placement	While he was still studying, he got a placement in a law firm.
get fired	Did you hear that Freddy got fired from his job last week?
get lost	Sorry I'm late – I got lost on the way here.
get ready	The actors got ready and waited for the curtain to go up.
get the impression	I always get the impression that Layla finds me a bit boring.
get the sack	I can't believe I got the sack just for being late.
get upset	Lucas got upset when I told him his exam results.
go abroad	Next time you go abroad, send me a postcard.
go bankrupt	Anushka went bankrupt when her business failed.
go crazy	Charlie's going to go crazy when he finds out what you've done!
go missing	Some money has gone missing out of my bag.
go quiet	The audience went quiet as the show started.

WORD FORMATION

Core word	Derivatives
employ (v)	(un)employed (adj), employer (n), employee (n), (un)employment (n)
finance (v/n)	financial (adj), financially (adv)
friend (n)	(un)friendly (adj), friendship (n)
neighbour (n)	neighbourly (adj), neighbourhood (n)
poor (adj)	poorly (adv), poverty (n), poorness (n)
satisfy (v)	dissatisfy (v), (un)satisfying (adj), (un)satisfactory (adj), (dis)satisfaction (n)
vary (v)	various (adj), (in)variable (adj), varying (adj), varied (adj), variation (n), variety (n), invariably (adv)
volunteer (v/n)	(in)voluntary (adj), (in)voluntarily (adv)

UNIT 7

TOPIC VOCABULARY | Words connected with *the arts*

Word	Example sentence
abstract (adj)	I don't really like abstract art – I like pictures to look realistic.
auction (n)	Every year at school we have an auction for charity where we sell things we've made to the person who will pay the most.
choreographer (n)	When he retired from dancing he became a choreographer.
conductor (n)	A conductor often doesn't look like he or she is doing much, but leading an orchestra is a big responsibility.
exhibition (n)	There's a new exhibition of Picasso's early work on at the gallery.
illustration (n)	I've always loved the original illustrations for *Alice in Wonderland* – they're beautiful.
installation (n)	I saw an amazing light installation in the street when I was visiting London.
masterpiece (n)	The ceiling of the Sistine Chapel is one of Michelangelo's many masterpieces.
producer (n)	George Lucas produced most of the original *Star Wars* films.
set (n)	The set for the play was amazing – a giant palace which turned around so you could see inside and out.
stage (n)	The stage was very small and we were sitting very close, so we had a great view of the actors.
studio (n)	His studio is a disaster area! Paint and brushes everywhere – but his pictures are beautiful.

PHRASAL VERBS

Phrasal verb	Meaning	Example sentence
draw up (Type 1)	prepare, draw or write a plan	The government has drawn up plans to evacuate the area.
edit out (Type 1)	remove parts of sth, e.g. a film, TV programme, newspaper article	It was a good film, but they could have edited out the scenes where nothing important happened.
grow on (Type 3)	start to like more	I didn't like that picture at first, but it's growing on me now.
sketch out (Type 1)	make a general plan or drawing with few details	Use a pencil to sketch out your picture before you start painting.
tear up (Type 1)	tear/rip into pieces	I realised I'd misunderstood the question, so I tore it up and started again.
turn out (Type 2)	develop in a particular way, have a particular result	I thought the play was going to be boring but it turned out to be excellent.

COLLOCATIONS | Collocations from the art world

Collocation	Example sentence
balancing act	Having a part-time job and studying for important exams is a very difficult balancing act.
be a difficult/hard act to follow	Mrs Bridges was a fantastic headteacher, so she'll be a difficult act to follow for the new one.
behind the scenes	They seem like a happy couple but, behind the scenes, they're always arguing.
blank canvas	We've got to write a poem for English. It can be about anything at all, so we've got a blank canvas to start from.
play a part/role (in doing sth)	Thank you for playing an important role in cleaning the beach.
take centre stage	I don't like to take centre stage at parties. I prefer to sit in the corner and talk quietly.

WORD FORMATION

Core word	Derivatives
access (v/n)	accessibility (n), (in)accessible (adj)
attract (v)	(un)attractive (adj), attraction (n), attractively (adv)
beauty (n)	beautiful (adj), beautifully (adv), beautify (v), beautician (n)
doubt (n)	doubtful (adj), doubtfully (adv), doubtless (adj), (un)doubted (adj), undoubtedly (adv)
ease (n)	(un)easy (adj), (un)easily (adv)
equip (v)	equipment (n), (un)equipped (adj)
mass (n)	massive (adj), massively (adv)
patience (n)	patient (n), (im)patient (adj)

TOPIC VOCABULARY | Words connected with *environmental issues*

Word	Example sentence
carbon footprint (n)	We're trying to reduce our carbon footprint by using our bikes more and the car less.
climate change (n)	We need to take climate change more seriously, or our world is going to become a very different place.
global warming (n)	If we don't do something about global warming, some islands are going to disappear under the sea.
greenhouse effect (n)	The greenhouse effect means our planet is becoming warmer than it should be.
ozone layer (n)	Although we can't see it, the ozone layer protects us from dangerous UV radiation.
renewable energy (n)	We need to rely more on renewable energy like solar panels to generate electricity.
sustainable development (n)	Governments are now more concerned about sustainable development, but they still don't do enough to control economic growth.
toxic waste (n)	There is a lot of industry there and the river and sea are polluted with toxic waste.

PHRASAL VERBS

Phrasal verb	Meaning	Example sentence
call for (Type 3)	require, demand	This situation calls for immediate action.
chop down (Type 1)	make a tree, etc. fall by cutting it	We decided to chop down the old oak tree in the garden.
clean up (Type 1)	make a place completely clean and tidy	Why don't you clean up your room before your friends arrive?
die out (Type 2)	become less common and then disappear	Does anyone know why the dinosaurs died out?
do away with (Type 4)	get rid of	They've done away with the traffic lights outside the school.
run out (Type 2)	if sth runs out, you don't have any more of it	One day, all the world's oil supply will run out. What will we do then?
throw away (Type 1)	get rid of sth you no longer want	Do you mind if I throw away all these old magazines?
wipe out (Type 1)	destroy completely	Wolves were wiped out in Britain centuries ago.

WORD PATTERNS | Words + prepositions

Core words	Example sentence
affected by	Were you affected by the recent floods?
exposed to	Young children shouldn't be exposed to cigarette smoke.
harmful to	Building another airport will be very harmful to the local environment.
protected from	Elephants need to be protected from local hunters.
threatened by	The local wildlife is threatened by pollution from factories.
waste of	Trying to explain something to Harry is a waste of time because he never listens.

WORD FORMATION

Core word	Derivatives
benefit (v/n)	beneficial (adj), benefactor (n)
industry (n)	industrial (adj), industrially (adv)
live (v/adj/adv)	life (n), alive (adj), living (adj), lively (adj)
ordinary (adj)	extraordinary (adj), ordinariness (n), (extra)ordinarily (adv)
origin (n)	originate (v), (un)original (adj), originally (adv)
signify (v)	(in)significant (adj), (in)significantly (adv), (in)significance (n)
storm (n)	stormy (adj)
tradition (n)	(un)traditional (adj), (un)traditionally (adv)

TOPIC VOCABULARY | Words connected with *literature*

Word	Example sentence
crime fiction (n)	My favourite genre is crime fiction. I love trying to guess who's guilty before the detective!
critic (n)	He's a good critic, but he can be a bit cruel in his reviews!
editor (n)	My uncle is the editor of the local newspaper and sometimes he writes articles too.
fantasy (n)	I think the best fantasy novel ever written is *The Lord of the Rings*.
graphic novel (n)	I like reading graphic novels to chill out – all the pictures mean you don't have to think too much!
historical fiction (n)	My sister loves historical fiction. She's reading a huge book about the Tudors at the moment.
legend (n)	The story of Robin Hood is a legend, no-one really knows if he existed or not.
novelist (n)	He wants to be thought of as a serious novelist, but he's most famous for his funny short stories.
playwright (n)	William Shakespeare is probably the most famous playwright the world has ever known.
romantic novel (n)	That must be a romantic novel – look at the cover. It's pink with little hearts all over it!
science fiction (n)	I don't really like science fiction. Stories about aliens and strange planets don't interest me at all.
tragedy (n)	The play is a tragedy, but although the end is very sad, there are some funny bits too.

PHRASAL VERBS

Phrasal verb	Meaning	Example sentence
bring up (Type 1)	mention	I'm not sure if now's the right time to bring this up, but have you thought any more about our holiday?
flick through (Type 3)	look at but not read in detail	I've flicked through your report but I'll study it in detail later.
get across (Type 1)	explain, communicate	We need to get across the idea that this product is the best!
go on (Type 2)	talk more than is necessary and become boring	I love my grandmother very much but she does go on.
put forward (Type 1)	suggest	Some of the students have put forward the idea of a trip to a castle.
read up about (Type 4)	get detailed information about something by doing research	I read up about the author before I went to hear him read extracts from his new novel.
spell out (Type 1)	explain something very clearly and in detail	I know it's not difficult, but I'm going to spell it out very clearly so I'm sure you've understood.
talk through (Type 1)	discuss something, e.g. a problem or an idea	Let's sit down and talk it through. I'm sure there's a solution.

COLLOCATIONS | Collocations with *say*, *speak* and *tell*

Collocation	Example sentence
say hello/goodbye/ goodnight	Dan, your cousins are going now, so come and say goodbye.
say sorry	You'd better say sorry to Annie for ripping her jacket.
speak against / in favour of sth	Some people at the meeting spoke against the proposals.
speak for yourself	Speak for yourself! You may be happy about having an extra 30 minutes of classes every day, but I'm not!
speak well/highly of sb	The new headteacher's doing a really good job – all of the teachers and students speak highly of her.
speak your mind	My mum always speaks her mind, which some people think is a bit impolite sometimes.
tell a joke	I'm bad at telling jokes – I can never remember the endings.
tell a lie / the truth	Angie told me that her uncle is a millionaire, but I'm not sure she was telling the truth.
tell a story	Our dad always used to tell us a story before we went to sleep.
tell sb a secret	If I tell you a secret, will you promise not to tell anyone else?
tell the difference between things	How can you tell the difference between a dove and a pigeon?
tell the time	I learnt to tell the time when I was about six years old.

Core word	Derivatives
able (adj)	unable (adj), (in)capable (adj), disabled (adj), (dis/in)ability (n), capability (n)
appear (v)	disappear (v), (dis)appearance (n), apparent (adj), apparently (adv)
know (v)	knowledge (n), (un)knowledgeable (adj), (un)known (adj), (un)knowing (adj), (un)knowingly (adv)
lonely (adj)	loneliness (n)
speak (v)	speaker (n), speech (n), speechless (adj), (un)spoken (adj), unspeakable (adj)
surround (v)	surroundings (n), surrounding (adj)
think (v)	thinker (n), thought (n), thinking (n), (un)thinking (adj), thoughtful (adj), thoughtless (adj), (un)thinkingly (adv), thoughtfully (adv), thoughtlessly (adv)
vary (v)	various (adj), variable (n), (in)variable (adj), varying (adj), varied (adj), variation (n), variety (n), invariably (adv)

UNIT 10

TOPIC VOCABULARY | Words connected with *spending money*

Word	Example sentence
bill (n)	Did the electricity bill come in the post this morning?
cash (n)	Could you lend me £10? I haven't got any cash on me.
cashpoint (n)	Excuse me, is there a bank near here? Or a cashpoint?
change (n)	I'd get a drink from the machine but I haven't got any change, only a €10 note.
credit card (n)	Some people say that using a credit card makes it easier to control spending.
discount (n)	I got an amazing discount on these shoes, they had 50% off.
PIN (n)	You shouldn't use the same PIN for all your cards and your phone, it's not secure.
receipt (n)	Shall I put the receipt in the bag for you?
refund (v/n)	Could I have a refund on this jacket, please? It's not my style.
till (n)	I'm sorry but this till is closed. There are two open at the front of the store.

PHRASAL VERBS

Phrasal verb	Meaning	Example sentence
carry on (Type 2)	continue	Please carry on until I get back.
decide on (Type 3)	choose one thing from various options	We arrived at the party late because my friend couldn't decide on what to wear.
pick on (Type 3)	keep treating sb badly	I wish you wouldn't keep picking on me all the time!
press on (Type 2)	continue doing sth despite difficulties	I was tired but I had to finish before the end of the day so I decided to press on.
put on (Type 1)	make a machine or piece of electrical equipment start working	I always put the radio on as soon as I wake up.
sleep on (Type 3)	wait until the next day to make a decision	I'll sleep on your suggestion and let you know tomorrow.
start on (Type 3)	begin to criticise sb	Don't start on me! It wasn't my fault.
switch on (Type 1)	make a machine or piece of electrical equipment start working	You need to switch the computer on at the back.

COLLOCATIONS | Collocations with *do, get, go* and *make*

Collocation	Example sentence
do business with	They're so demanding that I really can't do business with them.
get a bargain	You really got a bargain when you bought your new tablet in the sales.
go bankrupt	Anushka went bankrupt when her business failed.
make a fortune	Sarah made a fortune when she sold her company.
make a living	It's getting harder to make a living from photography.
make a loss	The business made a huge loss last year.
make a profit	This year, we've made a profit of over a million pounds!
make a purchase	We'll give you a bonus every time you use your credit card to make a purchase!

WORD FORMATION

Core word	Derivatives
desire (v/n)	(un)desirable (adj)
economy (n)	economise (v), economic (adj), (un)economical (adj), economically (adv)
grow (v)	growing (adj), grown (adj), growth (n)
nation (n)	national (adj), nationality (n)
revolution (n)	revolutionary (adj), revolt (v/n), revolting (adj), revolve (v)
stimulating (adj)	stimulated (adj), stimulate (v), stimulus (n), stimulation (n)
strong (adj)	strength (n), strongly (adv)
supply (v/n)	supplier (n)

UNIT 11

TOPIC VOCABULARY | Words connected with *travelling*

Word	Example sentence
arrive (at swh) (v)	We arrived at the airport at six in the morning and took a taxi to the hotel.
commuters (n)	There were so many commuters on the train to work that I had to stand all the way.
entrance (n)	I'll meet you at the entrance to the shopping centre at 7 pm, OK?
excursion (n)	We have a variety of excursions to local tourist attractions – there are half-day and full-day options.
fare (n)	Travelling by air is fast, but the fares can be very expensive.
fee (n)	Does the museum charge an entry fee or is it free for students?
flight (n)	The flight left very early in the morning, so we slept in the airport!
gate (n)	We waited at the gate for hours before they told us there was a problem with the plane.
get (to swh) (v)	We didn't get to the festival in time to see our favourite band, but it was fun anyway.
journey (n)	How was your journey to the office this morning? Was the train very crowded?
passengers (n)	A Boeing 747 aircraft can carry about 500 passengers.
platform (n)	Trains to London leave from this platform and trains to Brighton from Platform 3.
reach (swh) (v)	You can only reach the tiny island where we stayed by boat.
reception (n)	Please leave your key at reception when you check out at the end of your stay.
ride (v/n)	The train station is only a short ride from the hotel by taxi.
route (n)	Which route did you take to get here? The motorway or the local roads?
ticket (n)	Are there any tickets left for the excursion to Skellig Michael tomorrow, please?
travel (v/n/adj)	Air travel is actually the safest form of transport there is.
trip (n)	Enjoy your trip to the beach – see you in a few days!
voyage (n)	Everyone knows that the Titanic sunk on its first voyage.

PHRASAL VERBS

Phrasal verb	Meaning	Example sentence
check out (Type 2)	leave a hotel	We'll pay for the room when we check out.
drop off (Type 1)	stop to allow sb to leave, usually from a vehicle	The driver dropped me off at the hotel.
get away (Type 2)	go swh for a rest or holiday	We're planning to get away for a couple of weeks in the summer.
head for (Type 3)	move towards a place	When the fire alarm went off, everyone headed for the car park.
pick up (Type 1)	collect, often in a vehicle	My dad picks me up from school every Tuesday and Thursday.
see off (Type 1)	say goodbye to sb who's leaving on a journey	We all went to the bus station to see Kylie off when she went to university.
set out (Type 2)	start a journey	The explorers slowly set out on their journey across the ice.
turn round (Type 2)	reverse direction	The road was blocked, so we had to turn round and go back.

WORD PATTERNS | Words + prepositions

Core words	Example sentence
crowded with	The town centre was so crowded with shoppers that we decided to go home.
do about (-ing)	What are we going to do about planning the party?
interfere with	I watched your bags the whole time – no-one's interfered with them.
keen on (-ing)	I'm really keen on cycling, but I don't like playing team sports.
look forward to (-ing)	I'm really looking forward to going on holiday next week.
point in (-ing)	There's no point in complaining – it won't change anything.
separated from	I got separated from Helen at the concert and it took me ages to find her again.
upset about (-ing)	Don't get upset about having to change your travel plans, these things happen.
useful for (-ing)	This app's really useful for finding bargains nearby.
valid for	This exam certificate is valid for three years.
warn sb about (-ing)	I've warned you about being late before. If it happens again, you'll be in real trouble.

WORD FORMATION

Core word	Derivatives
active (adj)	inactive (adj), act (v), (in)action (n), (in)activity (n), (de)activate (v), activated (adj), activation (n)
apply (v)	application (n) applied (adj)
arrange (v)	arrangement (n), (pre)arranged (adj)
help (v/n)	(un)helpful (adj), helpless (adj), helplessness (n)
huge (adj)	hugeness (n), hugely (adv)
meaning (n)	mean (v), means (n), meaningful (adj), meaningless (adj), meaningfully (adv)
participate (v)	participant (n), participation (n), (un)participative (adj)
value (v/n)	undervalue (v), overvalue (v), evaluate (v), (in)valuable (adj), evaluation (n), valuables (n), valuation (n)

UNIT 12

TOPIC VOCABULARY | Easily-confused words

Word	Example sentence
achieve (v)	What things would you like to achieve in the next ten years?
earn (v)	I tried to earn his respect with hard work, but he just doesn't like me.
effort (n)	He made a huge effort and I think he really deserved that prize.
fail (v)	Always remember that it's better to try and fail, than not to try because you're afraid of failing.
famed (adj)	Cervantes was a famed writer and wrote what many people consider to be the first modern novel.
infamous (adj)	Al Capone was an infamous American gangster in the 1930s.
job (n)	Jo's got a new job. She's working at weekends in the café.
lose (v)	He lost the TV talent show, but went on to become a pop star.
miss (v)	She's incredibly hard working and has never missed a class.
succeed (v)	Van Gogh didn't succeed in selling many paintings while he was alive, but his pictures now sell for millions.
unknown (adj)	This piece of music is by an unknown composer, but I love it.
work (n)	I can't go out this weekend, I've got far too much work to do.

PHRASAL VERBS

Phrasal verb	Meaning	Example sentence
cut off (Type 1)	make a place difficult to enter or leave	The snowstorm completely cut off the village and no-one could get in or out.
finish off (Type 1)	do the last part of sth so it is complete	I finally finished off the jigsaw I had been working on.
log off (Type 2)	finish using a computer system	Make sure you log off when you've finished working on the computer.
rope off (Type 1)	prevent people from entering an area using a rope	The path was dangerous so the caretaker roped it off.
set off (Type 1)	make sth explode	We heard that somebody had threatened to set off a bomb in the city centre.
shave off (Type 1)	cut hair from part of your body by shaving	You should shave that ridiculous moustache off!
spark off (Type 1)	make sth happen	When I forgot to do the washing up, it sparked off an argument.
wipe off (Type 1)	remove sth by wiping	Let me just wipe my make-up off.

IDIOMS | Idioms with *keep* and *lose*

Idiom	Example sentence
keep sight of	If you keep sight of your aims, I'm sure you'll achieve them.
keep your head	Keep your head in the final and you could be the world champion!
keep your word	You can trust Alice because she always keeps her word.
lose track of	I completely lost track of time when I was playing my favourite video game.
lose your nerve	As we reached the top of the mountain, I began to lose my nerve.
lose your temper	Dad lost his temper when I knocked his cup of tea on the floor.

WORD FORMATION

Core word	Derivatives
able (adj)	unable (adj), (in)capable (adj), disabled (adj), (dis/in)ability (n), capability (n)
accomplish (v)	accomplishment (n), (un)accomplished (adj), accomplishable (adj)
capable (adj)	incapable (adj), (in)capability (n), (in)capacity (n)
celebrate (v)	celebration (n), celebrated (adj), celebrity (n)
child (n)	children (n), childish (adj), childlike (adj), childless (adj), childhood (n)
mathematics (n)	maths (n), mathematical (adj), mathematician (n), mathematically (adv)
program (v/n)	programmer (n), programming (n), programmable (adj)
wide (adj)	width (n), widen (v), widely (adv)

WRITING REFERENCE

AN ARTICLE | Example task

You see this notice in an international English-language magazine for teenagers:

> ### We want your articles!
> We're looking for articles about parties. Have you, a friend or a member of your family ever held a great party? Tell us about it – describe the occasion and explain what made it so great.
> We'll publish the best articles in a special issue.

Write your article.

> *Always give your article a title.*

Make a connection with the reader with a shared experience, or ask a rhetorical question.

THE PARTY OF A LIFETIME!

We've all been to lots of parties, but sometimes one stands out from all the rest. For me, it's my dad's fortieth birthday party.

We decided we would surprise him, so we all pretended we just wanted a quiet celebration at home. Secretly, we booked my dad's favourite restaurant and invited many relatives and close friends. As well as that, Mum invited some of Dad's old friends that he hadn't seen for years.

Use a variety of tenses and sentence types.

Use a friendly, conversational style.

On the big day, Mum asked Dad to call at the restaurant to ask about their new menu. When he got there, he got the surprise of his life! There were about a hundred people there! I'll never forget the look of surprise on his face. He was speechless for about a minute – a long time for Dad!

Use a good range of vocabulary.

Use exclamation marks to add a sense of excitement where appropriate.

We had fantastic food and danced to Dad's favourite music. He couldn't stop smiling all night. It was great to see him chatting to old friends and finding out what they were doing now. Dad had an enormous cake with 'Happy 40th' on it. He said it really was the party of a lifetime!

Use humour where appropriate.

USEFUL PHRASES

Making a connection with the reader	Linking words and phrases	Adding and ordering points	Describing reactions
We've all …, Have you ever …? *If you're like me, you probably …*	*For me, Personally, In fact, As a matter of fact, However, so*	*As well as that, Also, In addition, Firstly, Later, Finally, In the end,*	*speechless, surprise, shock, awesome, amazed, I absolutely loved/hated …*

You see this advert on a website for teenagers:

Local attractions – reviews wanted

We're looking for reviews of an attraction or event near where you live. Your review should include information about where the attraction is, what you can do there, and how expensive it is. Would you recommend this attraction to other people your age?

The best reviews will appear online next week.

Write your review.

> *Always give your review a title which clearly shows what you're reviewing.*

> *Address the reader directly to encourage them to read on.*

> *By the end of the first paragraph, the reader should know exactly what is being reviewed.*

ICE SKATING IN TAWSTOCK

If you live in the south and fancy ice skating this winter, head over to Tawstock any Saturday or Sunday in November and December. The local council has built a large open-air ice skating rink in the town centre.

> *Include all the information which the question asks you to include, plus any other relevant information. Use your imagination if you're not describing a real attraction/event/book/film/etc.*

Skaters can skate for one hour – though expect to queue for about 15 minutes. There is no entrance fee, so if you have your own skates, the attraction is free. Most people hire skates there, however. The cost for hiring skates is £3 for adults and £1 for under-16s.

> *A review is a combination of factual information and your own opinion. Use phrases such as In my view and To my mind to highlight that you're expressing your opinion.*

If you haven't skated on ice before, it's not easy. I held onto the side at first and slowly built up my confidence. In my view, it's definitely easier and more fun to go with friends or family than on your own. And make sure you wear warm clothes.

> *Summarise your general opinion in the final paragraph.*

> *Give advice where appropriate.*

Ice skating in Tawstock is great fun. There's a brilliant atmosphere on the ice, with people of all ages enjoying themselves. I would definitely recommend this attraction, whether you're a family with small children or a group of teenagers my age. Maybe I'll see you there!

> *Make clear who you would/ wouldn't recommend the attraction/event/ book/film/etc. to.*

> *A friendly tone makes a review more interesting and enjoyable to read.*

USEFUL PHRASES

Reviews of shops/hotels/places/ attractions/events/etc.	Reviews of gadgets/products/etc.	Other expressions	Useful adjectives
… is situated in/near, location, service, range, overpriced, reasonable prices, entrance fee, offers, aimed at, designed for, perfect for	use this device/product for, features, design, upgrade, the best on the market	What is most impressive about …, My only criticism is …, On the downside, Overall, In conclusion, To conclude, To sum up,	badly/well organised, disappointing, fascinating, impressive, surprising, unusual

AN INFORMAL LETTER/EMAIL | Example task

You have received an email from your English-speaking friend, Andy:

> I play in a volleyball team and we've got an important match on Saturday. The problem is that I've been invited to a birthday party on the same day. All my school friends are going to be at the party. If I go, though, it'll upset my friends on the volleyball team.
>
> What should I do?
>
> Andy

Write your email.

Use an informal greeting with your friend's first name.

Ask after your friend and refer to their letter/email.

Use informal language, including contractions and exclamation marks where appropriate.

Use linking words and phrases to connect your sentences and paragraphs.

Use modals to talk about possibilities and to give advice.

Use informal closing expressions.

End the letter/email with your first name.

From: Vladimir
To: Andy

Hi Andy,

How are you? It was great to hear from you. I understand your problem. You don't want to upset your friends on the volleyball team, but you also don't want to miss the party with your school friends! It sounds like you have to make a really difficult decision.

First of all, I would say that you have to decide what is important to you. Are you planning to stay in the volleyball team for a long time? If you are, then it might be a bad idea to miss the match if it's really important. Just remember that there will always be more parties, although this time you'll feel like your school friends are having fun without you.

On the other hand, you might decide that your school friends are more important to you. In that case, I suggest you explain the situation to your teammates. See what they say. Don't be surprised, though, if they become a bit annoyed!

Anyway, good luck with your decision and let me know what you decide!

Write soon!

Vladimir

USEFUL PHRASES			
Starting the letter/email	**Referring to your friend's letter/email**	**Linking words and phrases**	**Ending the letter/email**
Dear Andy, Hi Andy! How are you? I hope you're well. How are things?	*It was great to hear from you. I'm glad you passed your exam / had a good birthday / etc. I was very happy to read that …, Great news about your …, I understand your problem.*	*First of all, To begin with, On the other hand, By the way, One more thing, Anyway, …*	*Let me know …, I have to go now. Got to go. Take care! Write soon! Love, Lots of love, Best wishes, All the best, Yours,*

You have seen this notice on your school noticeboard:

School End-of-term Event

We will be deciding shortly what event to hold for the parents and students on the last day of term. In previous years, we have successfully held school concerts, school plays, science demonstrations, art exhibitions and singing competitions.

If you would like to suggest what we should do for this term's event, please write to me by the end of Friday.

Alan Dart

Headteacher

Write your letter.

> *Read the question carefully. Sometimes you will know the name of the person you are writing to (e.g. your headteacher). At other times, you might not (e.g. the editor of a magazine).*

Dear Mr Dart,

I am writing to make a suggestion regarding this year's end-of-term event. I propose holding a talent competition.

> *Clearly and politely explain your reason for writing in the first paragraph.*

> *Use linking words and phrases such as: however and in my opinion where appropriate.*

In previous years, as you said, the school has held singing competitions. However, we have never held a general talent contest. In my opinion, this would be more enjoyable and entertaining than just a singing contest as there would be more variety, including dancing, comedy and perhaps even magic acts.

> *When writing to an adult, or someone you don't know well, your tone needs to be more formal than when writing to a friend. Don't use exclamation marks or very informal expressions. For example, in an informal letter/email, you might write: Hey – how about getting the mums and dads to do something too?! That style is not appropriate in a letter/email to a headteacher.*

I would also like to suggest that parents are encouraged to take part in the competition too. Perhaps there could be two prizes – one for the best student and one for the best adult. You might even want to consider allowing teachers to enter as well. In terms of judges, we could either let the audience decide, or we could invite local people to judge the competition.

In short, I believe an event like this would be a fantastic celebration of the different talents which people at this school have, and would be great fun.

> *The final paragraph is usually short. (It's fine if it's only one sentence.) It should encourage the reader to take action, and show that you are willing to continue the discussion.*

Please let me know if you have any questions, or if you wish to discuss it further.

Yours sincerely,

> *Use an appropriate word or phrase to express respect.*

Jenny Hawkins
Year 12

> *End the letter/email with your first name and surname. Include any other relevant information, such as your school year.*

USEFUL PHRASES			
Starting the letter/email	**Formal words and phrases**	**Final paragraph**	**Ending the letter/email**
Dear Mr + surname, (for men) *Dear Miss/Mrs/Ms + surname, (for women)* *Dear Sir/Madam, (if you don't know their name)* *Dear Editor, (for a newspaper editor)*	*regarding, with regard to, in terms of, I would also like to, I would be grateful if you would/could, you might wish to consider*	*Please let me know … if/should you have any questions / if/should you wish/want to discuss it further. I look / I'm looking forward to hearing from you.*	*Yours, Regards, Best regards, Kind regards, Yours sincerely, (if you know their name) Yours faithfully, (if you don't know their name)*

You have seen this announcement in an international magazine for teenagers:

Send us your stories!

See your story in our magazine. Your story must begin with this sentence:
Grace ran to the window to see what the noise was.

Your story must include:

- an accident
- a surprise

Write your story.

Always give your story a title.

Read the instructions carefully. If they tell you not to change the sentence you are given, make sure you use it exactly as it appears in the question.

Don't start writing until you've planned the plot. Here are the writer's notes for this story: Grace hears a noise – a car accident – the drivers argue – Grace recognises one of the drivers – it's her lost uncle

A LUCKY ACCIDENT

Grace ran to the window to see what the noise was. A moment before, she had been reading when she had suddenly heard a loud bang. Looking out of the window, she could see that two cars had crashed into each other. She raced downstairs and into the street.

'You weren't looking where you were going!' shouted one of the drivers.

'I was! You were going too fast!' replied the other.

Grace looked at the first driver. He looked familiar. The drivers started to take each other's names and addresses.

'George Mills. 121 Park Road,' said the first driver.

Grace stared at him. Mills was her own surname. She looked at the driver more closely and then spoke. She was sure it was her uncle who nobody had seen or heard from for years.

'Excuse me. My name is Grace Mills. Do you have a brother called Alex?' The man looked at her for a moment.

'Grace? Is it you? I've been abroad and unfortunately, I lost touch with your dad when you moved house. I can't believe it! It's good to see you!'

Use a range of tenses and grammatical structures.

Use direct speech to show what people say. Start a new line for each speaker.

Use a range of different reporting verbs.

Vary the length of your sentences, occasionally using short sentences for dramatic effect.

Make sure you include everything the question tells you to include. Here, the writer has included an accident and a surprise.

USEFUL PHRASES			
Time phrases	**Creating drama**	**Reporting verbs**	**Describing actions**
A moment before, At first, Then, Later, After a while, Eventually, Some time later	*Suddenly, All of a sudden, Just then, Without warning*	*answer, ask, cry, reply, scream, shout, tell, think, whisper, wonder*	*more closely, for a moment, quickly, slowly, happily, sadly*

In your English class, you have been talking about pets. Your teacher has asked you to write an essay for homework.

> **What are the most important factors someone should consider when choosing a pet?**
>
> **Notes**
> Write about: 1 time spent with pet
> 2 geography and space
> 3 .... (your own idea)

Write your essay using all the notes and giving reasons for your point of view.

Create a formal tone by using formal grammar, vocabulary and punctuation. This is not an article for your friends. It's a piece of academic writing for your teacher.

Give examples, and use appropriate phrases to do so.

Make contrasts, and use appropriate phrases to do so.

A new pet can bring much happiness to a home. What is more, having to look after a pet can teach children important lessons about responsibility. However, choosing a pet is not a decision which should be taken lightly. It is vital to choose one that is appropriate for your lifestyle.

Make sure you include the two ideas you are given, and come up with your own idea.

One factor is how much time family members spend at home. If everyone is away for many hours, then pets that need lots of human attention may be an unwise choice.

Give examples, and use appropriate phrases to do so.

A second factor is the place and its surroundings. If you have a garden, your house may be ideal for a cat. A tiny apartment, however, with no outside space, may not be, as cats like to explore outside. Thirdly, there is the issue of safety. For instance, there are some breeds of animals which you must not leave with young children because they are too dangerous.

Come to a conclusion and summarise your main point in the final paragraph.

Give reasons, express results and draw conclusions as necessary. Use appropriate phrases.

To conclude, the best pet for someone depends on their circumstances. In my view, it is essential for them to consider all of the factors carefully before making such an important decision.

Use appropriate phrases to express your opinion, or the opinions of others.

USEFUL PHRASES			
Listing points	**Giving examples**	**Expressing contrast**	**Expressing results, giving reasons, conclusions**
First, Firstly, First of all, To begin with, Second, Secondly, Third, Thirdly, What is more, Additionally, In addition (to this), Apart from that, Moreover, Furthermore	*such as, like, for example, for instance*	*However, In contrast, Having said that, but, although, even though, in spite of, despite, On the one hand … On the other hand …*	*Because of this, Consequently, For this reason, As a result, so, Therefore, This is the main reason why …*
Expressing your opinion	**Expressing someone else's opinion**	**Concluding and summarising**	**Useful adjectives**
In my opinion, In my view, To my mind, As I see it, Personally, It seems to me (that) …, It is my view (that) …, I would argue (that) …	*According to, Some people say (that) …, It is said (that) …, It has been said (that) …*	*To conclude, In conclusion, To summarise, To sum up, In summary*	*appropriate, essential, particular, practical, relevant, vital*

IRREGULAR VERBS REFERENCE

Bare infinitive	Past simple	Past participle
be	was/were	been
beat	beat	beaten
become	became	become
begin	began	begun
bend	bent	bent
bite	bit	bitten
blow	blew	blown
break	broke	broken
bring	brought	brought
build	built	built
buy	bought	bought
catch	caught	caught
choose	chose	chosen
come	came	come
cost	cost	cost
cut	cut	cut
deal	dealt	dealt
do	did	done
drink	drank	drunk
drive	drove	driven
eat	ate	eaten
fall	fell	fallen
feed	fed	fed
feel	felt	felt
fight	fought	fought
find	found	found
forget	forgot	forgotten
get	got	got
give	gave	given
go	went	gone
grow	grew	grown
hang	hung	hung
have	had	had
hear	heard	heard
hit	hit	hit
hold	held	held
hurt	hurt	hurt
keep	kept	kept
know	knew	known
lead	led	led

Bare infinitive	Past simple	Past participle
leave	left	left
lend	lent	lent
let	let	let
lie	lay	lain
lose	lost	lost
make	made	made
mean	meant	meant
meet	met	met
pay	paid	paid
put	put	put
read	read	read
ride	rode	ridden
ring	rang	rung
run	ran	run
say	said	said
see	saw	seen
sell	sold	sold
send	sent	sent
set	set	set
shine	shone	shone
show	showed	shown
sit	sat	sat
sleep	slept	slept
speak	spoke	spoken
spend	spent	spent
spring	sprang	sprung
stand	stood	stood
steal	stole	stolen
stick	stuck	stuck
swim	swam	swum
take	took	taken
teach	taught	taught
tell	told	told
think	thought	thought
tread	trod	trodden
understand	understood	understood
wear	wore	worn
win	won	won
write	wrote	written

Macmillan Education
4 Crinan Street
London N1 9XW
A division of Macmillan Publishers Limited

Companies and representatives throughout the world

ISBN 978-0-230-48877-9

Text, design and illustration © Macmillan Publishers Limited 2017
Written by Malcolm Mann and Steve Taylore-Knowles

The authors have asserted their right to be identified as the authors of
this work in accordance with the Copyright, Designs and Patents Act
1988.

First published 2017

Designed by Designers Collective
Cover design by Designers Collective
Cover photograph by **Plain Picture**/Cultura/Peter Muller and
Shutterstock/zhu difeng (background)
Picture research by Penny Bowden

Authors' acknowledgements
Malcolm and Steve would like to thank the team at Macmillan and all the
many teachers and students around the world who helped make this
wonderful project possible.

The publishers would like to thank the Course consultant Karen Ludlow.

The authors and publishers would like to thank the following for
permission to reproduce their photographs:
123RF/scanrail p34(l): **Alamy**/ableimages p122, Alamy/All Canada
Photos p66(ml), Alamy/Simon Balson p87, Alamy/Todd Bannor p63,
Alamy/Blackout Concepts p100, Alamy/Blend Images p110, Alamy/
Simon Cowling p40(detective), Alamy/Danita Delimont p81(tl), Alamy/
Stephen Emerson p114, Alamy/F Fawcitt London Events Photography
p70, Alamy/Rik Hamilton p71(background), Alamy/Hemis p105, Alamy/
Hero Images Inc. p54(tr), 141(br), Alamy/imageBROKER pp81(tr), 106,
141(mr), Alamy/Brian Jackson p40(magnifying glass), Alamy/Tomas
Jasinskis p115(background), Alamy/Image Source Plus pp40(crime
scene), 120(bl), Alamy/Milko Nakov p132, Alamy/Nathaniel Noir p71,
Alamy/National Geographic Creative p74, Alamy/MBI p128, Alamy/
MITO images pp42(l), 117, Alamy/Nadezda Murmakova p54(tl), Alamy/
Andrew Paterson p92, Alamy/Pictorial Press Ltd p131, Alamy/Jochen
Tack p75, Alamy/Gregg Vignal pp65, 130(br), Alamy/Rob Whitworth
p76(mr), Alamy/wonderlandstock p49(tl), Alamy/World History Archive
p109, Alamy/Zoonar GmbH p103(mr); **Arsh Shah Dilbagi** p27(ml);
Brand X p99; **California State Science Fair** p27(ml); ©Classical Comics
p95(tl); **Tom Davies** pp118; **Andrew Federman** p125(c); **FLPA**/Reinhard
Dirscherl p80, FLPA/ Imagebroker/Bernd Zoller p37(butterfly); **Tobias
Fränzel** p33; **Getty**/Array p37(policeman), Getty/Thinkstock/Chad Baker
p38(background image), Getty/iStockphoto /Thinkstock Images/Ig0rZh
p125(lightening), Getty/iStockphoto/Thinkstock/ Roland Warmbier
p125(background); **Getty Images**/A-Digit p59(Silhouette), Getty
Images/AFP PHOTO p126(boat), Getty Images/Artie Photography (Artie
Ng) p129, Getty Images/Fadil Aziz /Alcibbum Photograph p72, Getty
Images/Andre Anita p81(ml), Getty Images/Nicolas Asfouril p86(tr),
Getty Images/B2M Productions p97, Getty Images/Sylvie Belmond
p9, Getty Images/Berezko p48, Getty Images/Alistair Berg p88, Getty
Images/Vincent Besnault p32(b), Getty Images/ Blend Images – KidStock
p143, Getty Images/EyeEm/Norbert Breuer p84(tl), Getty Images/Celo83
p96(header), Getty Images/Steve Debenport pp66(tr), 108, Getty Im-
ages/Echo pp14, 34(r), Getty Images/Flashpop p7, Getty Images/ Patrik
Giardino p130(bl), Getty Images/g-stockstudio p42(ml Getty Images/
Daniel Grill p15(tl), Getty Images/Gromit702 p102, Getty Images/Im-
age Source p54(mr), Getty Images/Hero Images pp10, 52, 55, 141(ml),
Getty Images/David Hogan p81(mr), Getty Images/KidStock p17, Getty
Images/Jutta Klee p4, Getty Images/Roy Mehta p145, Getty Images/
Douglas Menuez p6(br), Getty Images/Tom Merton pp94, 138, Getty
Images/Mixmike p59, Getty Images/Pamela Moore p56, Getty Images/
Peshkova p78(background), Getty Images/Monty Rakusen p39(r), Getty
Images/Matthias Ritzmann p119, Getty Images/Rubberball p38, Getty
Images/Blend Images/Pete Saloutos p51, Getty Images/Marcelo Santos
p50, Getty Images/ Robyn Breen Shinn p8(unicyling), Getty Images/
sturti p64, Getty Images/Tim Tadder p76(ml), Getty Images/Troy Aossey/
Taxi   p18, Getty Images/Art Vandalay p8(juggling), Getty Images/
VioNet p84(tr), Getty Images/william87 p120(ml), Getty Images/Forest
Woodward p62(tr); **Hartwood Films Ltd** p41; **HarperCollins Pub-
lishers Ltd** p95(mr); **The Kobal Collection**/Sony Pictures p124; **Luke
Jaden/Wallace Michael Chrouch** pp5; **Macmillan Publishers ltd** p53;
BRAND X PICTURES p6(cr); **IMAGE SOURCE** p37(bicycles); **PhotoDisc**
p49(background); **Plain Picture**/Johner/Stefan Isaksson p127, Plain
Picture/O. Mahlstedt p58, Plain Picture/Design Pics/Ingrid Rasmussen
p44; **Professor Daniel Nettle**, Newcastle University p37(eyes); **Rex
Features**/Isabel Infantes p11(tr), Rex Features/ITV p39(l), Rex Features/
Nature Picture Library p82, Rex/SIPA/CROPIX/PLAZIBAT p115(br), Rex
Features/c.Col Pics/Everett/Shutterstock p107; **Science Photo Library**/
Victor de Schwanberg p83; **Shutterstock**/Africa Studio p98, Shutter-
stock/Alexander Demyanenko p103(mr), Shutterstock/Amble Design
p86(mr), Shutterstock/Iakov Filimonov p103(bl), Shutterstock/Myroslava
Gerber p103(header), Shutterstock/Lenka Horavova p104; **Skateistan.
org** p125(b); **Kelly Simonds** p27(tr); **Superstock**/Ingram Publishing
p115(stamps); **Tamara Rose**/Earth Guardians p125(d); **The Shoe That
Grows** pp31; **West Yorkshire Police** p43.

The authors and publishers are grateful for permission to reprint the
following copyright material: Extract and quotes from *What It's Like to
be a Teenage Filmmaker* by Luke Jaden © 2015 Luke Jaden. Reprinted by
permission of the author (p5).
Extract from *Adolescents and Sleep: a summary of what researchers know
about teenagers' need for sleep and why sleep affects memory and learning*
by Sarah Spinks © 2014 Sarah Spinks. Reprinted by permission of the
author (p15).
Extract from *Macmillan Readers: Vanity Fair Upper Intermediate Reader*
retold by Margaret Tarner © 2006 Macmillan Publishers Ltd (p93).

Printed and bound in Lebanon

2021   2020   2019   2018
10   9   8   7   6   5